Onigiro.com

Thank you very much for choosing my book!

If the spine of the cover is not perfectly aligned with the
other volumes, and therefore the design is not harmonious,
or if you simply want to protect the book from wear, I have
created a PDF dust jacket that you can get for free and take
to your trusted printing store.

You can download the PDF dust jacket at my website address
onigiro.com/cover
or by scanning the QR code below with your mobile phone

Enjoy the reading!

Four Seasons in Japan

Autumn

VALENTINA SGAMBATO

Translated from the Italian by Sophie Henderson

Koi gathering -

autumn takes shape

peacefully

Ogiwara Seisensui

First published in Italian in October 2021 as
'Un anno di Giappone - Autunno'

First English edition: October 2022
Second English edition: July 2023

Translated from the Italian by
Sophie Henderson

ISBN: 979-12-210-1508-9

Also available as Kindle eBook

Edited and curated by Gabriele Curzi

Illustrated by Giada Lucchi

To Gabriele,
who has never stopped believing in me.

To life,
which has never stopped being wonderful.

Index

How to Use this Guide-Novel

Four Seasons in Japan is a series of four 'guide-novels' combining the informative aspects of a travel guide, with the aim of providing an itinerary rich with ideas and practical information to those who love to travel, with the narratives of an autobiographical account in which the adventure intertwines with the personal and sentimental story of the main character. The reader is accompanied on a physical journey, following typical routes for each season, as well as an inner journey full of emotion, observations and background scenes.

Although the two aspects coexist and complement each other, the book is designed to be consulted independently by two different types of reader. The reader mainly interested in the more informational and assimilable elements of the travel guide can easily and rapidly identify data relating to the itinerary, places, travel and cultural aspects of the country by reading specific sections of text.

In the **chapter dedicated to the season**, at the beginning of each book in the series, the writing becomes an enjoyable journey of discovery of the peculiarities of Japan in that season, including aspects of nature and landscape, holidays and main festivals, recommended activities, seasonal foods and likely weather.

Detailed studies within each chapter focus on the cultural and historical-geographical aspects of events, specific trips (e.g., castles, temples, shrines, parks etc.) with food as central protagonist.

Travel notes, at the end of every chapter, contain information on places visited such as how to get there, points of interest and principal annual events, as well as a daily itinerary and a list of recommended souvenirs and typical local products.

Finally, the **QR codes**, a completely new dimension to the editorial project, are useful both for anyone organising their own trip and the reader wanting to immerse themselves 360° in the places being described. Once scanned by a Smartphone, the codes enrich the reading experience with the contents of the website **Onigiro.com** where, for each destination, there are photo galleries, related content and official links to services and attractions, as well as further continually updated information.

And for the passionate reader... **watch out for the details in the novel!** From each chapter's opening data to the descriptions of experiences in the different cities, the book provides lots more information on each trip, from scheduling and descriptions of little-known local festivals, the name of secret roads, shops to wander into or a delicacy that absolutely cannot be missed.

Enjoy the book, but above all... enjoy the trip!

Behind each volume, direct travel experience and the collection of information compiled in situ is combined with a listing of books, guides and Japanese websites that cover the cultural aspects (festivals, folklore traditions, seasonal events and cuisine), and multiple places of interest to be visited (temples, gardens and historic sites).

Each itinerary lasts about three weeks, depending on the experiences and events held in those periods. Information such as the dates and cost of events, train times, restaurants, shops and attractions refer to our own trip and may vary over time. As a result, despite our commitment to providing the most precise data possible and regularly updating the content of the Onigiro.com website, we nonetheless advise you visit official websites and do up-to-date research when organising your trip.

1. Shirakawa-gō

2. Takayama

3. Kanazawa

4. Nagoya

5. Okayama

6. Hiroshima

7. Itsukushima

8. Himeji

9. Takamatsu

Map

10. Niihama

11. Beppu

12. Fukuoka

13. Kyōto

14. Kōbe

15. Ōsaka

16. Hakone

17. Tōkyō

Scan Here

Author's Note

All words of Japanese origin in the text are shown in *italics*, as are imported words integrated into everyday Japanese. When a Japanese term appears for the first time, it is accompanied by the corresponding characters 「kana/kanji」 and a footnote, if the meaning has not already been explained in the text.

Furthermore, the QR code on the side links to an online glossary that is always updated and contains an explanation of all these terms.

Words such as tempura or matcha are given in a literal transcription of the Japanese deriving from the relative kana/kanji, or rather *tenpura* and *maccha* in these two examples. Similarly, accent marks are not present in the Japanese writing, so words like saké are reported as *sake*.

For anyone unfamiliar with the Japanese language, here is a brief description of the most frequent pronunciations:

- vowels are read as short vowels in English, like the *a* in *cat*, *e* in *edge*, *i* in *igloo*, *o* in *octopus* and *u* in *umbrella*

- the diacritical macron mark doubles the vowel sounds, like *ā* in *rāmen*, *ē* in *karē*, *ō* in *Tōkyō* and *ū* in *Kyūshū*

- *f* is pronounced more like *h*

- *g* sound is hard, as in *pig*

- *j* is pronounced *gi*, so words like *momiji* and *jinja* are respectively pronounced *momigi* and *gingia*

- *r* is something akin to *l*

- *u* is silent if following an *s*, so words like *desu* are pronounced *des*

14

Introduction

When, at the age of 26, I first set foot in Japan, unknown to me as a place but object of an affection developed during childhood, my second life began. It wasn't love at first sight, but the confirmation of an omnipresent affinity, of a love relegated to a corner of my existence due to the superficiality with which, too often, we listen to our heart and treat our happiness. It was much more than a first meeting, almost a reunion, a return to belonging and, even more, a start to existing where it was right I should. A little like the sudden and irrepressible blooming of a flower when the suffering plant it comes from has finally found the right place to put down roots.

For ages I blamed my situation or people, including myself, for waiting so long before the meeting that seemed destined to transform my future. Besides, we're used to being told there's a time for everything, even for dreaming, changing our life or realising our happiness. Only with time did I understand that the right moment, initially appearing the least appropriate, could not be better, and that in the short amount of time we have at our disposal, there's no precise time to be happy, we must simply try to be happy all the time.

After that first trip, I also had a greater awareness of the power of ties, in particular those that mould and encourage us to be better, influencing our very identity. It was through this type of tie that Japan amalgamated its places and world with me as a person, shaping me and my existence as a pastry cutter shapes soft mixture into biscuits.

Since then, this country and I have become inseparable, and the teachings transmitted to me by its places and people have been part of my rebirth, growth and new vision of existence. They have shown me how in fact there is no deadline to becoming what we want to be, and how, in our approach to life, there is always a way to go forward that is different to that dictated as right and unambiguous by our surroundings. An alternative route to take: the one following our heart's desires.

From my very first experience of Japan, what struck me most was the eastern world's approach to life, the passage of time and our surroundings, in particular with regard to people and nature.

In Japanese, one of the most common interpretations of the two lines that make up the ideogram for 'person', *hito* 「人」, is two people supporting each other, because we can't exist without the support of another or without being able to give support to those around us who need it. I like to think this ideogram is also the expression of reciprocal contact, the trigger of mutual perception, powerful and widespread, just as I experienced it in this country: from respecting others' emotions to feeling part of a system, that, precisely in that way, becomes the highest expression of what we can define 'society', a system where awareness and respect to our neighbour leads to total self-identification with them and as a result, to the altruistic and principled Japanese behaviour that so surprises us.

Equally powerful in Japan is contact with nature. A relationship built on scrupulous knowledge of and sensitivity towards all its expressions and changes, in constantly taking on its lessons, and above all in marvelling at its wonder. This close relationship is deeply influenced by Shintoism, the island's native religion, which marks the changes in the seasons with celebrations and takes stock of the continual alteration of shapes and colours. It is a peculiarity that does not go unobserved by the *gaijin* [1] 「外人」 who find it equally easy to be fascinated by the inexorable Japanese expectation and desire to honour the cycle, to discover the beauty in transformation and celebrate it through *matsuri* [2] 「祭」, seasonal foods, and themed activities and decorations.

The relationship the Japanese enjoy with nature and its seasons is the heart and leitmotif of this series of books.

Celebrating Nature

In the first months of the year everything begins with magnificent festivals dedicated to the snow, in front of a boiling *oden* [3] 「御田」 in the company of friends and family, waiting for white winter sleep to make room for reawakening colour. These are the months to cultivate personal relationships in the warmth of the home. Only hanging on to nice things, while casting out ugly ones before the new spring. As occurs in the *Setsubun* [4] 「節分」, when the family, to the children's' delight, throw soybeans out of the front door or at a member of the family wearing the mask of *oni* 「鬼」, the Japanese devil, to banish it and attract fortune into the home for the future.

Soon afterwards is the arrival of spring, when picnics in the park and walks are enjoyed to admire the fragile and overflowing explosion of the plum trees' white blossom and then the pink of the *sakura* 「桜」, the Japanese ornamental

---

[1] Literally 'outside person', used to indicate foreigners

[2] Traditional Japanese festivals, recurrent events in Shinto and Buddhist tradition

[3] Dish in which vegetables, eggs and tōfu are boiled in a soy sauce broth

[4] Festival throughout Japan between 2 and 4 February in which people throw fukumame, 'fortune beans', at each other to drive evil spirits from the home

17

cherry tree. This occasion marks the beginning of the school and working year in Japan, symbolising the triumph of life's beauty, of a new beginning but also of the fleetingness of existence and beauty, so much so that only a few weeks later it is just a memory of petals blowing in the wind or floating along on the rivers winding through city and countryside.

Then attention shifts to the flowering of immense wisterias, storms of lilac and white raining down colour until late evening when they are celebrated with nocturnal illuminations. We continually look up at the sky during *Kodomo-no-Hi* 「こどもの日」, the day dedicated to the happiness of children, when in the cities and countryside brightly coloured *koinobori*[5] 「鯉幟」 swim in the wind, strung up by families as a wish that their boy children, like the tenacious carp, will succeed in navigating upstream in the river of life and reach all their objectives.

This is followed by the moment to admire the hydrangeas, whose colours are made vivid by the incessant light rain of June and July, the rainy season in Japan that not even the ghost-like *teru-teru bōzu*[6] 「てるてる坊主」 manage to placate. Their voluminous flowers are so numerous that when in full bloom the custom is to cut them off and float them on the surface of temple fountains, in the spectacle of water and petals called *hanachōzu* 「花手水」. If you're looking for respite for the eyes at nightfall, you find that towards the end of June marvels never sleep among the cedars in the unspoilt woods, where swarms of fireflies dance between the high trunks.

---

[5] Cone-shaped flags depicting the determined carp, that according to Chinese legend, by swimming against the current manage to transform themselves into a dragon and fly to paradise

[6] Ghost dolls handmade in white paper or cloth. They are hung outside windows like talismans to counter the rain and invoke the sun

With the warm humidity - and the cult of cold dishes such as the ever-popular *zaru-soba*[7] 「ざるそば」 and the playful *nagashi sōmen*[8] 「流しそうめん」 - comes the most important season, the one announced by the unmistakeable and deafening rhythmical chirping of the Japanese cicadas. It begins with colourful paper strips carrying wishes and hung from bamboos during *Tanabata*[9] 「七夕」, continues with delicate glazes on the *fūrin*[10] 「風鈴」 jingling in the wind, and explodes in the overflowing shades of the *Obon*[11] 「お盆」.

From the end of July to the beginning of September, the country enjoys one long party, among coloured lanterns, decorated wagons, processions and *hanabi*[12] 「花火」, with joyfully patterned *yukata*[13] 「浴衣」 as their owners dance down the streets or wander between the food stalls in the evening. Every town, from the most remote to the most famous, has its summer festival in honour of the deities that live in the mountains and rivers and watch over the precious rice fields.

Just long enough to say hello to the end of summer

---

[7] Buckwheat noodles served cold, to be dipped into a mentsuyu sauce made of soy and dashi, garnished with scallions, sesame and nori seaweed

[8] Fine Chinese noodles in cold water running along split bamboos, to be caught with chopsticks as they go by and dipped into accompanying sauces

[9] Star Festival, the only night in which the stars Vega and Altair, generally separated by the Milky Way, unite and indulge their passion. To celebrate, tanzaku, or strips of paper or wood inscribed with hopes and wishes, are hung from bamboos

[10] Small glass or cast-iron bells that make a pleasant sound in the wind

[11] Main Buddhist festival, generally held in the middle of August, when people commemorate their ancestors, with dancing, bonfires and other customs

[12] Literally 'fire flowers', hanabi are fireworks. Displays are either as a finale to an event or the main parts of longer festivities, then called hanabi taikai

[13] Spring-summer cotton version of the kimono traditionally worn at festivals, anniversaries that take place in certain seasons and at hot springs

typhoons when autumn arrives and the decorations change again: artificial red and orange leaves invade the shops and lanes, in anticipation of the real ones that will paint the whole of Japan in a blaze unseen anywhere else. But before the *momiji-gari* 「紅葉狩り」 in November, the 'red maple hunt' when people pour into the parks and up the mountains to bag as many reds as possible, October is the month of the festivals to usher in a good harvest, accompanied by the incessant sound of the *taiko*[14] 「太鼓」, the smell of mushroom soup, and the sight of ploughed fields with rice left out to dry, of the impossible yellow of the ginkgo biloba and of that moon, so white and perfect that, celebrated in *haiku*[15] 「俳句」, we cannot but stop to contemplate it.

Then, when the temperature begins to fall and the Japanese take refuge in the steam of the *onsen*[16] 「温泉」, the last red foliage falls to the ground and the sky fills with the colours of Christmas, invading the streets and avenues even before the start of December. Illuminations unrivalled elsewhere, compete in beauty, and turn into the spectacular garment adorning parks and neighbourhoods for several weeks.

Hard on this mantle of colours comes the snow, symbol of the Japanese winter. There is a hint of it near the end of December, when the silence of the mountains dusted with chalky flakes brings a break in the year's celebrations. In reality, the pistes are overflowing with skiers and snowboarders from around the world; Christmas is fêted in small

---

[14] Traditional Japanese drum with a wooden barrel or cylindrical shape, used for festivals, in Kabuki and Nō theatres and for ceremonies at shrines and temples

[15] Form of poetry consisting in three short phrases that evoke images suggestive of nature, a rapid scene that describes details of the moment caught with intensity

[16] Japanese hot springs, public or private, often outside, rotenburo, or inside, uchiyu, and also to be found at hotels and ryokan

events and local entertainment, as we await contentedly the 108 tolls of the bell in the Buddhist temples, ringing out the old year and in the new.

During the first days of January everyone visits temples and shrines for *Hatsumōde*[17] 「初詣」, to collect new stamps and new hope, to buy *daruma*[18] 「だるま」, entrusting to future projects, and wander through the food stalls, drinking *sake*[19] 「酒」 and steaming crab soups.

So, at any moment of the year Japan turns into a celebration to honour the beauty of nature that takes the breath away: no sooner is one season forgotten, the decorations and ingredients put away for next year, than the next marvel is underway. It is this perpetual euphoria, this continual desire to be amazed that fills the air, to evolve into that simple, daily happiness, which when you arrive in this country is initially hidden, to be slowly unearthed as time passes. And once discovered it takes up residence in the heart and is impossible to wash away.

Describing the Japanese Seasons

The symbiosis with time and its passing, the love of observing what naturally transforms around us, and the desire to celebrate change in all its expressions, enchanted me from my first visits. It is a desire that throbs out of sight of the majority of tourists, but is slightly less hidden from the visitor who looks beyond the appearances of more well-known

---

[17] The first visit to temples or shrines in the new year, usually in native towns, to pray for good health and make resolutions for the year ahead

[18] Good luck talismans, or small red dolls modelled on the Bodhidharma, founder of Zen Buddhism, sold with blank eyes. One eye is coloured when the owner makes a wish, the second when the wish comes true

[19] Japanese alcoholic beverage made from fermenting rice with kōji-kin mushrooms. The quality varies according to how refined the rice is and how much alcohol is added. It is drunk warm or cold depending on the occasion

places, and chooses the path less travelled. At a certain point in my life, with no warning, I began to find relief in this sensibility, of which I had felt the lack. I found comfort in the incredible simplicity with which the Japanese manage to relish happiness and experience stupor through the quotidian made up of all this, filling themselves with beauty and hope for the future, of love for life and good resolutions for their existence.

Narrating this - the passing of seasons on a journey through this many-sided Japan - soon became a necessity, a need to show how profound and often unfamiliar these places are, how much we have to learn in our relationship with the world and nature, and in pursuing a wealth so different from the materialism to which we are accustomed. Recounting how pain, being a part of existence with such naturalness, can be transformed into a hymn to life and how much that happiness, seemingly unattainable, is really always present in what surrounds us, and even more, where we would never imagine it to be.

This book aims to be a travel guide to famed places in Japan, but above all a glimpse of hidden places, by means of the festivals, colours, smells and tastes endlessly running after each other through the different seasons.

And then, with a light touch, it aims to do something else too: in unexplored corners of wonderment and a culture that is a world apart but intimate and familiar, to accompany the reader in the search to know their inner self, towards their own serenity and self-realisation. A short guide, as it was for me, along the many roads that lead to happiness.

 ← Find out more about the seasons of Japan

Autumn in Japan

Sparkling air combines the smells of moss and ocean in the same way the delicious hot broths mingle the secret ingredients of the season. The thousand shades of maple red and perfectly uniform gold of the ginkgo squabble against a bright sky. Paddy fields, shining out between their borders, are dusted at night with silver from the finest moon of the year. To the rhythmic sound of drums, the festivals convey a deep, intense call to the deities to protect their harvest. It is autumn in Japan, the season admired not only by its inhabitants, but also by travellers and photographers seeking views, ingredients and experiences in unattainable colours.

The short review that follows contains useful information for an autumn visit, but is only a peek at a country that loves to reveal itself little by little. Only by walking along its paths and ways, living places, knowing people and traditions immersed in local culture, do we discover the wonders hidden behind the season of the red leaves: a shower of nuances to seek out, ready to admire with heart full of emotion...

Nature

Autumn in Japan is synonymous with colour: from north to south the wave of autumnal foliage fire devours the entire country, ignited in mid-September on the island of Hokkaidō to blaze in December in Kyūshū.

In November, the eternal cedar woods perching on the mountains experience this absolute wonder beneath their very needles, when all the reds and oranges of the deciduous trees burst into an unparalleled explosion. It is the time many Japanese city dwellers, like the visiting tourists, travel to the countryside to hunt red maple leaves, or *momiji-gari*, which takes its name from *kōyō* 「紅葉」 when it is no longer just the maple leaves to be admired but all the trees whose leaves have turned into a palette of glorious colours. By shop windows and streets decorated with maple branches, windows of houses and schools decked in garlands of dry leaves, children and adults are tempted into the gardens and parks to admire the spectacle of that explosion of colour.

Next to the spring cherry blossom period, which is shorter and less predictable, the autumn colours are more stable and last for longer, allowing for simpler planning for a trip, above all if it involves going a fair distance around the regions of Japan. The fire of autumn's lazy pace makes it possible to admire it for a period of around 50 days, from the tinges of pink that counter the green in mid-October to the blood red that lights up the gentle November sun. And just like *sakura-zensen* 「桜前線」 the progress of the cherry blossom in spring, the autumn *kōyō-zensen* 「紅葉前線」 is reported on the national weather channels with forecasts and precise locations according to species of broadleaf.

In November the gardens stay open until late in the evening, offering suggestive *raitsu-appu*[20] 「ライツアップ」 with games of light beneath the vault of red leaves. As in the garden at Okayama, where lanterns mark the wide paths in the darkness of night, or in cities like Kyōto and Himeji.

Autumn is the season when walking in the city parks is a tonic for the eyes and heart. In the areas of woodland on the edge of Kyōto where markets open up at the weekend, the

---

[20] Suggestive lighting from below to enhances trees, landscapes and monuments

smell of moss and colours of the maples and other trees combine with the sweet smells from the stalls of chestnut desserts and local craftsmanship; all presiding over a carpet of red stars that gradually shrivel beneath the feet. While in Tōkyō you can heal the soul by standing in the silence of the gentle rain of leaves in Yoyogi-kōen Park or nearby Meiji-jingū Shrine.

In the cities you only have to skirt the skyscrapers and apartment buildings, and in the unexpected complexes of temples and shrines sewn into the city fabric you find the immense ginkgo trees, centuries–old witnesses of the human passage of time, and unchanging if not in their seasonal attire. Late October brings these giants' metamorphosis: like a butterfly drying its wings in the sun they quiver with colour, the leaves of the ginkgo let the autumn air and light dry and dissolve their green, deconstructing and transforming it into that clarion yellow that pulsates through archaic veins until it becomes a shower of gold in the house of the gods. And then, as at the Iwato-Ochiba-jinja Shrine, in the mountains to the north of Kyōto, at the end of October and beginning of November age old ginkgoes spread a golden cloak over everything.

Far from built-up areas, in the mountains or on the paths to remote shrines lost among the tall Japanese cedars, the moss swells with dew and grows out of all proportion, climbing over the bark of the cedars, cherishing the new life of small conifers and mushrooms, engulfing the stone of lanterns and fountains with green, breaching the confines of the gods up to the brink of the temples and altars, while the sound of the *shishi-odoshi*[21] 「鹿威し」 accompanies the last dance of the leaves falling into the fountains.

---

[21] Fountains in Japanese gardens where the water accumulates in a bamboo mo-bile that, emptying regularly, makes a certain sound as it pounds against the rock

Between ploughed areas that appear like battlefields of water, mud and birds, clumps of rice like rows of fallen troops on wooden stilt platforms lie exhausted to dry in the sun. Marking one plot and the next is the salmon coloured tinge of the persimmon trees that, hurriedly dropping their leaves, by December stand clad in large, vivacious orange fruit. While the plum and *sakura* trees live a second spring in October, when their leaves turn into pink petals to be admired in castle parks and city gardens.

To feel the season advancing you only have to look around you, day by day, in the simplicity of any street, in town or country while people wait to see flowers and plants sprout. Among them, the clover with its small pink flowers appears at the roadsides, but also in many of the flowerbeds and the wedges of landscape in miniature that are the private gardens at the doorways of people's homes.

Cosmos and anemones invade the fields with the same impetuosity as daisies in a spring greenhouse, indisputable symbols of the march of the season through countryside and rural villages. The coastal Hitachi Kaihin-kōen Seaside Park, in the town of Hitachinaka, north-east of Tōkyō, is literally taken over by them, as well as by kochia, another plant that charms the sight in this season: an entire valley of the park is blanketed by the roundish bushes of this shrub, that in autumn takes on a reddish purple colour so vivid that it looks like a layer of raspberries on a massive cake.

Chrysanthemums and *higanbana* 「彼岸花」, known as red spider lilies or equinox flowers, appropriate vast areas of park and garden in autumn, and sit in small vases outside houses so that any passer-by can enjoy their crisp red glow. From the end of September, these flowers evoke a profound beauty with a hint of sadness and melancholy, much like autumn itself and the inexorable passage of time. In this period people visit the graves of their ancestors, leaving gifts of *ohagi* 「おはぎ」, rice sweets covered in delicious *azuki*[22] 「小豆」 jam, and contemplate the lawns around the graves often covered in these flowers, thus associated with a death that, like autumn, is part of the cycle of nature. Parks such as Kinchakuda Manjushage-kōen in Hidaka, in Saitama Prefecture just outside Tōkyō, let you lose yourself in a spectacle that seems like nothing on earth.

Of all the autumnal flowers, pampas grass, *susuki* 「薄」 in Japanese, is often the most visually moving, especially in the late evening light. It belongs to the marvellous *aki-no-nanakusa* 「秋の七草」, the seven plants that mark the arrival of autumn, and presents itself in majestic silver brushes growing wild along the mountain paths, in fields glimpsed from the window of a train, on the cliffs by the sea or beside the dwellings of ancient villages. Associated with the silver colour of the full moon in autumn, often their reflections are caught in the decorations of houses and stores. Autumn in Sengokuhara Susuki Sōgen at Hakone is mesmerising: an enormous field of *susuki* where gold and silver undulate and shine in the light of both sun and moon.

Events

In a season where the tourists are less numerous than spring and summer, the peace and quiet is suddenly interrupted by the atmosphere of the *matsuri* celebrating the autumn rice harvest, when, between late September and late October, the whole of Japan shines with brightly coloured floats and altars parading through the streets, day and night, covered in decorations, silks and lanterns. During these festivals, traditionally decorated and bulky towers can

---

[22] Red beans originating in East Asia and widely used for bean paste in many Japanese pastries

be seen in all their glory gliding between roads and temples, sometimes taking part in competitions of beauty and strength, as the wooden structures ram each other to the yells of encouragement from their respective teams.

Every area has its own manner of expressing gratitude to the deities, adorning floats and filling the streets with *yatai*[23] 「屋台」, the classic street food stalls that puff out steam and smells on the cool autumn evenings. *Taiko* music can be heard at all hours along the festival routes as they swell with good cheer, and there are processions under the nigh dormant ginkgoes, and lion dances between the centuries-old cedars of the sacred temples.

This happens in Takayama at the start of October, when attention is focussed on this small town high up in the mountains for one of the most important feasts of the year, with processions and daytime markets, as well as nighttime parades when the floats studded with lanterns move like jewels among the stalls crowded with visitors. Niihama Taiko Matsuri, on the island of Shikoku, is particularly picturesque. Every year dozens of floats compete for precedence day and night, holding enormous *taiko* drum players in their wooden bellies. In Nagasaki, ancient Kunchi Matsuri is among the most famous for the dance of the dragon and floats in the form of sailing ships.

Whilst when Kyōto remembers the city's foundation with a parade in traditional costumes from the Imperial Palace to the Heian Shrine during the Jidai Matsuri, to the north of the city in the village of Kurama, one can witness the ancient rite of youthful passage sealed by the magic of fire. Finally, the Doburoku Matsuri at Shirakawa-gō distinguishes

---

[23] The term mainly refers to street food stalls during festivals and mobile restaurants in the city of Fukuoka. However, it can be used to describe some types of Japanese festival float

itself with traditional customs, lion dances and a 'prohibited' tasting of the cloudy local *sake*. In short, come autumn Japan explodes in dozens and dozens of *matsuri*. The autumnal festivals are small and unknown to most, brief summers concentrated in the countryside and warmed by the embracing heat of the trains bringing red leaf hunters, both foreign and Japanese.

And yet there is much magic in autumn, in the cooler evenings when the Japanese seem to want to harness the beauty of the season's colours in the lanterns strung up around the towns and villages in the countryside. Nihonmatsu Chōchin Matsuri, which takes place at Fukushima in the first days of October, is one of the three biggest lantern festivals in Japan, with its 300 oil lamps hanging from floats that move through the night, accompanied by the fragrance of incense, the sound of *taiko* drums and the mystical music of the bamboo flute. To experience similar splendours there are festivals at Hiroshima and Fukuoka, each with cloth and paper lanterns in traditional or abstract shapes, with distinctive scenery and designs to discover from one block to the next.

Unearthing these festivals isn't that easy, but perhaps it's part of the joy of planning your trip or of finding yourself unexpectedly in that unknown place just at the right moment as you were busy darting from one town to another. The autumnal *hanabi* are also worth experiencing, although they are rarer and less grandiose than the summer ones, once hunted down in the tangle of seasonal festivals and feast days they present you with evenings that are hard to forget. For instance, the famous Ōmagari Hanabi at Akita or the lesser-known Chōfu in the Tōkyō area, these *hanabi* delight the eyes and the heart with entertainment for as long as an hour of fireworks, often mirrored in the sea, or on a river or lake.

The festivals tied to seasonal farming activities some-times creep into the calendar on fixed dates and at others respecting the weekends in the month. However, as for every season, there are events that vary solely on the basis of nature and its continual transformations. For instance, from mid-September to the beginning of October they cele-brate *jūgoya* 「十五夜」, the night of the autumn harvest full moon, considered the largest and most beautiful moon of the year. On that night, but also those around that time, all over Japan they practise *tsukimi* 「月見」: contemplation of the moon. On this occasion the traditional ceremony of thanksgiving is celebrated and prayers said for a successful seasonal harvest, in particular for that of the new rice, ready to be reaped and threshed and laid out to dry from mid-September.

And the Japanese *susuki*, the pampas grass in flower then, which is hung here and there around doors and small gates, as its colour recalls the moon and the tussocks make you think of rice flower clusters, is the plant that accompa-nies that incredible contemplative moment of *tsukimi*.

Activities

Autumn is the season to cultivate tranquillity, to medi-tate on the irretrievable flow of time and on nature, that in a wealthy burst, lights up and shines before dying back.

Off the beaten track, if you like hiking among temples hidden in the autumn woods, any route in nature you take is a voyage of discovery in itself, through colours that ap-pear for the first time as you look. In particular, Momijidani-kōen Park on Miyajima Island, where the maples chase each other along the tourist route, in a river of fire reflected in the river of water below. You find it in the valleys by the famous national mountains and parks, for example in the national park of Daisetsuzan Kokuritsu-kōen in Hokkaidō, where nature is already going crazy by mid-September, showing itself off in such bright colours that they seem fake. And in the wilder lands of Tōhoku, in Nagano Prefecture along the Japanese Alps, in the sacred forests around Nikkō, on Mount Takao-san and in the area of Hakone near Tōkyō. Whichever natural path you wander in this season, your legs never get tired because your eyes are continually refreshed by a spectacle without parallel.

The *onsen*, which in summer are prey to suffocating heat and humidity, offer the most pleasurable shelter from the cold edge on the autumn air. For this reason, in autumn, leaving the big cities allows one to enjoy remote hot springs lost in the mountains and among woods dusted with red and yellow. In the secret *rotenburo*[24] 「露天風呂」, the turquoise steaming waters are immersed in the colours of the surrounding landscape, showered by the gentle rain of autumn leaves and scented with fresh moss that overwhelms the undergrowth in this season.

Until November, the temperatures at night make bathing under the autumn moon very enjoyable, and many Japanese are out late, strolling in *yukata* down the lanes near old thermal spas during *sotoyu-meguri*[25] 「外湯巡り」, going from one public spa to another, an incessant clatter of wooden sandals on tarmac as they go. From the orange woods of Hakone to the yellow willows of Kinosaki Onsen, escape to the *onsen* becomes a more intense experience at this time of year.

In smaller towns and in the countryside, relaxing leaves

---

[24] Open air hot springs, often immersed in nature

[25] Popular custom in small thermal towns in which clients make a tour of several onsen in one evening, walking down the lanes in kimono

room for pleasurable activities such as gathering autumn fruit, *kudamono-gari* 「果物狩り」, one of the open-air activities most loved by the Japanese: paying a few *yen*[26] 「円」 couples, families and school groups can enter orchards and greenhouses used exclusively for fruit picking, filling baskets to take home and/or choosing the best fruit to eat on the spot. In this way contact with nature's seasons is strengthened, here and nowhere else, working its way into the hearts of the smallest participants, who learn to love nature through play.

From October, it is possible to go apple picking in various parts of the country, such as the cold region of Tōhoku where Aomori Prefecture, thanks to its many orchards, has become famous for succulent apples, as has Takayama, where the city's morning markets display the delicious local varieties. In the region of Tottori, the autumn pears known as *nashi*[27] 「梨」 are nationally famed, with several farms near the sand dunes set up for picking and a museum entirely dedicated to them on the slopes of Mount Dai-sen.

If you'd rather participate in a grape harvest, the area of Yamanashi at the foot of Mount Fuji-san has various farm estates open to the public for grape picking. Alternatively, you can wait for the suggestive harvesting of the first persimmons towards the end of November, when the leafless trees seem to be decorated with bright orange Christmas baubles and the farms get ready to produce the highly popular jams and jellies. And for anyone who finds themselves in Japan too early for fruit or maples, the end of September is the best time to stay on one of the farms and help the owners in the arduous, traditional rice harvest followed by

---

[26] Japanese money. The Latinized symbol is ¥, while in Japan it is the kanji 円

[27] Variety of pear originally from Asia with skin much like that of a pear but the rounder shape of an apple, and a not very pronounced taste

laying the sheaves out to dry.

The fascination of autumn is alive in the cities too, where the lanes, shop windows and interiors of shopping centres and stations are decorated with garlands of maple leaves, acorns and chestnuts. In a Tōkyō that seems light years from the surrounding countryside, it is a surprise to wander along the narrow, picturesque alleyways of Omoide-yoko-chō in Shinjuku or Nakamise-dōri Street in Asakusa passing beneath vaults of maple boughs covered in orange leaves.

As in other cities, after school the children hurry to the big parks to 'hunt' for the finest maple, while photographers, amateur and not, trawl the best-known gardens, such as those in the outskirts. Hiroshima, city of maples, celebrates the season with hundreds of shop windows decorated for the occasion, Kyōto lights up the great station stairway with a mass of dancing red leaves, and at night the foliage around the Kiyomizu-dera Temple is lit up, as is the black mirror of water in the garden of Kōdai-ji Temple.

Next on the agenda, from mid-October, the large cities prepare for Halloween, a western event that is keenly enjoyed in Tōkyō, whose streets, such as Takeshita-dōri, are entirely dressed to the theme, and for several days kids in ghoulish costumes parade around the neighbourhood. In the same way, the Kagurazaka Bakeneko Festival held around mid-October is known throughout Japan for its masked parades and celebrations, all rigorously to a feline theme.

From the beginning of November, in the middle of *momiji-gari*, there are large urban gatherings to turn on the first Christmas lights and many towns put on incredible light displays in certain areas and in the main streets. At this time of year, you can marvel at light shows over entire parks, such as the floral parks of Ashikaga, north of Tōkyō, or Nabana-no-sato near Nagoya, and they are typical and widespread throughout Japan as the winter months draw on.

Seasonal Dishes and Foods

With the arrival of the first cold weather, the local dishes multiply in number and appear from all over the place, turning the country into a larger full of ingredients and recipes that vary from place to place, depending on altitude and climate, on wild herbs, and proximity to woods well stocked with mushrooms or the sea with its special bounty. On the other hand, the street food from the autumnal *matsuri* is a constant over the country, the food stalls groan with roasted sweet potato, *yaki-imo* 「焼き芋」, which kids devour from steaming paper bags. And then the fruit of the ginkgo, gathered when the leaves turn golden, appear along the sides of roads done up for celebrations and are on sale in the izakaya, served with rice, fried or simply on skewers. In honour of the autumn moon, whose shape and colour they echo, we see the sudden appearance of the sweet or savoury *dango*[28] 「団子」, often grilled during events and served on skewers to take-away, alongside piping hot pumpkin croquettes called *kabocha* 「南瓜」 cooked in fine breadcrumbs, which crunch in the mouth like autumn leaves underfoot.

Away from the frenetic atmosphere of the festivals, the typical seasonal dishes *kisetsu-ryōri* 「季節料理」 turn up in people's homes. Between the end of September and the middle of October the table is lavished with large bowls of delicious *tsukimi udon* 「月見うどん」, the *udon*[29] 「うどん」 in

---

[28] Sweet dumplings made from glutinous rice flour, often served with green tea, arranged on skewers when roasted and served with different sauces

[29] Thick noodles often made from wheat flour originally from Japan

broth with a bright floating raw or poached egg, an eye-catching visual representation of the shining autumnal moon that most children adore. While on household shrines it is always the *dango* that is offered to the gods and later enjoyed as the ideal snack while admiring the splendid night sky. Around the full moon, the grocers and pastry stores sell specialities and moon-themed sweets, and you often find restaurants dedicating a dish on the menu to the occasion.

This is the period when, besides *rāmen*[30] 「ラーメン」, hot food is generally begins to be eaten more frequently at home, as in restaurants and *izakaya*[31] 「居酒屋」. *Nabemono* 「鍋物」, one-pot steamed dishes and soups served during the colder seasons, are often cooked at the table over a small stove, in pans to which you gradually add ingredients while cooking. There are many types of *nabemono*, flavoured with typical seasonal ingredients, and in autumn the soups are cooked in terracotta pots, *donabe* 「土鍋」 that can maintain the heat for longer. In the cold months the Japanese like to eat *oden*, a *nabemono* rich in varied ingredients such as boiled eggs, *daikon*[32] 「大根」, fish fritters and *konjac*[33] 「蒟蒻」, submerged in *dashi*[34] 「出汁」 broth and soy sauce. Given the simplicity and the popularity of this poor man's dish, it

---

[30] Noodles served in thin meat or fish-based soup and flavoured with soy or miso sauce, usually accompanied by chāshū and nori seaweed

[31] Small, inexpensive Japanese pub, where people meet after work to drink sake and beer alongside grilled skewers and other appetizers

[32] Large white elongated winter radish used in Japanese cuisine

[33] Edible Asiatic tuber similar to the potato, made into a jelly used in many dishes and from which shirataki, transparent noodles, are made

[34] Broth made of konbu seaweed and dried tuna

is sold at *konbini*[35] 「コンビニ」, as well as the temporary stalls set up for festivals and the mobile kitchens at the evening *yatai* at Fukuoka, where you might easily find large stainless-steel cauldrons in which the ingredients float, set up as if they were a fishing game for children.

There are other soups and broths typical of the autumn, such as a soup from *matsutake* 「松茸」 mushrooms, a prized and rare type of aromatic mushroom that only grow beneath certain pines in this season, usually served in a small teapot called a *dobin* 「土瓶」. Mushrooms and pumpkins are also the seasonal ingredients most used in vegetable *tenpura*[36] 「天ぷら」, to the point of being placed as appealing golden crowns on *donburi*[37] 「丼」.

In a country that loves and knows its fish inside out, the *sanma* 「秋刀魚」 grilled in salt and served with soy sauce, *daikon* or lime juice, it is a wholly autumnal speciality. The *sanma* is a small blade-like fish found along the north-east coast of Hokkaidō in this season and popular as a delicacy in all Japan, even more than crab, which appears in coastal towns towards the end of November and is considered a winter speciality.

In Japan, the autumn is also the season for chestnuts, *kuri* 「栗」 in Japanese, used as the basis for many recipes, the fragrance spreading down the streets where old people sell cones of them heated up on small piles of burning charcoal. One of the season's most famous dishes is Japanese chestnut

---

[35] Store open 24 hours a day whose name derives from 'konbinience' the Japanese pronunciation of the English word 'convenience'. They sell a range of ready made and packaged foods, and toiletries, but also act as newsagent and chemist. They often have an ATM and sell tickets for events

[36] Commonly called 'tempura', it is a cooking method that consists in covering pieces of food, in particular vegetables and seafood, in frozen batter, to then fry them in sesame oil to obtain a light, crunchy result

[37] Japanese rice-bowl dish with a wide variety of condiments and side dishes

rice, *kuri-gohan* 「栗ご飯」. The boiled chestnuts with their bright yellow colour stand out against the pure white of the rice, echoing the shades of autumn foliage. In its simplicity, the recipe is very popular in Japanese homes, where it is enriched with ingredients such as *sake* and soy sauce, and traditionally prepared using *shinmai* 「新米」, the recently harvested rice typical of autumn. While the battle of colours begins outside, in the homes of the Japanese, a plate of fragrant steamed *shinmai*, flavoured with ginkgo nuts, sweet potatoes or chestnuts, is the nicest thing to eat 'en famille'.

Besides the delicious *kuri-manjū* 「栗饅頭」, soft sweet nuggets filled with chestnut cream, other traditional Japanese autumn pastries are made with this filling. For example, a generous windfall of *momiji-manjū* 「紅葉饅頭」, appears in the windows of the pastry shops between Hiroshima and Miyajima Island: made from buckwheat and rice, they are confectionary shaped like a maple leaf. Usually filled with *azuki* jam, cream or chocolate, in autumn more than the other seasons they are as ubiquitous as the leaves fluttering around the stores all over Japan, and often filled with chestnut cream too.

Likewise, all the fresh fruit of autumn, that seems to take on the hues of the mountains of Japan in mid-November, becomes the main ingredient for many fresh and manufactured desserts, such as jams, jellies and ice creams.

While green tea drunk hot is even nicer than cold in the summer, there are also other drinks that are best in this season. *Sake,* for instance, is usually produced in winter from new rice, pasteurised and aged through spring and summer, and the autumn is the best time to drink it, above all in the types that can be drunk at room temperature. Then there are typically autumnal varieties of *sake* like Doburoku, Hiyaoroshi and Akiagari, only to be had in this season.

Climate

Autumn is a season keenly awaited by the Japanese after summer months that don't so much have fiery colours as fiery temperatures. The high humidity and rains gradually make way for pleasant cool weather that give the Japanese the chance to enjoy going for a walk at all hours of the day, often leaving them uncertain about the right way to dress, so you might well meet people in t-shirts walking alongside people wearing winter coats.

However, the dry season only comes to a close at the end of September, a month peppered with typhoons and summer heat, to the extent that in the south of the country one might not be aware of a change in season until the middle of October.

October is the month when layers of mist shroud the tall cedar woods, rather like the clothing we have to put on: thicker as the evening falls.

Then, in November, the woods, run through by a blaze of reds and oranges, are damp and cold, and in the hills the air tingles the skin. And while Mount Fuji-san shows off his new white hat of dusted snow, in Hokkaidō the first flakes settle in towns and villages and people put on extra warm layers.

In the month of December, the season embraces the full arrival of the cold: powdery snow will begin to fall on the denuded forests, transforming them into emaciated ridges of silver wedged between the sinuous profiles of the Japanese Alps. Then, with a bit of luck, in the last days of autumn some ski slopes are welcoming their first visitors, just before the season of mild colours definitively makes way for freezing white.

← Find out more about autumn in Japan

Shirakawa-gō
白川郷

*Lost in the day-to-day, here it is simplicity
that invades the heart and takes the name of serenity...
Here they teach us the incredible beauty of living simply,
and I'm happy to be here, in Japan with you*

Opening my eyes, I am wrapped in the warmth of an embrace, beneath the soft duvet and above one of the most comfortable *futon*[38] 「布団」 I've ever slept on. The air, steeped in the smell of *tatami*[39] 「畳」 , moves around a dust-filled beam, in a hovering silence like that of snow or water in a glass sphere.

I recognise the golden aura that makes this light different to any other in the world, and I'm happy that it has found a way to sneak into the house. To remind me where I am. Making this place and me intensely real.

It is only a few days since October opened the dance of autumn; only a few hours since I returned to the place I now call home rather than Japan.

I don't understand how the alarm managed to expand time, and one more minute under the covers turned into half an hour. Suddenly there is a whirlwind of clothes, backpacks and imprecations.

"I don't believe it, we're going to be late, on the first day

---

[38] Thin rollable cotton mattress laid on the floor at bedtime and put back in the cupboard the next morning so the room can be put to other uses, gaining a lot of space in the house

[39] Rectangular rice straw mats placed around the floor in a modular manner

of our trip!" Gabry exclaims as he hurriedly pulls on his trousers in a burst of newfound energy after the exhaustion of yesterday, when the journey from Narita to Takayama had transformed him into a ghost.

It occurs to me that taking a twelve-hour flight, and going through all the subsequent stages as you drag yourself around in a body that seems to have been stuck in an 800 spin cycle, must be true love. It is. It always has been.

When we realise that our plan to catch the 7:40 train for Kanazawa is looking unlikely, the nocturnal haze outside is making way for overbearing colour: the small tiles like sugar paper on surrounding roofs emerge vividly on the horizon and the mountain mist curled up around Takayama begins to dissolve. Gripped by the euphoria of running late, we quickly lay our first breakfast in Japan: caffelatte and *bāmukūhen*[40] 「バームクーヘン」, the sweet pastries that signify these places to me.

Sitting at the table, when everything outside has once again become familiar, suddenly the mad, undue, rush of before seems to stop and we let ourselves be lulled by happiness, which is transformed into silent looks and smiles between one sip and the next. On the walls around us the ivory coloured wallpaper glows, its silvery chrysanthemums swaying and gleaming as the sun gradually grows stronger after the night.

Stepping on it a bit, we can get to the station just in time to catch the 9:40 to Toyama, a stop on the way to Kanazawa, the city known for one of the most beautiful gardens in Japan. It seems just as the writer Mario Vattani describes it in 'Svelare il Giappone': this country appears to have a very

---

[40] Sweet pastry in the shape of a doughnut, made of thin layers of sponge cake pressed together, originating from Germany but very popular in Japan, where they sell many different flavours and shapes as well as the classic version

precise rhythm that incorporates us too. Suggestion, pause, implementation. After our initial breathless race comes the pause, the frivolity of the excitement we feel as we wait to get on the train that will take us to our intended destination, the implementation of what we've been planning for some time.

But then, asking for information from a guard, we find out that lines to Toyama have been suspended due to the recent typhoons. There is a replacement bus service that, crossing the mountains, would only get us to Kanazawa in the early afternoon, pretty much the time we'd have to turn round and come back.

I feel a bit let down by destiny - what sort of a welcome back is this? – and by Gabry's rebuke about my disappointment.

"We've been planning this trip for months, have you already forgotten the flexibility we talked about?"

Always so rational, come what may, sometimes I find it hard not to think he's a robot, as he automatically solves any problem we encounter. In a moment, today's destination turns into the village of Shirakawa-gō, helped by a country where if you miss a train you can immediately find another: where encountering a snag you find someone has already sorted it out for you.

At Takayama bus station, we set off on a journey of about an hour, pampered by unfamiliar comfort and enjoying the incredible and poetic beauty of the Japanese forests: an army of cedars and junipers, their ranks of slender, white trunks impaled with green hats so perfect that they look as though they've been drawn. Nothing is out of place in the wild carpet that cloaks the mountains around us, that gentle profile I dig out of my memories of Japanese drawings from a past exhibition.

There are bends in the road, tunnels, glimpses of limpid rivers and shy orange autumnal wounds cutting into the emerald forest, before we descend into the valleys with their harvested rice fields. I hold my breath as I gaze at the stretches of yellowing tufts, the new shoots from the coming season timidly emerging from the water, and walls of sheaves dozens of yards long standing out to dry in the most artistic manner imaginable.

I dust off an old lesson learned after several trips to this country: here more than elsewhere, setbacks can create the strongest ties to places that you didn't even know existed. It is enough to make me forget our tumultuous start: the bus is bang on time and at 10:40 we are getting off in one of Japan's most famous villages, near the Hakusan Kokuritsu-kōen National Park.

Shirakawa-gō welcomes us with an unexpectedly warm temperature of autumn clinging on to summer. Beneath the veil of a different light, we become aware that here autumn is offering something unique, duelling with winter, which has already dressed the shelters in white as in the postcard that is famous all over the world.

A few yards from the tourist information office belonging to this minuscule settlement, the first houses in *gasshō-zukuri*[41] 「合掌造り」 style pop up on the horizon, with their massif thatched roofs and clearly defined structure with small details to distinguish every dwelling, making it unique in its type. If it weren't for the fact that we have an entire village to explore, I would stop and spend the whole morning photographing the first house we find.

Here it is so easy to be drawn in by the atmosphere of the authentic, uncontaminated Japan, miles from any western

---

[41] Literally 'prayer-hands construction', in reference to the steeply slanting roofs that look like a pair of hands with the fingertips together as if in prayer

influence: the wooden houses with rice-paper panels at the windows, so thin that a fire is essential to keep warm in winter. But the charm of these farmhouses is in the detail: the windows with wooden grills, the *noren*[42] 「暖簾」 hanging at the entrance, the powerful thatched roofs that seem to be sitting on the houses like an interlocking model; all creating the timeless identity of these places.

As we stand marvelling at plant material that becomes more durable and practical than terracotta, we soon find our view filled with the loveliness at the heart of the village itself: after passing the first buildings, taken up by artisans' stores, before our eyes the mountains crowd around a small group of delightful thatched houses, undisturbed by time and haphazardly positioned among the weak new growth of the rice paddies.

The muddy tracks made by tractors interrupt the perfectly finished seams of the fields, darned with little irrigation channels that I imagine transformed into shining trails through the thick green rice beneath the summer sun. And yet, even on this autumn morning, the sun warms everything, from the houses dotted like buttons on the cloth of farmland, to the small lake full of lily pads, right into the tangle of high meadows full of fuchsia, pink and red cosmos, looking as if painted at the foot of the shelters, as numerous as in springtime. Some escaped from the pictures are now kept in the parade of pots beneath the window or growing on the strips of earth between one rice field and the next.

Dazed, we wander from one landscape to another, embracing the peace that fills our senses, so that if it weren't

---

[42] Traditional fabric dividers traditionally used in Japan to separate the areas of a house or at the entrance of shops and restaurants, bearing their name. They are hung from above and cut vertically to allow people to pass

Gasshō-zukuri 合掌造り

The typical style of houses in the village of Shirakawa-gō resulted in the area being named UNESCO World Heritage Site in 1995, and dates back to the 1700s in the region of Hida, in the Japanese Alps of Gifu Prefecture. With the passage of time, these rural areas were depopulated because of the extremely hard winter climate, and many houses fell into disuse.

In 1970, with the purpose of preserving them and facilitating their upkeep, many were moved from various parts of the region to an area encompassed by three villages: the village of Ogimachi in Shirakawa-gō, and those of Suganuma and Ainokura in Gokayama.

The gasshō-zukuri were lived in by prosperous families that produced silk and potassium nitrate, gunpowder, two commodities in great demand during the Edo period (1603 – 1867). The houses were built with the komajiri technique that does not involve the use of nails: heavy cedar beams are tied together with thick cord, making the structure very resistant to earthquakes. Typically, they have two or three floors, with the upper floors used for sericulture, with a storage space for trays of silkworms and mulberry leaves.

The roofs are thatched in *Miscanthus sinensis* straw and built at an angle of 60° in order to combat the heavy snowfall in the region and to make the rainwater run quickly off before it rots the straw. The name of the houses derives from the shape of the roofs, which recalls a pair of hands joined in prayer.

Inside each house there is an irori, a traditional sunken hearth, to cook on and heat the living space. The smoke rising to the floors above also maintains the thatched roof, keeping out damp and insects. The houses tend to face north and south, to reduce the effects of the wind to a minimum and to regulate as much as possible the heat of the sun so that the interior is kept cool in summer and warm in winter.

Every thirty to forty years the roofs are completely re-thatched. The cost of thatching is high, which is why many of the houses were abandoned in the nineteenth century. Today, thanks to government subsidies and thriving local tourism, it is possible to maintain this stupendous cultural patrimony.

for the path meandering through the village, we would lose ourselves entirely among the hypnotic bushes of Japanese pampas, with their flowering plumes waving in the wind, silver as the full October moon celebrated all over Japan.

Then we reach Wada House, one of the two largest *gasshō-zukuri* in the village and still open to visitors, sitting impressively beside one of the main irrigation canals. The water seems to run joyfully through its interior, caressing the gaudy green of the water moss and the bright red autumn leaves, now sunk and lying on the gravel bottom. In this setting, where every element and colour seem to coexist in an unalterable equilibrium, Shirakawa-gō lives in harmony even with the spider's web of canals at its heart: after centuries of watering its rice plantations by means of myriad little rivers entangled with rounded stone walls.

There are fields of eye-catching vegetables and houses covered in creepers between us and Kanda House, the second of the large *gasshō-zukuri*, surrounded by a pond where dozing orange and white carp languish. We are welcomed into the house's shadowy interior, impregnated by the smoke of a central brazier.

Slipping off our shoes in the *genkan*[43] 「玄関」 we can hear a tourist guide already telling the story of these houses to a small group of visitors. We follow them up to the floor above, mesmerised by the muffled sound of footsteps on smooth wooden floors. Up the narrow, creaking stairs with agricultural tools displayed about the place, we reach the attic, where the dark wood almost immediately swallows the dull light entering at the two large windows overlooking the village. From up here Shirakawa-gō is an enchanting sight exclusively created to be admired. After a while, the

---

[43] Entrance to Japanese homes with the function of allowing anyone entering to remove and put aside their shoes before accessing the inner rooms

acrid smell of coal combined with that of the wood, compels us to leave the panorama and get some fresh air into our eyes and nostrils.

The sound of a watermill, a murder of cheerfully dressed scarecrows, rakish straw hats, witty poses and expressions that incarnate the place's sense of time standing still, attract travellers looking for the lighthearted photo. Then we reach the Hachiman-jinja Shrine, to offer the first prayer of the trip to the *Kami*[44] 「神」. I feel the need to do this more than in the past.

More than a year has passed since my last trip, when life was at the mercy of a hurricane and the storm of events taking hold of me was too fierce for me to listen to the spirituality of these places. During that experience I met an Italian girl who is now in my thoughts, as are the words she said on a visit to a shrine in Kyōto.

"Excuse me, I must stop here," she said when we got to a small red altar on the road to Kiyomizu-dera, a raised temple overlooking the timeless city of Kyōto.

I watched her wander away from the flow of summer tourists, enter the small area around the altar and say her prayer, with the ritual used before the *Kami*: two bows, two claps of the hands, a moment of silence to address the deity, and finally a bow in thanks. When she comes back and we go on our way, she tells me about herself.

"Some years ago, before taking the step to become a travel guide, I decided to begin to pray. Every year I found it increasingly painful to leave Japan and I felt I couldn't live without it. So, I prayed with all my heart, asking the *Kami* to let me return again and again. And do you know what

---

[44] Term indicating a Shinto deity or a supernatural spirit. The Kami worshipped in Shintoism can be qualities, animals or elements of the landscape and forces of nature, as well as the spirits of ancient forebears

happened?" she asked me, noticing how interested I was. "Now I spend more time here than at home! I think sometimes too much. Since then, I pray to the Japanese spirits for two reasons: to thank them for my present life and to ask them to help me when I need to find balance."

Her story struck me so much that the following day, at Kyōto's Kiyomizu-dera Temple, I prayed deeply, isolating myself from the world around me, as I never have before.

Today I'm back in Japan, after a year of events that I could never forget. I pray and offer thanks with my heart brimming over, hoping the *Kami* receive my thanks and listen to my imperative need for balance.

Before moving on, in the silence of a shrine that belongs to the sound of nature alone, I hug the immense cedars that have stood there for hundreds of years, remembering that in Japan there exists what they call 'forest bathing', or *shinrin-yoku* 「森林浴」, a practice in which it is possible to receive beneficial energy through closeness to and contact with these massive, ancient trees. I don't know whether it is suggestion or not but the inner peace I felt after doing it is the restorative sensation that I was seeking.

Along the road to the river, some of the houses sell souvenirs and foods typical of the area. Among these last is the local *soba* 「そば」, the famous buckwheat noodles that are so popular around here. In these stores you can buy them dry or fresh, often hand produced by people from the mountainous regions.

Alongside the *soba*, the village stores are besieged by bottles of cloudy *sake* produced during the Doburoku Matsuri, the annual festival to celebrate the rice harvest and the production of *sake* held in Shirakawa-gō in mid-October. For a lover of local produce like Gabry, these places are inestimable treasure troves.

Soon afterwards, carrying our newly acquired spoils, we are standing on the long hanging bridge over River Shō-gawa: from here, without taking too much notice of the oscillations caused by the continual passage of visitors, we enjoy the panorama of the valley around Shirakawa-gō. On the opposite bank some families are sitting on the grass or walking along the pebbly riverbank holding their children's hands. This snapshot of serenity convinces us to do the same, and lying in the shade of a large tree, we let ourselves be soothed by the relaxing background sound of running water.

For a while I watch the water gushing among the rocks in a tumult of erratic twinkling and sparkling and sense the link this population feels for rivers, a metaphor for life running on without pause, in a flow that can never be curbed, only diverted. The Japanese river is also the place where carp swim against the current, making them the symbol for strength and perseverance, as they battle upstream or, spent, let themselves drift back down river.

I ask myself what type of carp I am at this point in my life: the tenacious one fighting against pitiless swells and currents or the tired fish meandering in tranquil waters. As usual, I don't come up with an answer, but contemplating this limpid Japanese river helps me feel a little more at peace with myself, a little more in harmony with the universe.

Not far away from us, a father is playing at piling stones with his daughter: in search of balance according to the art of zen from which the game derives. It's easy to wonder if that sight, so pure and oriental, is real or the fruit of my imagination, of my idealising a place that could not be otherwise for me. For here it seems so simple to rest the soul, as if every Japanese person, from childhood, is educated to cultivate harmony with nature and the world.

Time slides quickly by, much like the restless water in the river before us, in its age-old journey, made up of eras, going on eternally next to the minuscule fraction of time that we are given to live beside it, or in Japan, or in our own existence. And yet, sitting here in the October sun, as it disintegrates among the leaves of the tree it is watching over, even reflections on life seem rapid, easy, light, stripped of gravity.

Before moving on, I attempt to capture those sensations in photos: through the movement of water over pebbles, that harmony of flowing that I wish would penetrate my bones and my very existence. And between one shot and the next I convince myself that the fuzzy effect of photographic motion blur was created precisely to trap the iconic and ineluctable flow of Japanese nature.

On the as yet unexplored bank of the river, near the UNESCO heritage museum, a group of small dwellings and refreshment points arouses our desire to walk on and have our first Japanese meal of the trip. The temptation is prompted by various signs showing the Japanese characters for *soba*, often accompanied by children's drawings of dark noodles splashing around inside a coloured bowl. Only an iron will keeps us from stopping before the planned destination for lunch.

Located at a distance from the other buildings, the restaurant Soba Wakimoto emerges like a great hooded hut with a solid sloping roof, looking out over an overgrown field beyond which we can just spot the river. As soon as we enter the restaurant, we are enveloped by the atmosphere of the Land of the Rising Sun, created by low wooden tables under which you cross your legs, the unmistakeable smell of *tatami* and the diffused indoor light, in marked contrast to the view of a radiant landscape stretching out beyond a transparent glass wall.

Perched on our square cushions in the large dining room, we breathe Japan in the sounds and fragrances around us. The *soba* is served in a cold soy soup with mushrooms, bamboo and *warabi*[45] 「蕨」. With the first mouthful, the broth hits the throat and the true essence of these lands explodes, the exact taste of a dish made by blending the surrounding mountains with the wood of the houses of Shirakawa-gō. Straight away there is the aftertaste of the noodles, rich as the perfume of hay left out to dry in the sun. We agree on the fact that this is the best *soba* we've ever eaten, the result of a splendid equilibrium between soup and the consistency of noodles.

As we say goodbye to this side of the river, without exploring it sufficiently due to the weather showing a lack of respect for our joyful intrepidness, we come across some unexpected, flowerbeds of beautiful flowering clover, little half spheres of green planted with protected and manicured pink flowers.

I reflect on how often, on the other side of the world, we are distracted and superficial when it comes to the beauty of small things, the very thing that each time makes me more in love with these places. This plant, for most of the western world, is nothing but a banal weed to uproot, while here, like so many of the simplest things, it is cared for and tended as though it were one of the most important. And in this way its beauty is enhanced, easily becoming accessible to everyone.

The sun is weakened by the autumn afternoon as we reach our final destination, the Shirakawa-gō viewpoint, the

---

[45] Generically known as wild mountain vegetables, they are shoots of the bracken *Pteridium aquilinum* gathered in spring, cooked in boiling salted water to be used in soups and condiments and also pickled

highest part of the village, from which you can see it nestling in the Japanese Alps. The steep path doesn't put us off, and unaware of the shuttle buses that leave at fixed hours, we begin our climb.

By the first viewpoint you already feel catapulted into a watercolour painting: the village with its thatched wooden houses, the fields adorned by new shoots of rice and the sinuous river making its way undisturbed between mountains voraciously chasing after each other, seems painted by a brush soaked in pigment placed gently on a piece of card. And here, in the typical manner of sharing beauty, a Japanese couple - in English that is as courteous as it is awkward - suggest we carry on to the viewpoint further on.

In no time we are just above, in a small clearing where there are several food and souvenir shops. From here, Shirakawa-gō is an even smaller village, even more magical, just a handful of houses that seem to have been built by gnomes in their secret realm. From up here it is all too easy to define it humanity's heritage.

The sun sets and the cool damp advances along the lanes and across the fields, sticking to the roofs. A stamp in our travel diary is what remains besides the memories.

In Japan you often find collectable stamps at the entrance to places of interest, like temples and tourist offices, and the custom of collecting them in special books is very popular among adults, including the elderly: this sort of 'stamp hunt' makes you feel the eternal child, like so many other things in this country, so unlike the rest of the planet.

It is 5:30pm on the dot when, from the window of the bus, we are spectators of the punctuality with which staff at the tourist office finish tidying up, lower the blinds and lock the doors, with alien coordination and timing.

At 5:31pm the bus station goes quiet, the lights go out and our bus gently moves out of its parking bay to cross a Shirakawa-gō already abed. When did that happen? Exactly when did the village, teeming with life a moment ago, suddenly fall into deep sleep? After various trips, I realise there is no explanation for the strange pace of the day in this country: although in villages and some small towns busy streets seem suddenly to go silent, in the large cities, some neighbourhoods carry on right through the night.

Ordinarily the time most shops and small offices close is around 5-5:30pm, depending on the area, and you can quite easily find yourself suddenly in completely deserted streets, particularly in small towns. In some built-up areas a melody is played over the neighbourhood loudspeakers at the end of the working day, a little like the bell at the end of lessons at school, one of the many curious things you stumble across when you visit the Land of the Rising Sun. Such a punctuated and precise end to the working day has always been one of the aspects I find most fascinating and that I most envy about these places, and worth remembering in a country often criticised for its pace of work, hours of overtime and the suicides of those who haven't managed to make space for personal life alongside work.

Before travelling and living the reality of Japan, I used to wonder how it was possible that this nation, so dedicated to inner life and spiritual growth during their existence - a far cry from the rhythms and pursuit for success in the west - could be slave to an aspect as material as work and working achievement.

Then, as trip followed trip, I began to notice how Japan's working reality differed from that of the west and its increasingly widespread slavery. Leaving aside individual cases, the Japanese who work in large companies, often accumulating many hours of overtime, do it out of an immense sense of duty to their country and out of the continual feeling of not being equal to their job, their boss, or society as a whole; one of the peculiar anthropological aspects of this people.

This giving of themselves to society, in a manner so extreme as to push them to suicide in the case of failure, is certainly questionable, as are other behaviours that turn out to be common in the workplace, for example the requirement of staff to attend *izakaya* evenings with their boss or entrenched corporate chauvinism.

However, going further into a culture and a people reveals other aspects too: in the case of Japan, as in other developed countries, a large number of employees and shopkeepers end their working day at 5pm without erring by a second, immediately returning home to their family life, in other words to 'what really matters'.

I lose myself in these reflections on our return journey, full of bends swallowed up in the darkness of the mountains and woods. From time to time, we slow down for roadworks and the thousands of decorations lit up like Christmas, flickering in the night along the motorway.

I'm lulled by a sense of being protected that I haven't felt for some time: I listen to the driver talking to the passengers; he tells us where we are and how long until the next stop, in the low tone ideal for not waking passengers who are asleep. Then I watch his assistant, diligently making notes on a timetable and travel schedule. A society where every piece of the puzzle fits perfectly, a magnificent drawing where not even the joins show, a machine that instils a security that would be utopia across the ocean.

In a Takayama where there is no one out and about, along one of the main shopping streets we find a restaurant that's still open for supper: Takumiya Yasukawa, a restaurant on two floors hidden behind a sign drawn in *kanji*[46] 「漢字」. There we have a great opportunity to taste the typical meat of the zone, Hida beef, a breed of cattle related to the more famous Kōbe beef.

Each table in the restaurant has a gas fire bowl in the centre and a large grill on which to cook your own food. The menu includes cuts of meat of all types, accompanied by seasonal vegetables such as *shiitake*[47] 「椎茸」 mushrooms, peppers, onions and pumpkin, a bowl of rice and the ubiquitous *miso*[48] 「味噌」 soup.

Placing the little rectangles of meat on the grill, we laugh at the flames that every so often give off drops of fat, at the vegetables getting scorched here and there, and a portion of innards that, despite being very much appreciated in Japan, doesn't appeal to us in the least.

The meat is delicious, different from every other sort of meat I've ever eaten, just as our laughter is different on this first day together on the other side of the world: light-hearted, straightforward, genuine laughter, which perhaps we had both been expecting for a while.

There is a serenity about the sleeping streets of Takayama. The cool temperature throngs down from the mountains and descends on the city, slipping down the roads at small junctions. I've only been here a day and I already feel at home, as if I've walked down these streets a thousand times, as if I've lived all this before in another life. A student

---

[46] Logographic characters originating in China and integrated in the Japanese writing system in 500 C.E.

[47] Mushrooms native to the Asiatic east, with a pronounced taste of wood

[48] Seasoning made from fermenting soybeans, salt and kōji-kin mushrooms

in school uniform overtakes us on her bicycle, riding through the silence of the city alleyways. I watch her disappear around a corner, envying her and thinking how lucky she is to have been born in a country where she need have no fear of her city's deserted streets. I think of Japan and people born here as if protected by a bell jar: everyone seems free of most of the worries we are saddled with in our daily lives in the west; for instance, children and young people not knowing danger and the adult's continual anxiety of having to watch over them. I feel jealousy towards the ingenuity that is denied us from youth, in the road as in society...

At the start of my trip, in the land I call home, I still have so many observations to make, so many answers to find and so many spectres of which to rid myself.

And yet every step, from north to south, will help me to re-invent myself, to pick out the best bits and drop the less good. Because whispering about life's sad moments in these streets takes them away, far away, it separates me from them with the delicacy the first autumn leaves separate from their trees. In this way, through the beauty of places and their stories, I will free myself from the old and grow new leaves.

I enjoy musing on this as I lie curled under the covers on the *futon*, holding tight to Gabry, already aware that it won't be easy for me to leave all that I've just found again: the ability to be born anew these places offer me.

Seeking comfort in him that I cannot have, I hug him. Then sleep gently enfolds me, and with it the finest consolation: at the start of our journey, it is good to think of all the moments waiting to be shared together here. Of all the things still to be told and all the wounds to be healed.

Travel Notes

The village of Ogimachi, known by the name of Shirakawa-gō, is surrounded by the Japanese Alps in Gifu Prefecture, in the valley of the River Shō-gawa. Sitting among the mountains of the historical region of Hida and only accessible by road on the tourist bus from Takayama and Kanazawa, the village is subject to among the most abundant snowfalls in Japan from December to March, the period in which its characteristic appearance attracts many tourists.

The places of interest are split between the World Heritage Site, which includes the historical hamlet of gasshō-zukuri houses, and the nature area around the thermal villages of Hirase and Oshirakawa, rich with rural delights such as the hot springs at the foot of Mount Haku-san, one of the three sacred mountains of Japan, the virgin beech woods of Hakusan Kokuritsu-kōen National Park, and the Shiramizu-no-taki Falls.

The village lends itself to day trips, but you can also stay in one of the farms converted into B&Bs known as minshuku.

From Ogimachi you can take the bus to Gokayama, a less touristic rural area containing the small, charming villages of Suganuma and Ainokura, where the houses are also gasshō-zukuri.

Day Trip:
* Travel by bus from Takayama to Shirakawa-gō
* Visit one of the large gasshō-zukuri, Kanda House or Wada House
* Visit the Hachiman-jinja Shrine in the tall cedar woods
* Cross the wooden Deai-bashi Bridge suspended over River Shō-gawa
* Lunch on local soba and mountain vegetables
* Admire panoramic views from the Tenshukaku-tenbōdai Observatory, situated in the northern part of the village
* Return to Takayama

Typical Products and Souvenirs:
* Box of fresh soba with ready-made sauces, noren and other local souvenirs
* Doburoku, unfiltered sake

Takayama
高山

*All day is pure waiting for the rows of floats
coming to line the route to the temple.
Above them soar the wooden towers
reigned over by wrestling dragons and demons,
at war before nightfall.
The lions dance and snap their jaws
among the tall cedar woods of the shrine
while the stands follow the contour of the river,
a rainbow of gazebos, gazing down
on the wake left by the silent carp...*

The morning has a coolness smelling of the mountains. From a refuge of warm covers fragrant of *tatami* comes a courageous awakening to remind us Japan is waiting to be discovered, on a day whose importance seems palpable.

As on every 9 and 10 October, Takayama gets ready to welcome the season of the red maples and offer up prayers for a generous rice harvest. They are the days of Hachiman Matsuri, the autumn festival that draws visitors from all over Japan, one of the most popular annual events officially sanctioning the arrival of autumn.

The spiritual and physical relationship this part of the world maintains with regard to nature and its seasonal cycle is missing in the west today, bulging as it is with an increasing number of commercial holidays with no link that could be described as ancient, much less profound.

As we glide silently along the sleepy streets, I notice that subtle halo of mist ringing the mountains around us, seeping into the conifer cover in a special way I'd know in a million. I wonder when the majority of mankind stopped marvelling at the continuous and cyclical beauty of what surrounds us, turning instead to valueless, ephemeral and unsatisfying material and artificial goods, often the product of a thirsty consumption of the resources of the planet itself. Whereas here I walk shrouded in what they would call *shinryō* 「新涼」, new freshness, to celebrate the season of fire, as one last time it ignites nature with life before its winter sleep.

In the direction of Sakurayama Hachiman-gū, the shrine looking down over the city, something is stirring among the maple shades beneath the as yet feeble rays of the sun: preparations for the festival have begun. It isn't the moment for us to be grabbed by the growing advance frenzy; we feel the need to begin this autumn in a reserved daily routine of a place protected by the Japanese Alps.

So, we stroll along the peaceful, crystalline River Miyagawa where, like every morning, the market of the same name occupies the eastern bank, beyond Kaji-bashi Bridge. This small market, like almost all Japanese morning markets, or *asaichi* 「朝市」, is set up early in the morning and runs until about midday, with small stalls of fresh produce, raided for the most part by unassuming old ladies out to scoop the best vegetables. Here at Takayama, the Jinyamae-asaichi Morning Market is also famous, another nostalgic reminder of the Edo period when these markets prospered, famous for rice, mulberries and flowers.

The stalls follow the profile of the river, a progression of boxes with red, yellow and green striped awnings, covered in huge *kanji* writing and exaggeratedly comical drawings of Japanese foods. Beneath each of these charming stores, the considerate Japanese are struggling with their baskets of vegetables, with *takoyaki*[49] 「たこ焼き」 ready to pour into moulds and dough for pastries, or in the swift tumbling skein of *soba* on boiling hotplates.

Today, even the local artisans' stalls have been replaced by stalls selling street food or with fishing games for children, and the air is full of the smell of pancakes mixed with that of soy frosting as it evaporates from the hotplates. Everything smells of the joy of a keenly awaited day. We begin to zigzag from one stall to the next, curious to see the products displayed, on the hunt for Japanese specialities and typical nibbles to try on our day out.

A young girl with a kind smile invites us to buy three of her *takoyaki* at just under 200 *yen*. By now we are familiar with the defects of this exquisite dish, which in the original Japanese version, is cooked so that the batter is half raw and very runny, a trait much appreciated in the east but less so to our western palates. But in Japan it is almost impossible to turn down someone offering you something, whether food or simply a helping hand. In the end, as always happens, in exchange for a handful of *yen* we get more than we were expecting: a wave of bowing and thanks, and a small plate containing not three but six smoking balls with a liquid heart centre.

At the next stall we find pods of *edamame*[50] 「枝豆」 still attached to their sticks and leaves. Their emerald colour leaps out at us, and they unleash a taste that is quite different to what we are accustomed to. A little further on, an old lady is keeping vigil at a stall of Takayama apples the size

---

[49] Famous octopus balls, cooked in a special pan with semi-circular indentations, stuffed with octopus, ginger and leek

[50] Immature soybeans in pods boiled in salted water or steamed, often served with salt or other condiments as an appetizer or starter

of boxing gloves. Takayama and the surrounding area is the homeland of apples with a delicate sweetness and coloured an indescribable crimson red that almost brings to mind the maples found in the region too.

Then it is the turn of the 'seed pancakes' or *bebii kasutera* 「ベビーカステラ」 to the Japanese, unmissable desserts found at every festival and the morning markets, drawing queues of customers of all ages: we watch them puff up in their moulds before our eyes, to then roll around, still piping hot, in the bag you are holding tightly, like a child who has just been given a treat.

Children are having fun trying to catch the duck with the highest score at the game stall, while a couple of kids are smiling as they taste a sesame pudding they've just bought from a lady at her portable fridge. Life seems easy here, pleasurable in its absolute simplicity, as it was in the olden days, among stalls where you win little fish and carts full of sweet things, one hand in Mum's hand and one in Dad's.

I fish around for a *baby kasutera* in the paper bag, then I fight over the last one with Gabry, and suddenly the nostalgia of that image of past serenity is relieved by life in the moment. Never has happiness seemed so interwoven with an instant.

Near the Miyamae-bashi Bridge, an enormous cement *torii*[51] 「鳥居」 marks the entrance to Omotesandō Street, where, among the crowd snaking along the side roads, we make out the first floats waiting in a line along the avenue. In the background, at the end of the road, we can see the flight of steps up to Sakurayama Hachiman-gū, the main shrine of Takayama, sitting on a hill encircled by cedars.

We dive into the flow of people, an undulating

---

[51] Traditional gate marking the entrance to a Shinto shrine and symbolically the path into the sacred world. Walking through it represents an initial purification

procession pouring from the high ground in the direction of the river, gliding beneath the *torii* that peer down at us, invaders crossing the road belonging to the *Kami*. We fall into step, but not always into the current, and slowly approach the floats, eleven in all, each surrounded by their team, dressed in a uniform of a distinctive colour, the enormous *kanji* writing occupying the entire back of their jackets.

The majestic towers are perched on top of outsized wheels, attached to long wooden shafts that rest on the shoulders of the bearers. Right now the towers sit immobile, covered in removable panels that will permit the *taiko* and musicians to enter.

The beauty of these structures lies in the velvet and other golden fabrics that cover the panels, in the painted decorations in oriental patterns, in the garlands and the great hanging pom-poms of different sorts. The complex bas-reliefs edging the panels are made of finely sculpted wood, adorned with coloured stones, cloth and gold inlay, and lacquered in black in the famous local technique. Through these elements each float becomes a style guide to Nippon art and culture. It is nigh on impossible to chose a favourite decoration from among them, because the oriental shapes interweave and throng in such marvellous display. The towers, all decked out and topped with the typical sloping roof, vary enormously in shape and colour, so much so that they seem to compete to be the most opulent and elegant, and at their peak, on the minuscule parapet where the flautists stand, we find the distinctive elements that identify the float and its history: a rearing horse, a bird with its wings outstretched, and a Japanese doll with white cheeks.

As we near the time of the puppet show, *karakuri ningyō*[52]

---

[52] Mechanised puppets for entertainment. Among these the dashi-karakuri are large mechanised dolls used during religious festivals

「からくり人形」, the crowd gathers around the float on top of which we'll see the puppet dance, now well known to the public of Takayama and throughout Japan. The city's momentum towards the heart of the celebration appears much like an enormous shoal of fish moving in unison, but we are irresistibly drawn by the sound of the drum luring us to the shrine.

Once you pass into the shrine's enclosure, at the top of the flight of steps, the lions are already dancing, in their human appearance disguised in green cloaks on which sinuous ruby red clouds are painted. We enter almost on tiptoes, while the flowing of the cloaks and the fluttering of the blood-coloured manes seem to swim to the sound of the flutes, as if the air had unaccountably turned into water. The lion masks snap their jaws in time with the vibrant rhythm of a large drum, creating a perfect harmony with the entrancing orchestra dances. The dancers' performance is so fascinating we feel disconnected from the world, in mute adoration surrounded by the giant cedars standing tall around the shrine.

After the show, the secretly buoyed crowd doesn't detract from the spirituality permeating this place. As a background to the anthracite grey roofs of the sacred buildings, stand the conifers, immobile in their centuries-old beauty. Observers of us tiny men, they seem to watch over us in silence, inspired by that vital force pushing the lymph upwards dozens of yards. A little further on, an enormous maple can't hold back its craving for autumn: a brilliant pink advances over its green leaves.

Here, I give thanks to the *Kami* once again for every single instant of the present: I can even feel my prayer grow and spread through my body, budding as it joins my heartbeat, which speeds up in the silence of my dialogue with the spirits. Every prayer is self-contained, but the feeling of isolation and connection with every element in this country is recurrent when I am near a shrine.

"Perhaps..." I say to myself, in search of justification, "it's simply that Japan has taught me to pray..."

From the shrine steps, you can see a swaying sea of heads and colour invading Omotesandō Street, from where the floats and pillars of the *torii* emerge like beacons. Borne along by that ocean of people we reach a booth distributing information material for tourists: the Japanese working there inundate us with smiles, in less than no time they have removed our backpacks and coats, dressed us in festival jackets as if we were part of a team of pole bearers and enthusiastically deposited us in front of a white panel. They dazzle us with a flash and we hardly know what's happened before they thrust a complimentary postcard from the festival of Takayama into our hands: it's of us, standing in front of one of the colourful festival floats, wearing the expressions of people who, while happy, have clearly been caught unawares. And so comes one more of the many unexpected memories that are created every time I return to this country. And I find myself, once again, keen to thank people for an important gift, while we hold the photo tight, and I bow to them over and over, although it never seems enough. Thanks to their small present I have a snapshot of today's happiness, something that will grow in value over time, will grow old making us seem more beautiful and will one day, at the end of the journey that makes us all equal, constitute 'what really matters'.

In the midst of the torrent of people, a small wooden store is tirelessly distributing a product typical of the season and its festivities: the *dango*. These shiny white balls sitting on a skewer and cooked on the grill are among the delicacies

Takayama Matsuri 高山祭

Along with Gion Matsuri in Kyōto and Yomatsuri in Chichibu, Takayama's is among the most beautiful procession festivals in Japan and attracts numerous native and foreign visitors.

The festival is organized according to the calendar of the rice cycle, with two events taking place every year on the same dates: 14 & 15 April, for the sowing of the rice paddies, and 9 & 10 October, to correspond with the rice harvest.

Although the protagonists of the festival are the same eleven magnificent floats that are part of the UNESCO patrimony, the route taken by the processions, by day and night, varies according to the event: in spring, it is held to the south of the ancient area of the city, near Hie-jinja Shrine (Sannō Matsuri), while in autumn the gatherings and parades happen in the north, near Sakurayama Hachiman-gū Shrine (Hachiman Matsuri).

Besides the display and parades of floats, various other events take place during the festival: lion dances at the main shrines, Goshinko parade of mikoshi, an altar on which the god is carried along the city streets, and the performance of karakuri ningyō, a XVII century puppet show on a dedicated float.

The most eagerly anticipated and fascinating event is the nocturnal parade on the first evening of the festival, when the city's illuminations are lit and the floats process, covered in hundreds of lanterns, accompanied by flute music and the deep boom of the taiko drums.

For both days of the celebration, stalls of street food, games and souvenirs are set up along River Miya-gawa, in the typical atmosphere of Japanese festivals.

Near Takayama station you find brochures with a map and the programme of events, whilst during the rest of the year, you can see four of the eleven festival floats on display at the Takayama Matsuri Yatai-kaikan Floats Exhibition Hall.

snapped up at the autumn festivals, not least for the fact that in this season they celebrate the finest full moon of the year, the *tsukimi*, with which the *dango* are associated in shape and colour. There are different variants of this food, from the sweet versions, sometimes spiced and with different flavours, to the simpler version, dusted in salt and scorched on the fire like the ones in front of us.

The walk along the riverbank is an oasis of tranquillity in the midst of the festival tempest raining down on Takayama. It is rather like a painting by Van Gogh where, like the messy painter's palette, the emerald green moss cushions are stained with the velvet purple of the ipomeas growing above them.

In the crystal clear water, orange, black and white carp 'brushmarks' flare and then fade in the current, creating endless pits of colour around a pensioner bent over to crumble bread into the water. Intentional colours and images that seem meant to give pleasure to the eye, as often happens in this country.

On our way back to the flat, chance leads us to one of the city's secret places: Kokubun-ji Temple, the Buddhist complex with a three-floor pagoda in dark wood with white carvings, unique in the whole region of Hida, it includes a majestic ginkgo tree that is 1,200 years old and more than 90 feet high. It is the first ancient tree I've encountered on this trip, and as always, I can't help being amazed by its immense framework of branches reaching up and the bright green of the leaves seen through the sun's rays. I stand there, inundated by the fragments of light dropping from the canopy, splinters that the Japanese tongue describes with the word *komorebi* 「木漏れ日」, 'light filtering through the leaves of the trees'. Because *komorebi*, as soft in sound as it is in ideogram, seems to condense within it the tiny glints that are now needling my face, the marvel that bears fruit to drop from that blend of green and gold, bathing everything it finds beneath the foliage.

In Japan, the language originates from the beauty all around, and their words are the ideal way to translate it onto paper. As I mull over this I wonder if there is an equally fine and fitting word to indicate the way in which the tree's wounds are protected from the elements by small terracotta tiles; or a word that can describe the trunk, too vast to be captured in one glance. A trunk marked by ancient scars, now lived in by little statues whose meaning I'm unfamiliar with, probably protective deities such as the Buddhist *jizō*[53] 「地蔵」, statues that, in their best sense, accompany and protect travellers.

I stand beneath the canopy for a while, envious of anyone here in November seeing this giant forefather entirely dressed in gold, and walk on a carpet more precious than any metal in existence.

It's so easy to come across trees like this one in Japan: in the temples, parks and even in the city. Creations conserved over time and generally cordoned off by white rope with paper lightning bunting hanging off it, attire that is a reminder of the sacredness they possess. Because the Japanese nurture excessive but sometimes disputed respect when it comes to nature. This holds for inanimate objects like stones, but also for plants and animals, which are often revered and safeguarded like existential primary figures, at other times victims of inexplicable cultural mores, such as the absurd whale hunts, now on the wane.

---

[53] Small statues of Kṣitigarbha, the bodhisattva (Buddhist monk who has reached awakening but not nirvana) who protects the dead and premature babies in cemeteries, or travellers along the road

A brief rest before the Goshinko parade in the afternoon, the daylight procession of floats through the streets around Omotesandō, on these days enhanced by bright lanterns and coloured Japanese umbrellas.

We choose our vantage point in a side street, surrounded by local people, next to an old man holding a child by the hand. From beneath the boy's little red hat, lively dark eyes survey the road, awaiting the arrival of the first men dressed in tunics and complex headgear. Both the man and child are living the joy of anticipation, one with the patience learnt of experience, the other with the excitement that comes of innocence and curiosity towards the world. A generation holding another generation by the hand, sharing the same values, the same focus on tradition. A love for the past that becomes more precious as time goes by. Found here and perhaps in other parts of the world too. Something I miss at times, like fresh air in a lift full of people invisible to each other.

To the sound of drums and flutes, the procession appears at the corner of the road, spearheaded by a plethora of small, smartly dressed children awkwardly leading the way hand in hand with their parents. I notice the latter smiling with unaccustomed pride, totally lacking any sense of boasting towards their neighbours, but bursting with the happiness of seeing their young take part in the story of a people, in a tradition that sketches out its identity. Then, following on is the first float. Elegant and powerful at the same time, it advances regally on its wheels, great wooden beams that press without crushing the men entrusted to steer it.

We stop to gaze at the display of sound and colour for about half an hour, observing the stately gait of the gorgeous Jimma-tai, the float carrying a white horse rearing on top of the tower, and soon afterwards another float, somewhat 'drunk', to the extent that it nearly gets caught in the network of electric cables hung across the road, while the spectators initially watch in horror and then burst into laughter.

This parade is a first taste of the evening display that the city looks forward to more than anything else, and we sneak silently away from the wall of spectators, choosing to enjoy the true pageant at sunset, and head for the centre of Takayama, to the three roads that make up Sanmachi-suji district.

The beautiful Yayoi-bashi Bridge paves the way. There the historic Kusakabe Mingei-kan Folk Museum looks out at an angle over the small canal, accompanied by a Japanese pine with slender locks about to dive into the water and by an *Akita-inu*[54] 「秋田犬」 sitting still as if it knew it was playing an essential part in the Nippon scene.

Beyond the bridge, a lattice of small roads snares a number of shops selling products made of wood, a material that the city is renowned for. The prices aren't cheap, especially for black and gold objects lacquered using an antique artisan's technique for which this region of Japan is famous.

However, among the prestigious stores, a small one peeps out displaying sheets of Japanese *washi*[55] 「和紙」 paper, incorporating flowers and bamboo leaves, or green and autumn-red maples: bringing together the edges of these sheets of paper, you can make lanterns that, lit from the inside, produce enchanting effects, expressions of the simple but stunning Japanese art of paper-making. Choosing the most beautiful piece from among the hundreds of fantastic and unique pages available is not an easy task.

---

[54] Breed of dog typical of the prefecture of Akita, in the north of Japan

[55] Literally 'Japanese paper', handmade from natural fibres, sometimes incorporating elements such as leaves, flowers and twigs

Sanmachi-suji, a small traditional district centred around three main parallel roads, is the city's historical area, a jewel hiding stores in Edo style, buildings with two floors constructed entirely in wood and sliding entrance doors surmounted by colourful *noren*. Here, shopping assumes a totally new form, and in an ancient and peaceful atmosphere, steeped in the fragrance of wood and its welcoming colours, we experience an almost meditative moment during which every shop window I gaze into and every object I closely contemplate seems to be more beautiful than the last.

In one of these streets the small store Kihachiro Honten, sells the best *nikuman* 「肉まん」 in the city. These soft buns made of steamed white bread have a very particular consistency, and are served hot and full of local meat spiced with onion and ginger.

"I think I could eat four in a row!" I exclaim, while I devour a second, warming my hands on the bag. In the bamboo basket at the entrance to the store, more *nikuman* are cooking, white as snowballs and laid out over boiling water among puffs of steam smelling of the Japanese cedar the steam cooker is made of. The white buns are laid to cool nearby on a table covered in a carpet of blood red maple leaves.

We go up and down the neighbourhood, wandering along its characteristic streets, scattered with pots of yellow chrysanthemums and delicate ipomeas with large lilac flowers climbing up the porches of the little shops.

Sifting through the shops with the aim of finding the best value for money, we come across a couple selling both *sake* and craftwork. Inside, I fall for so many things, again and again, as I look for the perfect collector's piece to take away with me: from small, engraved wooden bowls for *miso* soup, to a set of rough porcelain *sake* cups in varied shades of green, to a small cask of *sake*, a reduced version of those enormous works of art, each with their own features, depending on the label and area of production, with their own designs, cordage and painted *kanji*.

When a light rain begins to fall on the old part of the city, the windows warm up with gentle light as lanterns are lit between one store and the next. Around 5pm, the narrow entrance to Suzuya is already lit up and the kitchens are open and serving the speciality *hōba-miso*[56] 「朴葉味噌」 made from the famed beef from the Hida region. In the restaurant, which is intimate and very unpretentious, our table is laid up with two grills, on each of which is an enormous, aromatic magnolia leaf the colour of copper. On top is the *hōba* 「朴葉」, and on that, exhibited like treasures in a museum, strips of ruby meat are just immersed in a velvety carpet of golden *miso*, crowned by a mountain of soy sprouts, onions, fresh vegetables and ivory coloured mushrooms with thin stalks, referred to as *enokitake* 「榎茸」. At the peak of this perfect, entirely Japanese, culinary display, waves the ever-present leaf of the *shiso*[57] 「紫蘇」. Once the flame of the grill is lit, the magic is accomplished in exactly the time it takes the grill to go out. The meat begins to colour, while the boiling *miso* flavours it and softens the vegetables. At the point when the last spark bends and is extinguished with a thin puff of dark smoke, the leaf is empty and we have already finished eating one of the masterpieces of Japanese cuisine.

---

[56] Rich dish comprised of meat, mushrooms, vegetables and konjac flavoured with dark miso, served on a hōba leaf and cooked at table over a small grill

[57] Known as Chinese basil, in its red and green variants it is widely used in cooking. Also known as ōba, 'large leaf', it has fragrant leaves and anti-bacterial properties and is used in tenpura and sashimi, and shredded in other dishes

*When night has fallen, the city pours out
to invade the streets, drawn by the deep sound
of the drums, seduced by the tender rhythm of the flutes.
The army of floats advances beneath a cuirass of lanterns,
marking out the march to the beat of the taiko.
Just as autumn belongs to Takayama,
we feel we belong to the wonder of this country*

At 6pm Omotesandō Street pounds to the dull, unmistakable thud of Japanese drums signalling the approach of the night parade of floats. Now hung with shining hearted lanterns, the streets become surreal lands, paths suspended in time holding their breath before the celebration begins.

On a night that is never silent, illuminated by so many colours, I feel myself more alive than ever before. Alive, as my steps fall in with the drumbeats, alive, when Gabry takes my hand in the swelling crowd. Alive, when at the end of the street I spot the first tower move onto the night stage, ready for the great show.

There it is, stirring slowly, heavily garlanded and almost weighed down by the hundreds of little, shimmering lanterns hanging around it from top to toe. I find it unrecognisable from its daytime attire, now wrapped in an enchanting aura, as it flaunts a surplus of luminous jewels and yet somehow doesn't fall into vanity, simply evoking pure admiration. I watch it, trying to engrave the moment on my mind's eye, the lanterns piercing the night, the flute and *taiko* music that is only found here and nowhere else.

Then, from the position we've struggled to secure at the junction between two small roads, we watch enraptured as the cortège sets up and heads off before our very eyes. Float after float, the street is transformed into one endless dragon with glowing scales, and this October night seems to belong

71

entirely to Takayama.

I feel part of the rejoicing universe, part of its deep meaning, part of thanksgiving for the harvest offered up to the *Kami*, who are nothing more than Mother Earth for other peoples. I live this, my first Japanese festival, as if I had lived it before, as if in life I couldn't have done otherwise. I hug Gabry and can't but abandon myself to overwhelming emotion.

"Thank you... for being here with me."

We dive into the stream of lights, letting ourselves be carried along; excitements wildly accumulating: a photo taken beneath a float, two *korokke*[58] 「コロッケ」 bought at food stalls besieged by the gala populace, the jangling of ancient instruments accompanying the litanies of the flutes, men dressed in ceremonial garb escorting the vast towers, a lantern left lying in the centre of the road.

At around 9pm the crowd begins to disperse, and the last float leaves the main road to head for its evening billet. Next day some of them will be returning to the city's museum, while others will be kept in the large wooden hangars dotted around the city, where they will be seen to and lovingly prepared for the next event.

Many of the festival-goers accompany them to their final destinations, whereas we, exhausted by an overload of beauty and happiness, head for our bedrolls, roaming through a Takayama that no longer exists, other than for objects venerated on this autumnal evening.

And yet, along Dekonaru-yokochō Alley, the *izakaya* are lighting their lanterns. Nightlife is kicking off in the little groups of venues crowded together and linked by rows of lights jumping from one roof to the next over the few yards

---

[58] Deep-fried breaded potato croquettes, stuffed with meat, fish or vegetables

in between. I can already see ranks of customers sitting at the counter in front of a cold beer and a piping hot *rāmen,* their backs pressed against the window of the *izakaya,* each with their four stools and space for a pat on the shoulder. Hushed voices, the smell of frying, a bicycle in a dark alley, and some young people who have just left the festival on the hunt for more action. I'd stroll around these streets until dawn, waiting for the very last lantern to go out. In my travels here, I became aware that all lights warm the eye and the heart, whether they be lanterns or signs. One could spend hours gazing at them, as though the eyes feel the need. It is a need for warmth, to feel a sense of security, to be at one with the world. To feel at home.

The nostalgia of a present that will so soon be past urges me to commit an embarrassing plunder of Japanese pastries at the nearby *konbini.* However, before I manage to slip through the cash desk with literally dozens of Japanese nibbles, Gabry convinces me to offload the large part of my booty from this life across the ocean.

"You can't try every single new pastry whenever we come to Japan," he reproaches me, having a dig at a weakness of mine. I leave the store feeling grumpy. But then there's his embrace, and Takayama's evening perfume.

"You can buy some more tomorrow, we've got the whole trip ahead of us."

More pastries like more moments. The Takayama Matsuri and the nighttime *izakaya,* opening their eyelids of light and fragrance, as if they were other ways to feel part of this country, other ways of feeling at home.

Travel Notes

Takayama, in the Japanese Alps in the region of Hida, north Gifu Prefecture, is easily reached on the JR trainline of the same name that divides the region vertically. This small city, known for its festivals, has important old areas to the north and south of Yasukawa-dōri Street.

In the old town in the north, home to Shōku-ji Temple and Sakurayama Hachiman-gū Shrine, there are also private residences in the Ōshin-machi District where you can visit the traditional houses Yoshijima and Miyaji, as well as museums such as Hida Takayama Karakuri Shishi-kaikan, Takayama Matsuri Yatai-kaikan Float Exhibition Hall, Kusakabe Mingei-kan Folk Museum and the rice cracker museum, Yume Kōjō Hida. On the other side of Enako-gawa Canal, the Shimo-ni-no-machi District is a leap back into feudal times, with old commercial activities, wooden houses and tortuous roads. In this northern area there are numerous local artisans' shops selling Hida-shunkei lacquerware, made with a gold lacquering technique over 400 years old.

Day Trip:
* Stroll through the morning market on River Miya-gawa and the stalls at Takayama Hachiman Matsuri
* Visit Sakurayama Hachiman-gū Shrine for the lion dance and watch the karakuri puppet show
* Walk down Omotesandō Street to see the floats exhibited
* Join the Goshinko day parade of mikoshi and floats
* Wander around the old town as far as Sanmachi-suji district to find artisan products and try Hida nikuman
* For supper, try the local speciality, Hōba miso
* Evening parade of illuminated floats through the old town

Typical Products and Souvenirs:
* Sake from the old distilleries of Sanmachi-suji district
* Hōba-miso with Hida beef, miso, mushrooms and onions

* Hida-shunkei, utensils in lacquered wood
* Yakimono, various styles of local ceramics
* Kami-ema, lucky tags with a hand-painted horse made with washi paper

Takayama
高山

You only sense the power of these places
when you let the spirituality
of a walk along a temple path and silence
heal the noise of your own existence

The following day is peaceful in the city that has welcomed autumn. At our table, an instant coffee brings renewed awareness of where we are, and perhaps it is our surroundings that makes it taste better than you would expect from a packet of flavoured powder. A moment on my lips and I recall my love for a Japanese imperfection: instant coffee.

Today, our second day in Takayama, we've got no timetable to stick to, and no anxiety about trains to catch. It is a day to discover the city, its typical dishes and local craftsmanship. Besides, we've seen Takayama dressed in its best for the autumn festival, but we imagine it must be beautiful the rest of the year too.

So, after a quick stop-over at the station, where I stand hypnotized in front of the now famous Japanese tourist survey 'Put a sticker on your country's flag', we are afoot again, heading for Sanmachi-suji district, still half asleep, the shops closed, the streets emptied of the hustle and bustle of the day before, of the warm lights emerging from behind sliding doors.

The vestige of now slumbering liveliness can be seen in the parade of drapes at the entrances to the old stores and the picturesque *sakabayashi* 「酒林」, spherical cedar signs hung above the bolted doorways of *sake* distilleries. This old neighbourhood acts as a pass through to the north of Taka-yama where the city's famous panoramic walk lies, the Hi-gashiyama-yūhodō.

Naka-bashi Bridge with its distinctive red balustrade gives us the first sight of the old private dwellings in the north of Takayama, some of which today house ceramic workshops, maintaining to an extent the atmosphere of the rich commercial centre that flourished in the Edo and Meiji[59] periods. Here the roads intersect silently, quiet as the Hida Gokoku-jinja Shrine surrounded by a pond and linked to the road by the exaggerated curves of a white bridge, an attempt made by stone to throw itself towards the world of the *Kami*. The city's historical museum sits immobile in the early morning, providing glimpses to passersby of a slice of its Japanese garden, a lure to see the treasures within. A solitary, minuscule stall appears next to the doorway of a house: on it, protected by a large umbrella, some wooden boxes display handfuls of eye-catching vegetables. On a blackboard hanging near it are the prices in *yen* and the words 'Organic Farm' with the invitation to help yourself and leave the money in the wicker basket sitting on the table. When I encounter examples of trust in one's neighbour like this one, I always feel bewildered, disoriented and slightly guilty, and involuntarily distant from a culture educated in mutual respect, the result of a deep-rooted collectivist conscience that is far less common elsewhere.

Having failed to pay attention to the directions for the Higashiyama-yūhodō Walking Course, soon afterwards, we catch sight of Hokke-ji ahead, one of the temples dedicated

---

[59] The Meiji Period (1868-1912), corresponds to the Imperial Japanese period, following the Edo period, or Tokugawa (1603-1867), in which Japanese feudalism was under the rule of the Tokugawa shōgunate and 300 regional daimyō

to the sacred army that is based along this route, both spiritual and panoramic. In the courtyard there's an enormous Japanese bell that looks quirky next to a minute pond with a moss-laden little bridge.

Palpable silence reigns among these buildings, even more than before, permeated with a sacred and primordial aura. A cemetery behind the complex contributes to the atmosphere by climbing the landscaped higher ground dotted with small columned gravestones adorned with fresh flowers. Even the graves consumed by time, with dates way back in the past, have flowers whose flamboyant colours shine out from the grey stone.

It's a steep climb if you want to explore the place made in honour of those who are no more, where antecedents are not put to one side to rest, but left in a charming place like this, looking down on the city of Takayama. Perhaps as a gift from the living to repay those who have honoured them by passing down values that here in Japan seem to last longer through the generations, in a changing world. From up here, beside the magnificent temple with its vast and sinuous wave of black tiles, we can see the hills embracing the small houses down in the valley floor with their slender sugar paper roofs. Takayama, 'tall mountain' in the language of the Rising Sun, reveals its name as it looks down on the living, and the Higashiyama-yūhodō Walking Course watches over the city nestling in the Japanese Alps.

Just a few steps from the previous temple we reach another complex, Zennō-ji Temple, a constellation of sacred buildings joined to each other as if by astral lines. The glimmer of the beautiful white gravel zen garden in the internal courtyard dazzles the eyes. In this perfect universe enclosed in a few square yards, I am saddened to see some tourists ignoring the established route and trampling on the smooth

Higashiyama-yūhodō 東山遊歩道

In the hilly area to the east of Takayama, beyond Sanmachi-suji district, is the neighbourhood of Higashiyama-teramachi with its many temples and shrines, symbol of the days when the Kanamori clan governed the city, building numerous sacred buildings to imitate the Higashiyama area of Kyōto. Picturesque footpaths linking them together run alongside Enako-gawa Canal and lead south to Shiroyama-kōen Park where, inside a wood of tall cedars, you find the ruins of Takayama-jō Castle.

The Higashiyama-yūhodō Walking Course, which many Japanese and foreign tourists follow as a genuine pilgrimage, takes about 2 hours (almost 5 km) and begins at Hakusan-jinja Shrine (4) to then head south. In order, you can visit the temples of Kyūshō-ji (2), Eikyō-in (1), Unryū-ji (3), Daiō-ji (5), Tōun-in (6) and Sōgen-ji (7). From here, a small ascent through the imposing maples leads to the Shinmei-jinja Shrine (8) before going on to the temples of Tenshō-ji (9), Hokke-ji (10), Zennō-ji (11) and Sōyū-ji (12). Some of the temple's interiors can be visited for a few yen, others have zen gardens, ponds and bridges that can be accessed free of charge. Some complexes are linked to panoramic cemeteries welcoming the remains of people linked to the history of the city and offer a wonderful view as well as natural trails.

The hike is really delightful in autumn when, in November, the maples begin to take on their bright red hues. If you walk south you get to Seiden-ji Temple (13) and Nishikiyama-jinja (14) and Ena-jinja (15) Shrines before crossing Hikage-bashi Bridge (16) and entering Shiroyama wood, with Dairyū-ji Temple (17) standing as its guard.

By accessing the wood, you can visit the ruins of Takayama-jō Castle (18) to then conclude the hike at Shōren-ji Temple (19) and Shiroyama-kōen Park (20) in which, in April, you can admire dozens of blossoming sakura, or cherries, under which Japanese families lay out their picnics.

Should you want to take a shorter walk, after visiting Sōyū-ji Temple (12) you cross Sukeroku-bashi Bridge (21), go past Hidagokoku-jinja Shrine (22) and finish your walk in the woody area to relax in nature at Shiroyama-kōen Park.

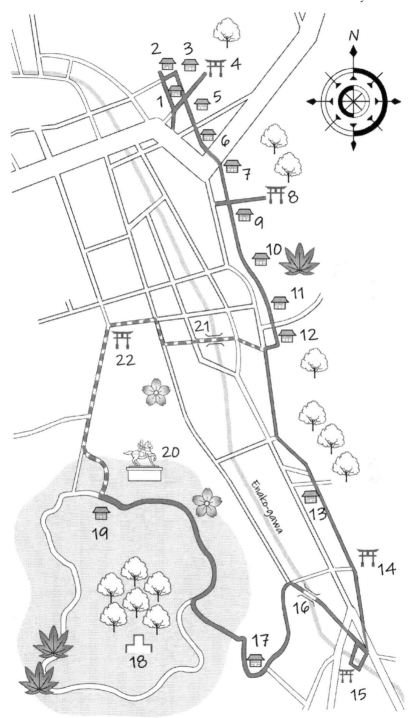

Takayama

surface of the stone pond, brutally destroying its harmony.

Nor can I remain indifferent faced with the now broken beauty of the concentric circles dug around a gravel cone. In its recent perfection it might have represented Mount Fuji-san, now collapsed on one side, surrendering to the footstep of a visitor's inexplicable carelessness. I wonder how it's possible to come to these places without becoming part of it all and holding all possible respect and care for it... Here, where past and present interlace, where silence nurtures the spirit and exalts the perception of the world.

Sōyū-ji, the next temple, welcomes us with quivering black pines, whose branches resting on wooden supports seem to dance in the air with the finesse of a ballerina en pointe. Distinctive Japanese conifers pruned to look like skewers of green tufts decorate the courtyard. Behind it the temple hides a small garden that can only be visited on special occasions, it is along a high path through the woods dotted with warning signs saying 'Beware of bears' and a new cemetery safeguarding the grave of someone who was clearly important in the area.

As we leave the main path, we become aware that we've only enjoyed half of its wonders. In the handful of miles between temples and hills in the woods around Takayama, the Higashiyama-yūhodō Walking Course is not just a walk but an immersion in spirituality that we promise ourselves we will one day come back and walk from beginning to end.

The road through Kasuga-machi District, a rural zone around Enako-gawa Canal, leads us to a short-cut across rice fields and through a vegetable garden tended by a Japanese couple bent over under large straw hats and wearing faded pink wellies, who take no notice of us as they remove invasive weeds. I stand and admire them at their silent toil, in a field that is a work of art: rows of luxuriant vegetables spaced out between clusters of brightly coloured zinnias, marigolds and nasturtiums. The recreated balance of beneficial co-existence between flowers and vegetables underlies organic growing, where no chemical products of any sort are used. It was the peoples of East Asia, close observers of nature, who were among the first to conceive and plant vegetable gardens where the crops grow and are protected by being intercropped with varied plants and flowers, and by the use of natural weed and plant pest killers. The result is a delight to the eye, a corner of paradise where the long silvery strands of spring onions alternate with yellow daisies and fuchsia anemones. I could gaze for hours at the resulting harmony, in the chaotic jumble of species that defines its beauty, and at the same time, its functionality. As soon as I move on from that joy, another awaits: a newly scythed rice field, where the bundles of long stems are standing out to dry in a wall of straw to admire beneath the autumn sky.

The walk leads us towards the last remaining traces of old Takayama-jō Castle, surrounded by a wood of tall cryptomeria, battered by recent storms, and Dairyū-ji, a hidden temple whose charm resides precisely in it lurking in the forest. The steep path toward the centre of the park, where once the imposing fortress soared, pierces the dark wood to suddenly open into a large clearing where Shiroyama-kōen is located, a park filled with dozens of *sakura*. I try to imagine it in an explosion of pink and white, with families sitting on their picnic rugs beneath a shower of soft petals as they eat *onigiri*[60] 「お握り」 and cherry cakes, although now, under an autumn sky studded with white clouds, it is the violent red of the acers that is devouring the green of the leaves. A group of schoolchildren larks about with their young

---

[60] Famous rice balls wrapped in crunchy seaweed with various fillings, sold in all convenience stores or made at home to eat with family and friends

teachers: an agitation of little yellow and red hats with soft, piping voices. With them comes the joy of being able to play beneath this Japanese autumn, to eat beneath the next unforgettable spring...

In the afternoon, far from the rural face of Takayama, Sanmachi-suji district is an ancient city bathed in rain. Small lanterns hanging outside the stores light up early, reflected in the mirror of water covering the historic roads, the smell of wet wood invades the air, and we find the distilleries have opened their doors for *sake* tastings.

Taking refuge in one of them, we pass beneath the great straw sphere habitually hanging over the entrance to these workshops where rice is transformed into Japan's most famous drink. Once inside I lose Gabry between one rack and another, as he is focussed on finding the right *junmai-daiginjō* 「純米大吟醸」, a fine variety of *sake* with no added alcohol and an incredibly delicate taste.

In part to warm myself up, in part for pleasure, equipped with the small ceramic cup the distillery gave me at a cost of about 300 *yen*, I try several different *sake*, and end up wondering if I will be able to walk all the way home. I am saved by Gabry and two piping hot *nikuman*, which we eat not long afterwards on the banks of the river, a necessary snack to soften the effects of alcohol and hunger.

We stay listening to the quiet murmur of the water until the swishing rain needling the surface becomes deafening. Then the food tents set up for the recent festival give us shelter once again: in the good company of some steaming *yakisoba*[61] 「焼きそば」 and cuttlefish skewers, as the rain

---

[61] Wheat flour noodles stir-fried on the griddle with kale, carrots and other ingredients such as meat or fish, then mixed with sweetish yakisoba sauce. A speciality of street food typically found on Japanese festival stalls

beating down on the roofs of the stall fails to dull the smell of cooking or the comfort found among huge pots of *oden,* on the contrary intensifying the colours and the unstoppable life twirling around.

It is Japanese rain, which doesn't cause irritability and chaos as it does on the other side of the world, but adds a filter of wonder to everything. It was what I loved from my first day, in a not too distant summer, when I arrived in a vivid and rainy Tōkyō that smelled of the recently passed storm, of the ocean and of home.

"Why are you buying another one?"

As a child, whenever I was chided without understanding the reason, I would stand there for a few seconds, feeling guilty about something I was unaware of.

"Don't you think one for home might be enough?" Gabry is looking at the grill I'm holding, the *shichirin*[62] 「七輪」, identical to the one in the shopping basket he's carrying. Only then do I understand his question, the chiding that hides the sweetness of an important change.

The events of the last year have been the result of painful choices, turning some things into memories and others into my present. It was understanding how, at the point where you realise you are drowning, you have to face up to a new beginning if you want to survive and breathe freely again. However, just as we decide to rise to the surface, the lungs burst in uncontrollable pain. Above all, the pain stems from the fight with ourselves, from seeking to accept the desperate egoism that urges us to follow our own dreams. Our own happiness.

I'll get the chance to tackle the pain, here, in the country

---

[62] Small, light-weight diatomite grill for cooking food at table

where just a few years before I discovered a new life, another way of finding myself and the joy of existing. But now is not the moment. I put back the little grill, realising that certain changes hurt us, but in one way or another they help us to move forward, to make a new beginning. For example, I must begin to think that possessions aren't mine but ours, to be shared in a physical space, created with shared passions, dreams and projects.

I don't know if this is the path to serenity, but I like to think so, then outside the store Gabry hugs me and plants a kiss on my brow. In my hand, neatly wrapped, the single little grill, memory of a shared Takayama. Of a wound that is still fresh but that the air here seems to be healing swiftly.

In the late afternoon, Suzuya welcomes us, full to bursting as the day before, and dishes that, as in every Japanese small restaurant, are the pure essence and representation of surrounding places.

Today we are keen to try two more local specialities, *sukiyaki* 「すき焼き」 and *shabu-shabu* 「しゃぶしゃぶ」, both based on Hida beef and cooked at the table over typical small gas stoves. Using different methods, both are cooked in a special container, the ingredients are added in a precise order and flavoured with a soy-based sauce, to create a delicious broth to be eaten at the end of the meal. Gabry opts for a *sukiyaki* cooked in a wok, while I choose the *shabu-shabu*, which requires more water and is cooked in a pan.

"I think this has become my new favourite Japanese dish!" exclaims Gabry at the first taste of his successful medley of ingredients. Whereas I am struggling with a pan of boiling water where, due to my lack of skill, the broth seems to be having difficulty absorbing the flavours, with the result that we laugh our heads off and spend the rest of the meal enjoying our joke: "This *shabu-shabu* is truly... *sciapu-sciapu!*"[63]

On the way home, the consolation for my rather bland supper is found by evening shopping at Takumi-kan. This store on two floors in the heart of Takayama knows how to send you into raptures, literally, thanks to its fantastic selection of Japanese artisan products in wood, porcelain and fabric. With reasonable prices, you can find objects in elegant and sophisticated or more rustic styles like those sold in Sanmachi-suji district.

The rain is getting chilly, and Takayama will soon be a memory. Back at the apartment, which has become the Japanese home in a life that hasn't started yet, we gaze out of the window at the impenetrable darkness outside: a few matters of business, a load in the washing-machine, a warm shower and one more day before moving on.

We are still here and yet almost feel we're on our way, a little like one of our cases, bursting with fragile souvenirs, which is already travelling to the next destination, entrusted to the *Takkyūbin*[64] 「宅急便」 courier service.

For here it is so easy to hand over to others, knowing people will take as much care as they would if it were their own. Whether it is a case, or oneself. I adore this serviceability, the ease with which we can trust and rely; a thing that is impossible elsewhere, in that now lack of trust towards others is a constant in society and people.

I want to go on for a bit longer feeling protected and pampered by this house, these places, by Gabry's hug, by a daily routine that has become crisp autumn evenings,

---

[63] The Italian word 'sciapo' – pronounced shapo - means tasteless

[64] Leading Japanese courier company: highly reliable, useful for tourists to send bags between hotels and recognizable by the black cat symbol

steaming cups of tea and another chocolate *bāmukūhen* bought from a traditional pastry shop near Omotesandō Street. I want to hand over my pain to these places, to their spirituality, so it can heal invisible but deep wounds.

"I know I shouldn't think about it, after all it's only our third day, but do you know what else I'll miss when it's all over? The sweetness of this doughnut, almost a pudding really... to be able to eat one, just like that, any time I want..."

"I promise you; when we are back on the other side of the world I will make you a perfect 'doughpudding'!" exclaims Gabry with that eternally playful boyish look of his that dispels every shadow.

I want to believe him, to think that everything will carry on like this, that a homemade doughpudding will be the same as a *bāmukūhen*, but I know that returning will catapult us back into our problems and fears, the difficulty of putting the pieces of the past back together to build a future with this happiness tasting of doughpudding.

Besides, if it's true that happiness often follows sacrifice, it might be all right to have sad days without doughpudding... before it becomes a daily possibility.

It might be all right to live the pain before finally healing from it.

Travel Notes

The old district to the south of Yasukawa-dōri Street was a very prosperous commercial area from the time the Takayama Jinya was built, 300 years ago, used then as a government residence for samurais, and still visitable today. This zone includes the Sanmachi-suji district, still well preserved in its traditional buildings and the homes of the wealthy merchants constructed in fine woods such as cypress and cedar, at one point banned and therefore stained in soot to remain hidden from the authorities. Today the dark colour of the timber persists as does the Sanmachi Yosui, the water that runs along the canals at the side of the roads and was once put to domestic use.

Besides the famous red Naka-bashi Bridge, with its magical nighttime illumination, and the Jinyamae-asaichi Morning Market, there are several art shops and museums, among which the excellent Hida Takayama Machi-no-hakubutsukan Town Museum.

In the three streets comprising Sanmachi-suji district, today in part populated by souvenir shops, cafés and restaurants, you can still feel the vibrancy of the old emporiums full of local ceramics and sake production premises. The area of Takayama is well suited to making sake thanks to the excellent quality of the rice and the mountain water, with several internationally renowned distilleries where you can taste many different types.

Day Trip:
* Visit the Jinyamae-asaichi Morning Market and the old city by crossing Naka-bashi Bridge
* Take the Higashiyama -yūhodō Walking Course, a journey through nature and temples
* Lunch at the stalls at Takayama Hachiman Matsuri
* Spend the afternoon visiting museums and local stores
* Dine on shabu-shabu, sukiyaki or yakiniku with Hida beef

Typical Products and Souvenirs:
* Ichii Ittō-bori, sculptures made of wood from the Ichii, a yew tree common in the region
* Shichirin, small diatomite grills
* Sarubobo, red doll good-luck charms

Kanazawa
金沢

In autumn, everything is fired
with new life before the end,
every colour is beauty making way for what will come.
So the maples are gripped by a thousand fiery shades,
the moss heaves with emerald hues.
This time of year, I thought I knew so well,
yet everything is new, showing itself afresh.
And even a sudden rain is fragrant with joy

A white sky rests on the high, sinuous shoulders of Taka-yama, swathing it in a light rain that breaks up in the air. A day of autumn in the annual procession towards winter.

I feel a wealth of newfound love waking up in this poised, peaceful world, listening to the rhythm of the water jangling in the gutter as I sip my new Japanese coffee. On the other side of the planet, a rainy day meant the worry of city traffic, an incomprehensible irritation towards our fellow man consuming us instead of these gentle sounds. Uncontaminated. Indispensable.

Sliding the glass doors open I go out onto the balcony and find the fog sitting in layers on the wood, and a child wobbling his way around the puddles, raincoat shielding his schoolbag from the rain; and his mother holding a transparent umbrella. Here is the beauty of the autumn rain that I can just recall from my childhood. Back then, gazing past the faded yellow walls of the classroom, how happy I was admiring the windows decorated with autumnal paper leaves. Colours that seemed almost too bright against the grey sky, against the raindrops on the pane joining into rivulets to chase each other.

Today it is as beautiful as then, and I can't help but love it even if it means visiting one of the most famous gardens in Japan in the rain, Kenroku-en in Kanazawa. To get there requires various train changes and long waits for connections that for many might seem a waste of time; for me it is one of the most cherished aspects of the trip. The moment I discover that I am travelling through the secret Japan I can fall in love with again as if for the first time, the moment I sit and gaze at the mountain's profile and its woods, the rivers and paddy fields, is the moment I implant the shapes and colours in my memory to carry them 6,000 miles away, the moment in which everything becomes feelings and then words written on paper.

The replacement bus service for the train cancelled due to storm damage leaves on time, early in the morning, in the direction of Inotani. The rain has swept a dusting of fog through the mountains that seems to sit on the pointed tops of the cedars like sprinkled icing sugar. A spell of primitive ruggedness exudes from the landscape of unspoiled Japanese mountains wrapped in mist that photography has made famous throughout the world.

It doesn't matter how much Japan has changed in recent decades, how many electricity cables cut across ridges or how many villages have crawled up the slopes of sacred and inviolate mountains. What I see out of the rain-scratched window is for me still an unusual, unknown and genuine beauty waiting to be shared.

During the two hour coach journey, even the man-made landscape offers interesting discoveries, such as the slow lanes on the roads, where the heavier vehicles, like our bus, can take their time while letting the queue of cars behind overtake. In face of such a simple solution, I reflect on a world in which globalisation is on everyone's lips, whilst in many of its more positive aspects, completely inexistent. How many accidents could be avoided by constructing a few more of these 'banal' slow lanes? It must be the knotty problem of focussing on one's neighbour and the 'everyone' that will prevent this world ever becoming truly global-ised...

We change at Inotani, a town lost in the mountains with no more than a dozen houses and a miniature station, and yet equipped with a heated waiting room. In this small space - or ageing glass box - is the umpteenth unexpected thing to marvel at: alongside the inevitable drinks machine is a small wooden bookshelf with a hundred or so books, the best gift with which to while away the time in hidden places. I reach out for a worn spine, by an author between one journey and the next, maybe imagining other places and other lives. A little like me now, sitting in my bright pink mac that simply won't blend in with the autumn col-ours, just as my eyes can't read this waterfall of vertical sym-bols on the page. Pages of that longed-for life in another place, which is right here, of the life in which the thoughts, musings and tales of an old book found in a station written in a language of pictures, would finally make sense to us as we wait between trains. Pages that for now seem to be filled with mysterious signs so achingly beautiful and untoucha-ble.

The shining wet train for Toyama arrives and in ten stops we change to catch the voracious *shinkansen*[65] 「新幹線」

---

[65] High-speed Japanese train, also called 'bullet train' due to its tapering shape, capable of travelling at speeds of up to 220 miles an hour

bullet train. After a journey lasting four hours, the station at Kanazawa welcomes us in the commotion beneath Motenashi Dome, a covered entertainment area at whose entrance the modern Kanazawa *torii*, Tsuzumi-mon Gate, rises majestically in a timeless design that is a melding of archaic and futuristic and seems to come alive in the contorted movement of its harnessed beams. If I had to imagine the magnificence of an ancient *torii* moved into the future, I couldn't do a better job.

The rain gets heavier and only now do I realise how important it is in Japan not to leave your galoshes at home. In an attempt to avoid the rain we duck into the famous Ōmichō-ichiba, the large covered market where, among fresh fish and seasonal vegetable stalls, you can try Ōmichō-korokke, the city's traditional *korokke*.

Near the west entrance to the market, where this last store is located, we have the good fortune to happen upon a genuine Japanese fish exhibition, with two enormous yellowfin tunas weighing over 20 kg displayed on stainless steel tables surrounded by a mass of people in raptures. Lots of those present are just passersby, intrigued as we are by such an unusual sight, others are restaurant owners waiting for the bidding to begin to secure the best bit.

"I should think a tuna of that size could easily swallow you in one bite..." jokes Gabry, as I think about what it might be like to stumble across an animal of that size at sea, pretending it's just a simple, innocuous tuna.

Having caught our outsized souvenir, we leave the rows of adoring Japanese behind us to throw ourselves into another crowd, jostling along the market's narrow aisles. Ōmichō-ichiba, where hundreds of small shops hug one another in an explosion of colour, aroma and light, turns out to be full of character due to the aisles that look like a modern reconstruction of old Japanese roads: stores on two floors from which signs of every type protrude and a glass ceiling to mimic the coloured awning of a local stall. It's almost as if Kanazawa, with its immortal *torii* and market harking back to a long-gone era, were playing with time, clinging to the past that makes this country unique in the world.

We find the famous deep-fried croquette seller, easily recognisable thanks to the enormous sign in the shape of a croquette smiling so sweetly that it has lost any resemblance to food. At the counter there is a continual to-and-fro of hands as clients quickly grab their favourite *korokke*, and we stand there among the businessmen, old ladies and mothers with children, complicit in the age-less tradition living on at Ōmichō-ichiba Market.

Visiting this picturesque place gives me a glimpse of the east that I had experienced a year ago at the Nishiki-ichiba in Kyōto: narrow passageways, a whirlwind of people peering at products displayed on laden stalls sticking out in front of the stores; colours, shapes and smells alternating ceaselessly in the middle of a mass of signs and cards showing prices and *kanji*. In Japan the typical multicoloured disorder of the oriental bazaars and markets has evolved, acquiring unique features like those here at Ōmichō-ichiba.

In the perpetual chaos we find vegetables of the strangest shapes and colours, carefully placed on ceramic plates, boxes full of mushrooms, divided by type and size, large display cases holding cuts and qualities of meat arranged in graded tones of red from light to dark. And again, lotus roots, pocket-sized pumpkins and Hawaiian fruit at exorbitant prices laid out like exhibits in a museum. Even the fish area, where the smell isn't as strong, looks like a chessboard in colours inspired by the coral reef.

Whilst Gabry is busy taking photos of a very sweet group of schoolchildren in fuchsia berets, I can't help but lose myself in front of a wall of seed packets for local plants: from silvery spring onions to Japanese leeks, from bright orange chubby carrots to phosphorescent green *wasabi*[66] 「山葵」, I stare and stare at a canvas of many-coloured elements the market has to offer.

We lose ourselves for a little longer in those colourful passageways, feasting our eyes before going out into the Kanazawa autumn, with its pale sky and washed-out landscape seen through drizzle that keeps on and on.

The park belonging to the city castle, destroyed by the great fire of 1759 and only partially rebuilt in later centuries, sits on a perfectly mown lawn stretching almost as far as the eye can see to the entrance of Ishikawa-mon Gate, national inheritance and final door to a story now lost. From here, crossing the bridge that leads out of the park, we finally reach one of the seven access paths to what is one of the most famous gardens in Japan, Katsurazaka-guchi, the northern entrance.

I forget how easy it is in this country to enjoy beauty until, for a handful of *yen*, we enter that incredible landscape, and find Lake Kasumiga-ike, a mirror of water on which ancient pines seem to levitate and reach out while vermilion acers gaze down at their mirror images. One surreal setting encompassing the two symbols of the garden of Kanazawa, historical elements of the Japanese garden tradition: the Kotoji-tōrō stone lantern on its svelte legs, appearing to perch in the water with the delicacy of an aquatic insect, and the

---

[66] Sharp-tasting spice made from the roots of the green horseradish, or Japanese radish, a plant originating in Japan that grows in mountain streams. Given its antibacterial properties, the root, grated or crushed into a wasabi paste, is used to flavour sushi, sashimi and meat

Kenroku-en 兼六園

Kenroku-en, in Kanazawa, is considered one of the three most scenically beautiful gardens of Japan, along with Kairaku-en in Mito and Kōraku-en in Okayama. Planted over more than two centuries, it was designed to be the garden for Kanazawa-jō Castle, the fortress destroyed by fire in 1759 and only partially rebuilt. Open to the public since 1851, the name means 'Garden of the Sublime Six' referring to the six attributes that make up the perfect garden according to the canons of beauty of Chinese landscape: spaciousness, solitude, artificiality, abundance of water, antiquity and extensive views.

Entering by the north entrance you immediately encounter the garden's two main lakes, Kasumiga-ike (1) and Hisago-ike (2), fed by a complex hydraulic system that includes Japan's oldest fountain operated by natural pressure (3). On the bank of the former lake is the iconic Kotoji-tōrō stone lantern (4), standing in a unique manner on two legs, and Karasaki-matsu (5), the pine tree planted from seed in the thirteenth century. Lake Hisago-ike, on the other hand, has the small waterfall known as Midori-taki (6), which connects the two lakes, and the stone six-level pagoda, Kaiseki-tō (7). Following the small waterway (8) dotted with bridges and stone lanterns, you reach the central section of the garden, which turns pink in late April when the marvellous kiku-zakura (9) cherry trees explode in their blossom of masses of little Chrysanthemum-like petals. Again in the central area is the immense Neagari-matsu pine (10), whose roots rise up over six feet thanks to soil being removed decades after the tree was planted, and the sacred islet of Sekirei-jima (11), tied to the legend of the ballerina of the two creator deities, Izanami-no-Mikoto and Izanagi-no-Mikoto.

The south of the garden is rich in maples and chestnuts that burst into colour in mid-November, giving breathtaking views from the heights of Yamakazi-yama (12), a panoramic point where you can relax in the pergola on benches for that very purpose.

In this garden with a thousand vistas, even winter is amazing thanks to the yukitsuri, traditional winter structures like enormous tents made of ropes that protect the garden's ancient pines from the weight of the snow, in particular the Karasaki-matsu. Besides which, from the end of February you can admire the plum tree forest (13) in flower, contemplating the many varieties of trees from gardens all over the country, sent from Kairaku-en in Mito and from the Kitano Tenman-gū Shrine in Kyōto. In this area you can also see the tea ceremony performed at Shigure-tei (14), the teahouse.

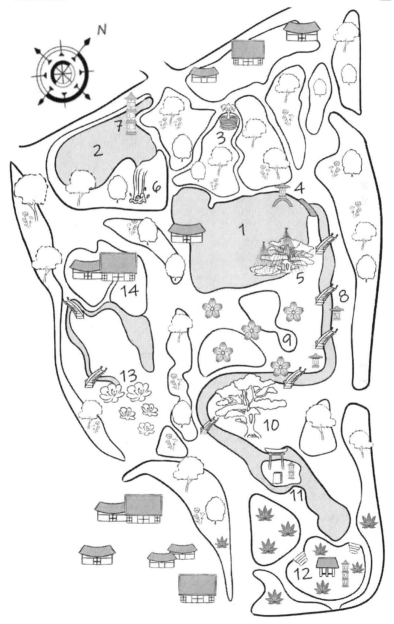

delicate Niji-bashi Bridge.

In this season there aren't many tourists who venture there, so the pond is left immersed in its tranquillity, under the murmur of the rain that distorts and mingles the oranges and greens mirrored on its surface.

Today I'm grateful to the rain for amplifying every whisper of Kenroku-en Garden, and every colour of its autumnal character. As we walk along the paths the noise of the rain on the tree leaves and those lying on the ground dominates everything else; and we are struck by the vivid black of the wet tree trunks, dark roots emerging like veins, the fresh green of the moss swollen from the downpour, and the air heavy with the smell of autumn. The autumn guise of the Karasaki-matsu pine tree is notably different. The most famous tree in the garden, its branches dart out black as pitch against the background of white sky. They wave about sinuously, as yet un-shrouded by the *yukitsuri* 「雪つり」, long lengths of rope that splay out over the tree from a point above to protect it from heavy snow, an extraordinary sight in this garden from next month onwards.

Despite the rain, skilled gardeners bring scale to the varied patterns of branches as they prune the trees sprig by sprig with great care. It is the attention to detail and extreme dedication to the trees on the part of the gardeners - who think of their job as a mission – that year after year helps to form the inimitable shapes of these gardens and this Japan.

We pause to take a rest beneath a particularly ancient pine whose tired limbs are leaning on wooden supports so as not to touch the ground. Here, near a small, solitary teahouse, we eat our *korokke*, sheltered from the rain by the canopy of needles smelling of resin and moss. Three of the four *korokke* are so delicious we eat them straight off, while the fourth, a taste that is new to us, *mentaiko*[67] 「明太子」, we like much less.

"Perhaps that is why it's the flavour that wasn't selling!" exclaims Gabry struggling between feelings of amusement and shock.

By now my feet are soaking, the rain simply hasn't stopped, and the *mentaiko* is the first culinary trauma we've experienced in Japan. And yet, under our umbrellas on which the tick-tick of raindrops is unrelenting, wrapped in my bright fuchsia coat and the warmth of Gabry's laugh, I wouldn't be anywhere else.

The garden of Kanazawa also treats us to maples clad in the first throbbing bursts of red, to winding streams and the oldest fountain in Japan, which works from the natural pressure of water. There are miniature zen landscapes created on carpets of moss, among fallen ruby leaves and shining rivulets of rain, a view of the main pond from the small peak Sazaeyama, and the *sakura* garden before our last goodbye, where autumn seems to have replaced the glory of spring blossom with yellow and salmon-coloured leaves.

After all, Kanazawa has always been, throughout the year, one of the most splendid gardens in Japan.

"A piping hot *rāmen*!"

A hot *rāmen* is what I desire more than anything else in the world right now, as my feet are swishing about in cold-water shoes. This is my answer to Gabry when he asks what I would eat on a day of rain and spectacular Japanese sights. Because a bowl of good *rāmen* would be the umpteenth spectacle of many colours, with its moss of spring onions,

---

[67] Alaska pollock roe marinated in various spices, originally from Korean cuisine. Considered a gourmet condiment, it is traditionally eaten raw with steamed rice or as a filling in onigiri or korokke

its foliage of *nori*[68] 「海苔」 seaweed, its rocks of *chāshū*[69] 「チャーシュー」 meat and all those autumn colours exploding among the egg yolks and colours of the broth. Topped with a mist of hot steam, these dishes are nothing if not paintings of the countryside around.

You could define the Ippūdō chain of restaurants a sort of Japanese *rāmen* fast-food outlet, and their *tonkotsu rāmen*[70] 「豚骨ラーメン」 is really exceptional. It's not uncommon to find their restaurants full of Japanese having a delicious bowl of *rāmen* outside the conventional mealtimes, as they are open all day.

So, we flank the city's memorial park, full of splendid monumental trees, to then pass the Museum of Contemporary Art, reach the nearest restaurant and finally enter the warm, dry dimension I've been longing for.

Sitting before my thick, white *rāmen*, having shaken off the cold and wet, I abandon myself to the unmistakeable smells, tastes and consistencies that, from the first time I became aware of them, have remained unaltered in time and place. Each *rāmen* is different and each *rāmen* is like the others, with a special taste that you only find in this country.

It is late afternoon, Ōmichō-ichiba Market is already a locked casket, plundered of its colours and hubbub, as if exhausted by the day's incessant drizzle. Out of our delicious take-away *korokke*, only a frightened few remain, here and there behind the counter, and decidedly more of the

---

[68] Dried seaweed of high nutritional value, often roasted and sold in leaves to wrap around sushi or onigiri rolls

[69] Loin pork, roasted and browned in the pan, typically flavoured with soy sauce, sake, mirin and sugar, and served sliced in rāmen

[70] Rāmen originally from Fukuoka, also known as Hakata rāmen, whose dark broth derives from the lengthy boiling of the pig meat and bones. Served with chāshū and other ingredients. The customer can often choose the consistency of their noodles

mentaiko!

Once we reach the station, I can't decide if it's the autumnal weather that has reshaped and redefined everything today, even blurring our sharp sense of timekeeping so that we miss the *shinkansen* meeting the last bus back to Inotani. However, standing close to Gabry recalculating our route with the speed the station screens rattle up the changing departures and destinations of the trains, I'm not worried about setbacks.

"The Rain, mentaiko, soaking shoes, missing korokke, missed trains."

Not long afterwards we are on the local train to Toyama, where we have an hour to wait for another train to Inotani. I'm still inexplicably buzzing. We while away the time in the shopping mall near the station, buying puddings, a *bentō*[71] 「弁当」 with Hida beef and rice, some *onigiri* from the *konbini,* and at 9pm we are back in a gloomy Takayama that has just shaken off the rain.

"Do you feel like a 'Chicken Teriyaki'?" asks Gabry in front of an advertisement for Japanese McDonald's.

"Are we really out of sorts enough to eat at McDonald's here in Japan?" I answer, surprised by such a suggestion.

"What does it matter... we must try everything, even the big Macs!"

As a result, fairly soon afterwards we are back home in the delightful warmth of our apartment with our burgers, trying a taste of the west that flattens everything, even,

---

[71] Ready-made take-away meal in a container with compartments, packed at home or bought in a shop. Based on rice and various side dishes, such as fish, meat, vegetables in tenpura or pickled. The ingredients are artistically arranged

somehow *teriyaki*[72] 「照り焼き」 sauce in a chicken sandwich. In the end, Gabry was quite right.

I come to Japan whenever I can to find out everything about this place, even to experience days like today, meteorologically speaking. It doesn't matter how much it rains, or how cold it is, nor how many trains are missed or meals don't turn out to be great. It's like being in love. Faults and differences don't come to light in the early days, when the object of passion is so precious for being desired more than anything else. They are discovered bit by bit, with time and a profound understanding of life's myriad situations. A connection can become deep and permanent if the differences can be accepted and embraced, if faults are smoothed over and accepted with a smile for the foibles they are. If the many difficulties and less enjoyable moments are tackled as our own, if what we don't like we come to know nonetheless and in the end like anyway.

"The Rain, mentaiko, soaking shoes, missing korokke, missed train, the nondescript sandwich."

So, in not such a distant past, the pain suffered in my life because of differences and irreconcilable dreams changed an important love into beautiful and nostalgic memories, at the same time, behind initial appearances, I also learned to love the faults and less enjoyable moments of these places. Not only the small banal ones, but those derived from a sometimes insurmountable cultural barrier, the contradictions of a people who are so very different, often even incomprehensible. My connection with Japan is still blossoming, it still has hidden sides and differences to get to know and accept. In the desire to try everything, even what is less pleasant, I can ensure this tie becomes as sincere and deep

---

[72] Japanese sauce made of soy, sugar and sake, used as a glaze on roasted or grilled meat, fish and tōfu dishes

as possible, and might glide through the years to become unbreakable...

Our last evening here in Takayama spent on the *futon* of an apartment in a coveted house. The city in the mountains welcomed us as though we already belonged to it. From here, between unforeseeable events and discoveries, we explored Gifu Prefecture and thanked the *Kami* for the rice harvest. Tomorrow Nagoya, on a new day, my birthday, and in a new place, where a connection may be made for a specific reason. Connections don't recognise place, borders or temporal walls. And above all, they win over diversity, over unforeseen circumstances and the limits that we all too often impose on ourselves.

When I consider I would never have thought it possible to be full of joy at the end of a day that went more than a little lopsided, or to spend my birthday in the pursuit of the deepest association, I become aware of how many limits I have already imposed on my existence. And, more seriously, on my happiness.

Travel Notes

Kanazawa, overlooking the Sea of Japan, can be reached from Tōkyō on the Hokuriku shinkansen line. Fascinating features of the city are its three historical teahouse districts.

East of Kenroku–en, Higashi–chayagai teahouse district was the main geisha entertainment area in the Edo period and home to sake distilleries, with wooden buildings, distinctive black slate roofs, and antique streetlamps. South of the garden, the minor Nishi–chayagai teahouse district hosts the Myōryū–ji Temple, aka Ninja–dera, the temple of ninja, due to its numerous hidden tunnels, secret rooms, and labyrinthine corridors and stairs, while the third, Kazuemachi–chayagai, offers an enchanting walk along River Asano–gawa. Whereas to the west of Kenroku–en, in the Naga–machi District, are the houses belonging to the rich samurai of the ancient feudal city. Having eluded fires and air raids, it still has narrow roads, the typical street water drainage system and the original tsuchikabe earth walls, protected in winter by straw mats.

Day Trip:
- ❋ Take the train from Takayama to Toyama and change for Kanazawa
- ❋ Visit Ōmichō–ichiba Market and try delicious ōmichō–korokke
- ❋ Visit Kenroku-en Garden via the park around the ruins of Kanazawa–jō Castle and Ishikawa–mon Gate
- ❋ Visit the historical teahouse districts
- ❋ Return to Takayama

Typical Products and Souvenirs:
- ❋ Kinpaku, edible gold leaves used in cosmetics, sake and sweets such as Kanazawa kasutera or yōkan gelatine
- ❋ Hanton–raisu, rice with omelette and fried cod
- ❋ Kaisendon, rice donburi served with sashimi
- ❋ Kanazawa–shikki, technique of gold lacquering
- ❋ Kaga–mizuhiki, decorative cords
- ❋ Ōmichō–korokke, stuffed croquettes
- ❋ Kutani–yaki, local ceramics

Nagoya
名古屋

How often we are directly responsible
for imposing limits on the happiness we desire,
blaming life for tying us to choices and failings that,
in reality, depend on us alone...
This is why I would never have believed,
on the day of my birthday,
I could walk under golden leaves,
taking in the unforgettable sight of
what has lived long eras,
listening to the flow of water
in all its varied fashions and
making love, illuminated by a world that,
mistakenly, I was certain I'd never find again

29 today.

Without opening my eyes, I reach beneath the soft covers. Patting the mattress I can feel the rough grass-like fibres. Then comes the smell of *tatami*. I open my eyes and here I am. It's all true. 29 years of age. Today is my birthday and there's no place I'd rather be.

For a few years now, I've been feeling the weight of all the responsibility life can throw at one. It's all there, squeezed into a timer running at breakneck speed. A responsibility that at times feels like a suffocating cloud, at others materialises into a persistent anguished question 'And now, what do I want to do with my life?'

From work to personal life, from family to realisation in

103

the things we most love to do. All at once, from the last year of university where everything was lightness and freedom to be or become, it acquired a different weight, turning into an enormous boulder.

Back then it seemed silly to pay heed to the widespread depression hitting kids around the blooming age of self-realisation, the yearned-for 30. Perhaps because, in truth, I hadn't yet got to thirty. Besides, after success at university and a largely serene private life in which everything seemed planned and sorted, why would I have to go through such sadness?

After my master's degree, and the smiles that hid fear and uncertainty, I began to doubt myself and my happiness, becoming aware, while gradually emerging into 'adult life', that nothing in the world that I had imagined up to that point corresponded to reality. I began to feel there was something amiss in my life, in the daily involvement in a society with a lack of the values and respect I grew up with and the fruit of unjustly enforced schemes, the pursuit of materialism and conformism aimed at nullifying the person, their identity and their dreams.

I make our last cappuccino in the house in Takayama while Gabry lays the table, putting out the delicious *bāmukūhen*, while everything that's happened in the last two years comes to mind: stifling the desire and resisting the opportunity to move to the one place where I could find my way, Japan, out of fear of failure that could be held against me by the world outside, always running after success; giving in my notice, a decision taken almost too late, from a company I had joined out of duty towards my family's pride and where, having suffered mobbing and a terrible work situation, my life had filled with pain and dissatisfaction; the awful awareness that, after more than seven years of memories and plans, the wonderful person I had at my side was perhaps not the one to spend a lifetime with. Then the new job as a waitress in a Japanese restaurant, the need to hoist myself out of the abyss into which I was falling, encouraged by the wonderful people I met on that occasion, and suddenly leaving that haven to risk another unwanted change, considered necessary by those near me.

In living a life and choices that weren't mine, I began to believe I was wrong wherever I went. The suffering and sense of inadequacy inside me grew at the speed of a black hole, devouring almost any desire to struggle on, worse still, to exist. It was the fear of this very thought that led me to accept the inevitable truth that I needed help. And so it was that I found myself a woman on the verge of 30 fighting depression while still trying to make sense of the world with the support of a good psychotherapist.

Torn from my life like a plaster ripped off an arm, I watched myself drift away, curling up small while I waited to rip myself off completely, as though it would bring relief from being unclear about who I was and what I wanted to do with my existence. And meanwhile, the world was still out there, shouting: 'You're a failure. Where is that great job and career, where is the money for a nice car and a house? And the prince charming come to marry you, have children and live in a fully material world? Why aren't you doing what everyone else does?'

I loathed every single word of that guide to false happiness that only now can I see in all its poverty, and yet I couldn't help but think of myself as precisely that: a failure. I felt a failure, and even more, I felt lost. We grow up in a world where giving value to the wrong things is instilled in us as children. We all set up our lives on the value of money and no one teaches us the value of time, the greatest wealth we have in our life but that is less than a sigh. We all know the value of exercising power over others and of possessing, but no one teaches us about the dreams and happiness of doing the things we most love, even if they are quite different from what went before.

I was searching for a way out of that nightmare, and in order to do it I necessarily had to pass through limbo. To soothe part of the soul's wounds, I sought to distract myself with what I love, and signed up for a Japanese language course. In that limbo I met Gabry, with his own story, like me hunting for elusive happiness, like me running from an inexplicable sadness.

After two years like this, despite a solitary trip last year, I was afraid that it would be hard to carry on making Japan part of my life. Like a noose around my heart, I felt the fear grow day by day. And the fear of losing a reason to be happy is the most devastating and unacceptable of all.

"Happy Birthday!" Gabry hugs me and places a pudding with a candle stuck in the middle in front of me. There are a few messages on my phone: on the other side of the world I would have already blown out my candle, but it probably wouldn't have had the importance it has now, in front of a white pudding smelling of milk, sipping instant coffee in the heart of Takayama, in the season I love the most. One of the many surprises of which life is capable.

We tidy our things and I arrange the futon as if we were staying another night. I clean the bathroom and leave the kitchen in order. As I close the door behind us, the house looks as lovely as the day we arrived. It is my thank you to this country, this people, for these wonderful days and the ones to come.

Walking to the eight o'clock train, the noise of our bags

dragging on the pavement and destroying the silence of a damp, drowsy morning, I reflect out loud on whether sooner or later I should share this trip from hell to paradise.

"Do you think I should try to tell my story?"

Gabry is walking ahead. He doesn't turn round but I know he's listening and has understood the words unsaid.

"I think you should give it a try. Not everything's that easy, but it's worth trying. You've been wanting to for a while, haven't you?"

"To write." To write about your own life and emotions. To write about the beauty of a place, a journey, a moment. About daily happiness, little things to snatch out of difficulties and disappointments. To write so that anyone lost and frightened on the day of their birthday, finds courage in the existence of beautiful things, in the conviction that, basically, happiness can be caught and kept in a place, person or moment. To write about rebirth, as you are achieving it. To write about your road to happiness, as it is revealed and you walk along it.

We reach the station gasping for breath and laugh heartily as we realise we've just dragged over 110 pounds of luggage on the umpteenth race to catch a train out of Takayama.

After only two and a half hours, Nagoya gives us a gentle welcome: at the exit to the heaving station, behind an enormous pastry shop window, shining steel skewers turn slowly; on top of them are carpets of fine sponge cake layered closely on top of each other, creating a roll of impressive dimensions. The production of a *bāmukūhen*, our favourite cake, is a fairy-tale spectacle worthy of Willy Wonka's chocolate factory.

It is this unexpected and delicious sight that ushers us into the city known for state-of-the-art commercial and technological strength. A city of high, slender skyscrapers, men in jackets and ties vanishing into taxis in the maze of roads between soaring crystal parallelepipeds, with advertising screens covering every corner. Here and there, crushed by shining giants, is a small, old house counting the days before a bulldozer uproots it to make room for yet another skyscraper. In this, Nagoya seems to have undergone a hurried metamorphosis, flashier and less elegant than that of Tōkyō, which it vainly tries to resemble.

The area around the station is swarming with affordable hotels and apartments, the homes of the businessmen that come and go more often than not stopping in the city just for a night. Here every hotel has rooms equipped with the bare essentials. Used to the spacious apartment we have just left, the typical rooms of the business hotels now seem like cells where we can hardly find space for our albeit overweight luggage.

We try our best to organise things so as to have at least minimal living space, to then plunge back into the indefatigable wave marking the station's regular rhythms, for the local train on the Tōkaidō line heading towards the outskirts to the south of the city. Jingūmae is our stop to visit the famous Atsuta-jingū Shrine.

Before entering the park, which wraps itself around its shrine in a way that recalls Tōkyō's Yoyogi-kōen Park and Meiji-jingū Shrine, I experience another glimpse of the swift transformation of the city of Nagoya: life has moved to the station, now the city's nerve centre, leaving rows of abandoned stores with fading signs and a desolate picture of modernity advancing.

Welcoming us at the entrance to one of Japan's most famous shrines is a lengthy avenue of ginkgoes on the point of turning gold. In the slanting autumn light hitting the intense yellow of the leaves, the avenue becomes an inde-scribable shower of colour and lazy dancing leaves. Walking beneath this, we are subjects in the presence of the majesty of nature.

Forest green scuffed by autumn tints opens out around the mighty Atsuta-jingū Shrine, now newly restored and smelling and coloured like living, newly cut wood. Today, purple and white cloth decorates the portico, much like the Japanese children's laughter enhancing the gravel court-yard: the boys in their elegant samurai tunics, the girls in their coloured kimono[73]「着物」 topped off by elaborate hairstyles. Both boys and girls seem mini adults in their cer-emonial dress, on the day they are probably celebrating 'be-coming big'.

Here are the proud parents patiently straightening their children's outfits, crumpled by their irrepressible desire to live. It is a tender sight, seen in the pink and green tunic of a boy with dark eyes and salmon cheeks, walking around bewildered on the day that is all for him. He turns towards my camera and I catch tenderness and innocence in one shot. One single shot of the country where I would have wanted to be a child.

I offer another prayer at the shrine, crowded but silent on this feast day. Desires and thanks that fly who knows where.

Perhaps it is curiosity to find out whether, behind that shell of beams and tiles, there is anyone or anything listen-ing to our mute words, which drives us to explore the whole complex, almost as impassable as the space separating us

---

[73] Japanese traditional garment and national dress. Generally made of silk and worn with a large sash, the obi, and with accessories such as zōri sandals and tabi socks. Today they are most often kept for formal ceremonies and festivals, apart from by geisha and maiko

Atsuta-jingū 熱田神宮

Atsuta-jingū was founded in the year 43 C.E. and is the second most important shrine in Japan, after Ise-jingū Shrine. The Shinto deity worshipped here is Amaterasu-Ōmikami, goddess of the Sun, represented by the sword Kusanagi-no-Tsurugi; one of the three sacred treasures of the Imperial throne and still kept in this shrine. Like the other treasures, the sword can only be seen by the emperor, as a direct descendant of Amaterasu, and by a small number of high-ranking priests. For this reason there are no photos or paintings of the sword, only hypothetical depictions.

The complex is immersed in a verdant park with more than thirty points of interest including ancient trees, cultural buildings, towers, altars, teahouses and other scenic elements. Entering by the northeast entrance, closest to the train station, you walk along beside the purification room Sai-kan (1) before reaching the Hongū (2), the main shrine dedicated to the 'Five Great Deities of Atsuta', all of them connected to the goddess Amaterasu-Ōmikami through the legends of the holy sword.

During the Meiji era, the main shrine was redesigned in the Shinmei-zukuri architectural style, like the Ise-jingū Shrine, where the steeply sloping roof culminates in decorative logs, the vertical ones called chigi, and the horizontal ones katsuogi. Behind the Hon-gū there is a path winding through the forest past picturesque shrines such as Shimizu-sha (3), and an ancient camphor tree dedicated to the gods.

Continuing to explore southwards, you find a second gigantic camphor tree watching over six houses where the tea ceremony takes place (4), the old imperial dwelling Ryōei-kaku (5) and the Bunkaden (6), the treasure room around which lots of roosters wander freely.

Not far from the stone bridge named Nijūgochō-bashi (7), you can try some excellent kishimen at the refreshment area, while further south there are more secondary shrines, such as Kamichikama-jinja (8), and a camellia that is over 300 years old.

Finally, in the southeast area of the grounds, besides several small altars, there is a gate that has been kept locked for over a thousand years, the Seisetsu-mon (9): legend has it, in 668 C.E., a Korean monk sneaked into the shrine through this gate and stole the holy sword. However, on his return to Korea, a storm caused his boat to sink, allowing the holy treasure to be recovered. From that day on, the gate has never been opened.

from the gods themselves. High walls and a steel barrier stretching right into the thick wood, in a setting that made us think of the electrified fences in Jurassic Park.

Gabry tells me how this shrine is the second most important in the whole country after Ise, in that inside is the sacred sword, Kusanagi-no-tsurugi, one of the Three Sacred Treasures of Japan. Legend has it these treasures were given by the goddess Amaterasu-Ōmikami to her descendants and passed down to Jinmu-tennō, the first emperor. No one knows what they look like, other than a few priests and the emperor, who receives them on the day of his enthronement.

I listen to Gabry eagerly and at the same time am drawn by the secret and untranslatable aspects of this country that make it fascinating and inexorably unique. Atsuta-jingū is imbued with sacredness: you can feel it in the silence around it, in the shade of the thick arboreal canopy broken by the sun's rays, in the beauty we find as we admire the smaller Shimizu-sha and Mita-jinja shrines. Located close to one another, the spirits of these two sacred spaces are respectively embodied by water and an ancient tree.

Shimizu-sha Shrine sits contemplating a pool whose bottom is full of pebbles beneath a few inches of clear water. The pool leads into a small cave at the entrance to which a larger stone is placed that breaks through the surface of the water. A ritual involves taking one of the classic bamboo spoons found at purification fountains, scooping up some water and throwing it on the protruding stone. If the water hits the stone full on it is a good omen for your prayer.

I have a go in my usual clumsy way, afraid of offending the spirits of this country by awkwardness that is unbecoming from a foreigner in a place belonging to others. The two old men who have just shown me what to do are unexpectedly thrilled when my first attempt is successful. Whereas Gabry has a tussle with his spoon and goes on defying bad luck until the water finally splashes on the centre of the stone.

Mita-jinja Shrine, on the other hand, other than having a wooden altar, has the appearance of an intangible place, with no palpable walls, water or stones. However, in front of the vast tree, we soon realise we are in a unique place, where the edges are pure energy, in the presence of something that can't be described, only perceived. The tree soars from the shadowy undergrowth and wraps itself upwards in its immense and formidable trunk, while the massive roots, after centuries of wresting the soil, plunge into it like a great marine monster, serpent like on the surface of a dark sea.

We gaze at it in silence because, faced with such an ancient being, we can't but feel awe, and think of ourselves as insignificant. We feel we should make an offering before asking it to hear our prayer, needing permission to stretch our hands out and touch its roots. I'm happy to find this tree here, in a land that seems to understand the importance of taking care of a witness of such a long time period. To be aware of the preciousness of time and respect it is a symptom of wisdom that scarcely survives today.

Among the paths through the park, in the deep green of the wood, there's a fragrance that immediately becomes the identity of this place. It's coming from a small eatery peeking out among the bushes, one of those secret places you only happen upon by chance. We glance into the tiny kitchen where various ladies are pouring soup into bowls.

"Miya Kishimen Jingū... I think it must be where they make *kishimen*, the delicious *udon* typical of the area!" Gabry painstakingly translates the name on the entrance sign. It's all that's needed to convince me that this is the very spot for lunch.

During my travels in Japan this often happens. You begin with a list of hypothetical places in which to try local specialities, found here and there on an internet that nowadays scarcely leaves space for adventure. Then, exploring or ending up losing your way, you find places you didn't know existed. Hidden, unpretentious, simple. It's in places like these that you eat best, and taste the best memories.

The sight of these extremely flat, long *udon* attracts us to the counter where there is a continual swamping of noodles coiled in bowls of clear soup before being served. Gabry prefers to order the cold version of the dish, where the *udon* are served alongside a soy-based soup at room temperature. As I adore *udon* even more than *sōmen*[74] 「そうめん」, I throw myself on the steaming *kishimen*[75] 「きしめん」, topped with vegetables and typical pink and white *naruto-maki*[76] 「鳴門巻き」. Both dishes, which we eat on long benches shared by Japanese noisily slurping their *udon*, satisfy our stomachs and our spirits.

We head into the little shop adjoining the eatery embedded in the woods: it sells packets of *kishimen* with various accompanying sauces, and given the more than reasonable prices, I can't help but buy a supply for Gabry, pretending that I've forgotten the lack of space and abundant weight of our luggage.

As we are about to leave Atsuta-jingū Shrine, it continues

---

[74] Very thin noodles made of wheat flour that originated in China, used inside classic rāmen

[75] Typical udon from the Nagoya area, very sticky, less thick but wider than the classic udon, classified as among the best in Japan

[76] Rondelles with a vortex design. A type of kamaboko, or fish loaf, mainly used as topping for rāmen

to give us sudden surprising sights. From among the trees, covered in grass and wire-like mosses that look as though they come from a fantasy world, an *ōkusu*[77] 「大楠」 appears, another giant of bark and leaves with its necklace of cords and lightning signs. Not far beyond there's a goofy monument representing a goddess: a lady, in the solitude of this hidden corner of the park, has stopped to pray to her.

There are many more temples and shrines, dotted around in the most improbable recesses of the complex, but we must leave the peace of this place to head to another. When I leave the temple of trees and spirits, my eyes are used to seeing the world in a new light, while outside the sun is already hot and blinding.

"Shirotori-teien is a smaller garden than its more famous and renowned Japanese counterparts, but I think it is just as fulfilling..." Gabry reminds me of the day when, planning our visit to Nagoya, we were in two minds as to whether to visit a garden that was held to be secondary. Fortunately, once again, we let ourselves be guided by a sixth sense.

This garden spouts out of the city's heart like the water flowing down its every slope, shaping eight vistas or small landscapes each with its own name and identity. Wonderful views lurk among the numerous waterways, pools and little rivers that intermingle and transform each other, often framed by vegetation. The sound of water is everywhere: always different and yet consistent as it runs through and joins all elements. Everything seems to stretch out and come together around a single, perpetual flowing.

We let ourselves be carried away by the different backdrops, with the same ease that the autumn leaves run along the surface of a stream, gliding out of sight towards who

---

[77] Literally 'large camphor tree'

knows what new landscape.

I am particularly struck by one panorama in this world of water and vegetation: it is the small raised landscape of Tsukiyama, the mountain of the moon, which recreates Mount Ontake-san with rivers running boldly down its slopes to represent River Kiso-gawa, flowing past enormous, honed rocks dotted around on its bed, with the ever-present rose-coloured autumnal acers stretching out over the surfaces.

Next we reach Seiu-tei, a group of teahouses built in the Sukiya style typical of tea ceremony houses, planned in the image of a swan, *shirotori* 「白鳥」 in Japanese, on the verge of lying on the water. The artificial lake into which the building is reflected as if planing across the mirror of water is something very special. Here, by means of spectacular jets of water arching over each other every 30 minutes, they simulate the tide coming in and going out, all by quickly moving a mass of water between different basins.

Before having to leave, we watch the tide change, and the water, with its continual flowing, transforming everything once again.

When we reach Nagoya-jō Castle, at 5pm, there is only an hour left before closing time. And yet we have just the right amount of time to explore the only visitable areas in the complex, the outbuildings, given that the castle, in all its unreachable grandeur, is currently a prisoner to restoration scaffolding: one of the downsides one has to come to terms with when travelling around Japan to see its many temples and ancient castles.

The building open to the public is Honmaru-goten Palace, a recently restored building entirely made out of wood, in which the large beams evoke live bark both in their golden colour and in the smell of resin from the cedars they are sawn from.

We remove our shoes at the entrance and stow them away in the special bags handed to us by smiling staff; then we begin the guided tour, walking on virgin *tatami*, down corridors flanked by sliding doors that are nothing more than enormous painted pictures. On the ivory and gold of the panels, garishly coloured tigers and leopards with enormous eyes woo each other, according to the Japanese belief that the latter were female tigers. They twist their bodies in furious movements that are harmonised into the sparse backdrops around them.

This is Japanese art in all its strength and wonder: few elements to pierce the spectator's vision, no detail left undefined or incomplete, while the whole remains suspended, left to the imagination of the viewer. A bamboo hedge, a waterfall, a pine that stretches and creeps along the line of the sea. Nothing else around and yet everything is there. It isn't clear where, what or why, and yet it's sufficient for us to recognise the Rising Sun in the picture.

Outside the golden Japan of Honmaru-goten Palace, Nagoya-jō Castle is a giant extending towards the sky. The two famous *shachihoko*[78] 「鯱鉾」 the colour of the sun, leap and hurl themselves at each other on top of the curved roof of the highest wave of turquoise tiles. There is a marvellous contrast between the unfathomable black of the façades beneath the arches of each wave, while the rest of the castle is white enough to make snow envious.

All about are the skeletal gardens of plum and *sakura* trees circling the fortress, easy to imagine as the white and

---

[78] Animal from Japanese folklore with the body of a carp and the head of a tiger, it can summon the rain and is used for good luck against the frequent and devastating fires of the past that destroyed castles, temples and shrines

pink cloud on which the castle floats every spring. I like to think that one day I will be free to dive into the sea of petals, and finally feel like the carp that has swum up stream, winning over with its strength, to reach the wave at the very top.

Evening closes in, and around the central station, Nagoya is a sunset of lanky skyscrapers beginning to palpitate with lights, their lifts appearing like galactic pods fired up and down. The neighbourhood lights up with neon, and people, their daily duties finished, pour out onto the streets and into the station. Everything comes alive under artificial lights.

I immerse myself in that alternative universe of windows, sound and colour, and I relive my love for the evening atmosphere of Japanese cities, one of the legacies of the unapproachable Tōkyō. I smile at my grandmother and my parents on the screen of my smartphone, showing them the sight of an unrestrainable river of stimuli: they are all surprised and almost scared of such a different and distant world capturing and swallowing up any familiar reality. Put simply, I feel part of it.

"*Koko desu!*"[79] the kind girl who left her store to accompany us to the restaurant we've been desperately searching for this last half an hour, finally points to our destination and we try to thank her with an outpouring of bows and smiles.

At Maruya Honten, a restaurant hidden on the ninth floor of the station's shopping centre, you can taste one of the best grilled *unagi*[80] 「鰻」 in town. And here, in Nagoya,

---

[79] It can be translated as 'Here it is!'

[80] Japanese eel, served as a delicacy opened down its length, boned, grilled and accompanied by its own sweet and sour sauce

the *unadon*[81] 「鰻丼」 is a truly famous dish in the *hitsuma-bushi* 「櫃まぶし」 variant, in which the eel is cut into small mouthfuls, laid on the rice and served with *nori* seaweed. The long queue meant a wait of over 40 minutes, but as always it's a good indicator of the quality of the food, and can be avoided by ordering a meal to take away.

Whilst outside our hotel window the city lights crash through the dark of an autumn evening, after hot showers, we are wrapped in white *yukata* and relaxing on white sheets that have a laundry smell very different to ours back home. Equally, the portion of grilled eel awaits us, lying on its soft, pure white bed of Japanese rice. To eat it is to taste something that you can only find here, like love in the night, with bodies coloured by intermittent city neon. A world of lights that never seems to want to cease existing but that, like every living organism, must sooner or later take its rest.

So, when our bodies begin to abandon themselves to drowsiness, flopping one on the other, outside the lights begin to go out too. I drift off before midnight, no longer awake to find out whether this city switches itself off in one go, hanging on to the bare minimum to call itself a city.

I go to sleep before my birthday is over. Before I remember all the times I've told myself I'd never be able to spend this day here, in a Japan that offers days like this one.

In the end, it's just like that: believing you can't grasp happiness and seize your dreams is the greatest limit that we can impose on happiness itself.

---

[81] Unagi donburi, or a bowl of rice with grilled eel on top

Travel Notes

Nagoya, located in the centre of the country and overlooking the sea, is one of the most industrialised and highly populated cities in Japan, famous for dishes based on ingredients such as miso and eel. Today, it is easy to reach by means of the dense rail network. After playing an important part in many battles in the Edo period, it became the native city of companies like Toyota and Mitsubishi. Because of its primary role in Japanese industry, at the start of the nineteen hundreds it paid dearly in airstrikes during the Second World War.

Besides museums of art, technology and cars, the city offers numerous points of interest such as the garden of Shirotori–teien with its eight aquatic panoramas, Atsuta–jingū Shrine, and the castle built by the legendary Tokugawa Ieyasu in the hopes of a lengthy shōgun dynasty, as indeed it turned out to be. In recent years, the port in the Bay of Ise has becomes a tourist attraction thanks to the public aquarium and fireworks displays held at specific moments of the year. The historic neighbourhood of Ōsu has numerous temples and shrines, among which the temples Banshō–ji and Hongan–ji. One of the most important is the Buddhist temple of Ōsu Kannon with its famous red paper lantern hanging from the ceiling of the main room to which pilgrims tie their prayers. In the surrounding streets there are many small stores selling artisans' goods and traditional foods.

Day Trip:
* ✳ Take the train from Takayama to Gifu, change for Nagoya
* ✳ Visit Atsuta–jingū Shrine and explore the park
* ✳ Lunch on Kishimen near the shrine
* ✳ Explore Shirotori–teien Garden's eight panoramas
* ✳ Visit Nagoya–jō Castle and Honmaru–goten Palace
* ✳ For your evening meal, try hitsumabushi

Typical Products and Souvenirs:

* ✳ Miso–nikomi udon, with vegetables in miso soup
* ✳ Miso–katsu, tonkatsu with miso sauce
* ✳ Hitsumabushi, local type of unadon
* ✳ Kishimen, typical Nagoya udon

Nagoya
名古屋

*In Japan, the time taken to reach something
is more precious than the thing itself.
Here time is pampered, enjoyed, lived fully.
While in the west it is a race to the outcome,
the East has learned that only by taking care of time
we do really feel satisfied with ourselves.
So, this is the country of patience and a slow pace,
of the richness of gestures and attention to detail,
the art of meditation and tenacity to our dreams.
The beauty of the moment
that shortly afterwards drifts into nostalgic memory*

I open the instant coffee sachet, freeing the paper label to place over the edge of the cup. I follow the instructions carefully, so that the filter is stretched at just the right point, like a little basket in which to pour the boiling water. In a few actions, as if by magic, my little filter machine is ready.

In Japan, every object, accessory or consumer good, is conceived to be as operational as possible, to guarantee the best experience for the user. Like the wrapping on the *onigiri*, to be opened in three simple steps, which allows the crunchy seaweed to adhere to the rice only just before being eaten, the instant drink sachet is fitted onto the teacup as though it were a little centrepiece, guaranteeing easy filtering to make better coffee.

Another thing I love about Japan: amenities, which are everywhere here; purchased goods, even the most discounted, continue to be cosseted during use; the experience of daily routine is made simple and enjoyable; with instructions that are a kind of joke and sweet pictures clearly showing how a thing should be used.

But there's more.

The right quantity of water slowly poured into the filter makes the coffee more concentrated and I love the time needed to make the coffee as good as possible. This unhurried pottering is among the qualities that I miss elsewhere. That elsewhere, the west, where conversely time is a fragment that flies away as quickly as possible, where every action must immediately be followed by another, where there prevails an impatience to get on, to accomplish. The impatience of being.

As a result, just as the morning coffee is drunk in five minutes without the slightest appreciation of the moment, so in life, work and family, everything must come about as quickly as possible. There is no space for the while, and no importance given to all those actions leading to the outcome. Engagement, effort, and the single daily activities carried out with care and intentness, with the right amount of time given to make the outcome better, to feel ourselves majorly fulfilled and conscious of who we are and want to be. None of this seems to hold any value in a west hasty to reward those who arrive first.

I live it on a daily basis, in the morning traffic when the most basic rules of the road and respect for our fellowman are useless against the necessity to hurry. I see it in the workplace, where the race is about time and quantity, where often the important thing isn't well programmed work and a job well done, but a snatching at the highest number, handing in sloppy work in the shortest time possible. The goal, without us even being aware, is to reach it before everyone else, at any cost.

Like this, everything slips away: the hours, days, months and years, and we find ourselves old and wondering what the race was about, when even the final result isn't that clear to us.

I reflect on my need to cultivate the moment, to enjoy it fully and give it a sense, in a world and society imposing the opposite. I think of the throngs of dissatisfied and empty people who have been chasing their whole life after the hypothetical final result without concentrating on the meanwhile and whom even if they did reach their goal, continue to feel unhappy because no final result of any real concrete value was really reached. I think of the regenerating and languid time spent in my little kitchen garden not far from the sea, in a little house bought by my parents with so much sacrifice. Both the time spent before you taste its first fruits, and fulfilling that small family dream. There is no fruit so sweet and satisfying to eat as that from a tree we have spent love and time cultivating.

Outside, despite the fact that it is only just seven o'clock on an autumn morning, a warm light is climbing gradually up the skyscrapers, now awake. The lines of the buildings become clearer and the blue is reflected on the crystal city. Down in the street, in the shadow of the tall buildings, there is already a hustle and bustle of black and white taxis opening their automatic doors to extract and deposit businessmen, freshly clad in jacket and tie.

We leave our luggage at reception before setting off in the direction of the Toyota Commemorative Museum of Industry and Technology, one of the city's main thematic attractions. The museum is a vivid testimony to the visionary genius of Kiichirō Toyoda, the entrepreneur who with time and dedication turned his personal dream into that of an entire nation. A second museum, the Toyota-kaikan, is located in the small town of Toyota, not far outside Nagoya and focussed mainly on the company's historical models.

To reach the complex belonging to the manufacturing plant that changed the automobile history of a country, we cross Noritake-no-mori, a small park where yellow ginkgo trees are interspersed with tidy, pot-bellied cypresses around a central fountain.

The square architecture of early twentieth century Japan at the start of its economic ascent, can be seen in the surrounding commercial buildings, clad in typical red brick to distinguish the industrial areas of this workaholic city. Equally, long, restored warehouses belonging to Toyoda, the initial name of the most famous textile factory in the country, founded by Sakichi Toyoda at the end of the nineteenth century, consist of a block of red brick buildings that once housed the company's thousands of textile machines, and still today, give the idea of the unstinting hub of the city in which they were transformed for Nagoya and the whole of Japan. A city within a city, so that within the limits of the age, the workers had all comforts in order to work for the great dream.

At the entrance to the museum, school children stand in groups near company employees on a visit to the place where innovation and progress became reality. One feels the magnitude of Kiichirō Toyoda here, and the desire for today's Japan to retrace his steps, to be inspired by his undertaking, his perseverance, his vision of the end result and the time needed to achieve it.

At pre-determined times the museum offers guided tours in English too, but Gabry reassures me that he came here on his last trip and understanding the explanations in Japanese is easy thanks to the interactivity of the visit itself and the numerous panels written in English along the way. So we decide to join a group of Japanese, to listen to the language whose sounds we love and be told about the great Toyoda venture.

Various interactive exhibitions, the original machinery and a wide variety of demonstrations one can watch, make the aim of this fantastic museum tangible: to bring back to life the spirit and talent of Sakichi Toyoda, his son Kiichirō, and the vision that transformed this textile factory into an automobile colossus.

As we follow our guide, we hear the whole story of the brand, watching entranced as we are shown how the early textile machines transformed tufts of rough cotton into huge reels of cotton. Before Toyoda automated the processes, the cotton was worked and woven manually, and to see in detail how hard a job it was for the operators to produce the textiles opened our eyes and minds to cultural and historical aspects and caused us to reflect deeply.

"Every child should be brought round a museum like this at least once!" I say to Gabry in the throes of a euphoria brought on by an awareness and curiosity towards a new world and its story. It is curiosity towards everything around us that, by animating humanity, should help to improve it, instilling itself in the young and stimulating their creativity and dreams.

During the visit, I am filled with emotion when I think of these men's ambition, their dedication and the courage they showed. Kiichirō is one of the most potent examples of commitment, sacrifice, effort and patience, and his story an example of the setbacks we encounter when we follow our dream. As an engineer, he travelled the world studying the early cars and trying to transform his father's textile factory into one of the biggest car manufacturers in the world. But above all he cherished his dream, in all its phases, all the time necessary for it to come true, which was many years.

In the museum we follow his objective and sense the perseverance typical of this people: from the sector of the weaving machines to the first cars ever produced, to the manufacture of vehicle parts, where you can only be amazed by the enormous presses making single metallic pieces of frames. And then the incredible car assembly line and the exhibition of new models with zero environmental impact that, given the spirit of the company, I would not be surprised to find already on the market in the next few years.

After a three-hour visit, we come away with more enthusiasm than we started out with, from one of the finest and most educational museums in the world, taking away as a reminder some beautiful rough cotton shoes produced by the factory itself. Mine are in the colours of the Japanese autumn.

Before leaving the city, near the central station, feeling menaced by the unstoppable rumpus we look for a slower pace in one of the restaurants belonging to the famous *tonkatsu*[82] 「豚カツ」 chain originally from Nagoya, Miso-katsu Yabaton, recognisable by the funny picture of a fat strutting pig you often see around the city. In their restaurants, besides the classic *katsudon* 「カツ丼」 in which the pork cutlet is laid on a bed of rice and kale, you can also try the delicious Nagoya *miso-katsu* 「味噌カツ」, a dish in which the meat is wrapped in a creamy red *miso* sauce and served, with cabbage, on a very hot stone that maintains its heat at table. We try both, tasting goodness that is even more precious because it is part of the desire to enjoy the moment to the full.

---

[82] Thick and very tender pork cutlet fried in panko, a particular type of Japanese breadcrumbs

Nagoya. The city that expands time, in whose relentless rhythm and pursuit of a fast-changing world, there is the stillness to savour time.

Teetering on the yellow line behind which I should be safe from the train pulling in, I think of the wealth of these few hours spent in the city streets, and of the placidity and slowness that places like Atsuta-jingū Shrine, Shirotori-teien Garden and the Toyota museum have managed to instil.

Time can't be curbed here either, but it feels easy to read the value of its single instants, those lived slowly to appreciate their intrinsic beauty, those that give meaning to its full flow.

**

Okayama
岡山

Time, forgotten on the other side of the world,
here articulates a people and a culture.
Because, afterall, is easy to understand:
there is nothing in our life
that has more value than time itself

The Hikari *shinkansen* sprints in silence to Okayama. Another train that offers more to its passengers by defying time over distance. Some are asleep and some on the phone, some eating their *bentō* and others working on their computers. The time spent on high-speed trains seems more precious, almost a gift. And as for me, I find here what I thought I had lost elsewhere and use the time to write my travel diary, wondering if one day time might even transform it into something more.

On leaving the station, Okayama reminds us of its closeness to the sea with a fountain whose jets imitate the shell of a sea urchin. Twilight is approaching and the purple and reds of the city's electric lights seem to melt into the jets of water. The absence of skyscrapers, sundown turning the buildings copper coloured and a wide avenue where the traffic is lessened by the vastness of the lanes propel us into a seaside town where we can almost smell salt in the air.

In front of us, an enormous fish-shaped sign marks the entrance to a long shopping arcade, Okayama Ekimae-shōtengai, a pedestrian gallery full of stores and restaurants running parallel to Momotarō-ōdōri, the main street in the central neighbourhood of Okayama.

So as soon as we reach the city, after only a few yards we come across a clear reference to *momo*[83] 「桃」 in the prefecture called 'land of sunshine'. With its mild climate and low rainfall compared to the rest of the country, it is indeed the ideal place to grow peaches, the symbol of the city alongside Momotarō, the boy warrior who, according to Japanese folklore, was born from a peach.

I look at the artificial colours of the sign and at the peach with its pale and delicate outside, soft as a Japanese model's skin dusted with salmon coloured powder: rather than whimsy it is perhaps the reproduction of the most popular variety of fruit that grows in the area, the white peach, Shimizu Hakutō. And if I had not come into contact with the extreme care, consideration and dedication of the Japanese towards even the smallest aspects of daily life, I would never have believed that peaches could be grown in paper

---

[83] 'Peach' in Japanese

bags to protect them from insects and the sunlight to which only the cheek that will become that inimitable pale pink is exposed. So, Shimizu Hakutō is the white peach par excellence, and thanks to the love of this people, the sweetest peach in the world.

A long walk separates us from our business hotel overlooking River Asahi-gawa, where the smallest possible living space in our room soon takes second place to the panorama from the window: Okayama-jō Castle shines out in the emerald of the enclosing night, lit up by green lights outlining carbon-black walls.

"You can keep your ocean sunsets, this is the romantic sight for me!" Gabry makes fun of me as I stand staring at a small marvel blossoming in the darkness, near the famous garden now drowned in a well of shadow.

I breathe in the sea again, on an unexpectedly mild city evening, the invisible garden of Kōraku-en awaits its magnificent November light show. *Raitsu-appu* is widespread in Japan to light up both castles and gardens; but while the former can usually be admired throughout the year, the evening openings for *raitsu-appu* in the gardens only happen at certain times: in summer during the August festivals; in autumn to admire the magnificent foliage; in winter for Christmas light events; and in spring for the cherry blossom. So, while Kōraku-en secretly hides its hues in the night, the castle watching over it palpitates with green over narrow Tsukimi-bashi Bridge, as big as a dragon with scales of tiles ready to glide over the city.

A jingling among the internal streets of Okayama, accompanied by the sound of the flute that we know well by now, echoes among lamps overflowing with golden light: in front us a small parade of children dressed in their best wriggles through the streets. Holding their parents' hands, and dozens of swinging Japanese lanterns, they remind us that even in this city, coloured by the sea, it is customary to celebrate the beauty of autumn.

And yet, it is still hard to believe it's October as we are immersed in a mild air with a hint of salt, in the lanes of Okayama full of dolled up evening spots and little bridges. Like the ones spanning the charming Nishi-gawa Canal, reflecting dozens of bicycles entrusted to the townspeople's honesty and where rows of willows dab at the ridged surface of the canal.

Not far from this area - a fair way from the station - is Okonomiyaki Teppanyaki Goemon, one of Okayama's best *yakisoba* and *okonomiyaki*[84] 「お好み焼き」 restaurants, despite being slightly off the beaten track. A bit like an improvised kitchen in the middle of a crowd of commercial warehouses, it welcomes us with a picturesque and slightly distressed atmosphere: suffused light, walls clad in sheet metal from which hang rows of kitchen utensils and the menu hanging on long rectangular cards, each with its columns of *kanji* naming and pricing the specialities they serve.

The restaurant has a long counter with a shiny griddle, a *teppanyaki*[85] 「鉄板焼き」, behind which a mother and her two children cook, smiling shyly at their clients.

We sit at the scorching griddle, entering a world that seems almost too different from our own, almost too humble, but in which we immediately feel at our ease. All we need to do is wait for our hosts to prepare the *yakisoba* and *okonomiyaki* in front of us to appreciate the care they take in laying out the ingredients and the coordination with which

---

[84] Type of fried food cooked on a griddle, made up of batter, kale and a choice of other ingredients, usually flavoured with okonomiyaki sauce, mayonnaise, seaweed and tuna. One of the most common foods at Japanese festivals

[85] Large metal griddle on which cooks prepare food for customers

they carry out one action after another, gradually giving our two plates colour and shape. Simple traditional dishes created as works of art. Here too, what is fundamental is preparation, not just the final result. Lacking care and the right timing, the noodles wouldn't frost over with soy, the kale wouldn't have the right consistency, and the bacon wouldn't be sufficiently crunchy.

Gabry is in ecstasy as he watches this dance of ingredients and movements. He quickly jots down in his notebook what he sees, what he recognises, and what he'd like to do himself one day; while after one bite I write in my diary, so as to remember what you feel when you eat something made with patience, time, and a few carefully chosen elements, the important things: whether they are ingredients, life or the love of this humble, marvellous family.

Enthused by what we've just eaten, I listen to Gabry wondering about the best way to start growing *shiso* as soon as we get back home, while we stroll peacefully along Shiyakusho-suji, to the shining neon signs and lights of the immense shopping centre next to the station. We take our time investigating the main street and smaller side roads that are still palpitating with life, in an Okayama autumn impregnated with sea and freedom, the euphoria of weather that is making me feel I belong here a little more each day.

"It's the time that you spent on your rose that makes your rose so important," the fox said in Antoine de Saint-Exupéry's 'The Little Prince', a book that in its handful of pages provides an answer to the meaning of human existence.

I begin to believe he's right. And that it goes for relationships as it does for life. That in the end happiness hides in the time we take to reach it.

Teppanyaki 鉄板焼き

The term teppanyaki, a particular style of Japanese cooking, is made up of the teppan kanji 「鉄板」, or rather a metal griddle, and yaki 「焼き」, which means grilled. This last kanji appears in numerous names of dishes, for example yakisoba and okonomiyaki, prepared in this style.

Teppanyaki came into being in Japan at the end of the Second World War in restaurants that seat their customers at a counter laid up with a large steel griddle heated by a gas stove beneath, with food prepared directly in front of them.

Teppanyaki foods are also widely used at festival stalls both because the griddles are easy to assemble and for the short time it takes to prepare cooked food in this way.

Yakisoba is perhaps the most famous of griddled street food, omnipresent at festivals held in the cold of Hokkaidō as they are in the tropical islands of Okinawa. It is an extremely simple and quick dish, consisting of vegetables mixed with meat or fish, cooked on a griddle, to which pre-cooked soba is added.

Everything is sautéed and browned, with the help of a particular spatula, mixing it all with yakisoba sauce, a sweet and sour sauce based on soy, sugar, Ketchup, Worcestershire sauce and oyster sauce.

Other teppanyaki-style dishes you regularly find at festivals are okonomiyaki, delicious fried kale and soy sprout pancakes with other additions and varied sauces, yakitori and ikayaki, respectively chicken and cuttlefish skewers, and sweets such as dorayaki and imagawayaki, sweet pastry stuffed with red azuki bean paste.

Teppanyaki is widespread in steakhouses too, in particular those of Kōbe, considered this cuisine's native city. To date, the city is full of teppanyaki restaurants that, thanks to Kōbe-gyū meat being famous throughout the world, every year attract thousands of tourists.

In general, the meat is cooked on the griddle with vegetables and mushrooms seared in the same way, so that it is all semi-raw inside and retains its beneficial properties.

Travel Notes

Okayama, located on the south coast of the main island of Honshū, is connected to the main cities by the San'yō shinkansen line and gives railway access to the island of Shikoku as well.

Renowned the world over for having one of the three most beautiful gardens in Japan, Kōraku-en, in Japanese folklore it is also famous for being the 'city of peaches' thanks to the tale of Momotarō, the young demon-chaser born from a peach and very keen on millet dumplings, or Kibi-dango.

Besides the scenic black castle, Okayama offers a very mild climate ideal for walks down its wide avenues, through modern neighbourhoods, such as near those of the central station and Omotechō-shōtengai shopping arcade, or in more picturesque areas such as along Nishi-gawa Canal, adorned with cherry blossom in spring and charming light shows in winter.

Kibitsu-jinja Shrine, a national treasure, is famed for its unique architecture and for a wooden terrace nearly four hundred yards long from which you can admire cherry trees, peonies and azaleas, as well as over 1,500 hydrangeas in the garden of Ajisai-en in June, during the rainy season.

Day Trip:
* Visit the Toyota Commemorative Museum
* Enjoy a meal of Miso-katsu at the Yabaton chain
* Take the train from Nagoya to Okayama
* Walk around the Nishi-gawa Canal area
* Eat your evening meal and have a stroll in the station area

Typical Products and Souvenirs:
* Murasuzume, small crêpes filled with azuki paste
* Ōte-manjū, sweet azuki pastries glazed in sugar
* Shimizu Hakutō, the high-quality white peach from Okayama, used in many sweets and drinks
* Bara-zushi, raw fish and mixed vegetables on a bed of rice
* Demi-katsudon, tonkatsu donburi flavoured with demi-glace sauce and peas
* Kibi-dango, sweet millet dumpling

Hiroshima
広島

I think of Tōkyō as an expression of the beauty
that man is capable of forming,
then I see Hiroshima as the city
carrying the signs of evil of which he is capable.
I ask myself how humanity can create
such marvel and horror at the same time...

I open the curtains of our little room by simply reaching a hand from where I've taken refuge beneath the covers. We are already missing the more spatial apartment of Takayama, but as with every trip, little by little we get used to the minuscule rooms in business hotels, transforming ourselves into travellers to be packed into essential spaces.

Outside there is a clear and impeccable blue sky, and in the sunlight the dark castle is more of a raven than a dragon. Patches of orange sully the green canopy stretching all around. Our first morning in Okayama is a riot of vivid and intense colour that fills the air with energy mingling with the slight saltiness that is always here, floating over the city.

Stunned by this strange brightness, we leave the hotel convinced we are heading for the station, taking Momotarō-ōdōri Street that goes straight into the network of platforms at Okayama station. When we realise we are going in the opposite direction, train times leave us few alternatives. We turn round and run at breakneck speed, our backpacks bumping up and down on our backs, desperately looking for a taxi, which all of a sudden becomes rarer than gold dust in a country overrun by them.

Only once we are on board the *shinkansen*, are the sighs of relief accompanied by laughter. For us, travelling in Japan is also this: sprinting down platforms, speed reading times and names riffling fast on shutter boards, trying to spot the familiar characters of a train or a city. From our mobile phones, the Hyperdia App always finds a solution to our mistakes, whether it's a new train or a new time.

Hiroshima. I wonder about the correct pronunciation of the name, and what we will feel visiting a city so irremediably marked by history.

Here, where the country is revealed every day in front of our eyes, Hiroshima cannot be just the 'atomic bomb city'. So, what else? What shape does life take on, or normality and daily routine, in a place that can no longer be the same? The fear grows in me for what I will see, the concern that in the end the perfect diamond of Japan will have a flaw.

Just outside the station, I photograph a manhole cover painted maple red. It has nothing to do with the season, but rather with the fact that Hiroshima is considered the city of maples. Perhaps because here the sun touches everything with a gentleness that turns the colours unique, for instance the maples, engulfed by the light, are illuminated in impossible reds. This different light seems due to a strange quirk of fate, as though over the ineffaceable past, the desire not to forget so as not to repeat leaves a patina that conserves but at the same time overlays.

There's no need for monuments or memorials to accompany this sensation: the nuances of a new autumn lie in the air, the umpteenth to reach Hiroshima like a gift, yet another to make the closing colours vivid and awesome.

Bicycles glide undisturbed along the streets, where life

rolls on as if it always has, and accompany us to the entrance to Shukkei-en, a tiny jewel of a garden in the city rebuilt to its original splendour, immediately after the end of the devastating war. The park, designed around a large central pond, is an enclosed place instilling an alienating serenity, an oasis aspiring to imitate the harmony of miniaturised landscapes in the famous garden of Xihu in China.

A small white arched bridge, the Kokō-kyō or Rainbow Bridge, crosses the water of Takuei-chi Pond, populated by hundreds of red and golden carp that light up under the warm sun. Here and there dotted around the surface are a dozen islets emerging with dome-shaped black pines on their moss green backs, like turtles floating in the placid water. Another irony is that the turtle is a sign of longevity in Japan and there are some here, in a place inextricably tied to the events of human time. On the circular shore the colours of the crown of acers reflect all around, ruby and all shades from salmon pink to bronze. The carp swim in their element under a vault sharing the colours of their livery, waiting for a visitor to pay a few *yen* in exchange for a packet of fish food to empty into their gaping mouths.

We follow a path in the shade, jumping on beautifully smooth rocks emerging beside a stream, enjoying the sight of a small grove of bamboos with silvery, perfectly ringed stems. Gabry is impressed by the wide circumference of the stems and wonders how the plant can possibly have such an incredible and lovely shape in a part of the world that is almost in the middle of the ocean.

At the top of a rocky flight of steps wedged among curvy knolls, as tradition dictates: the view of the garden in its entirety, with the white bridge in the background. While not much further on, we become aware of how this little park is so different from all the others: the only ginkgo tree that survived the bomb is stationary and silent in front of us, perhaps no longer aware of time. We wander up to this sole witness, leaves still mainly green, leaning in the direction of the explosion's epicentre to which it was sucked after the initial shock wave. A small distance from it, a memorial stone recalls the place where the first victim in the area was found. I brush my hand against the tree's black bark, wizened by time, and imagine the pain it still seems to be suffering. In the heart of the placid Shukkei-en, there is a ginkgo whispering through the coming gold of its leaves, as contorted by sorrow it seems to be saying 'That day I wanted everything to cease. But I decided to go on and to show mankind what it means to die.'

A skeleton that lives on. About twenty minutes on foot from the garden we find the Atomic Bomb Dome, icon of the devastation and entrance to Heiwa Kinen-kōen Park, another wound that is still bleeding. Further on is the Peace Memorial Museum, recently enlarged and modernised. Gabry went there on his last trip and tells me it was an experience that would leave a deep impression on anyone. They say the contents are powerful and touching, but we can't talk about it as though it were a film when it is reality. Strapped for time we've decided to put off the visit until our next trip. Because you need sufficient time for some things, to discover them and consider their existence properly, accepting that unfortunately the unacceptable does manage to exist.

The hollow dome and building gutted by the heat on that distant 6 August 1945 draws the eye, making a visual and inner impact that it is hard to find words for. It sits beside the slow river that once a year is a route to the sea for hundreds of lanterns, never tiring of giving shape to evil, to standing as its abode, amidst a stretch of perfectly kept, emerald green grass: immaculate frame in clear contrast to the most terrible sight.

I take a few photos, but then stop, realising the absurdity and paltriness of my action. I know I can't replicate what we feel in the photos, faced with this body of ruins, cement and metal that has withstood the tragedy as an emblem of the mere desire for life of the citizens of Hiroshima struck down at 8:15 on an ordinary morning.

We head through the park in the direction of the eternally burning flame, which is waiting to be put out when all nuclear bombs in the world are decommissioned. Around the flame two stylised hands lie open, perfectly lined up with the memorial altar on one side of the park and the dome on the other. One sight to tell of the world's evil and the perennial hope that it will end.

Afterwards we stroll through the city's re-born streets, now a long way from the past. In Hondōri-shōtengai, one of Hiroshima's shopping arcades, we come across an over-crowded *Shōnen Janpu*[86] 「少年ジャンプ」 store, symbol of passing time, of generations that have been spared that pain. Inside they buy gadgets of their favourite figures, of the popular tales about fair play or the happy ending where good triumphs over evil. An example of the relief in believing that things can change for the better, that in the end humanity aspires to improve rather than destroy itself, that the most famous *manga*[87] 「漫画」 of Japan's new era are stories about friendship, respect, loyalty, love and protecting the values of the collective good even at the cost of life.

In the spider's web of lanes in this neighbourhood we

---

[86] Official shop belonging to Shōnen Jump, the world famous weekly Japanese manga magazine that launched titles like Dragon Ball, Naruto and Onepiece

[87] Japanese style comic books and graphic novels, very different to western versions both in the drawings and because they are read from right to left

find Fumi-chan, a restaurant known for another of the riches that the past didn't take from Hiroshima, the *hiroshima-yaki* 「広島焼き」, the city's culinary speciality. This dish, now among the most famous countrywide, is a successful attempt at fusion between *okonomiyaki* and *yakisoba* and in Hiroshima, besides the famous Okonomimura building where more than a dozen small specialist restaurants exclusively serve the dish, this mingling of ingredients fried on the hotplate can be eaten in almost all the many eateries dotted around the city. However, as always, the locals serving a truly unforgettable *hiroshima-yaki* must be carefully hunted down with advice from local people, and Fumi-chan seems to have an excellent reputation among the inhabitants of Hiroshima.

After the experience of the previous evening, sitting at the counter in front of a hot griddle strikes me as life's greatest pleasure. For the Japanese, the counter is the place where you can eat in peace, enjoying your food prepared with greater calm and in a sort of solitary meditation. At the same time, it is the place where you can feel at ease in unfamiliar company, chatting with your neighbour or the cooks, in a less formal and friendlier context. In the course of my trips, and after yesterday's experience, the counter has become the place where you can first fall for a particular dish, to then do the same on tasting the second. Perhaps because witnessing a dish taking form is the best part, as if watching the cooks at work, seeing their technique, becomes a way to share and be included in this world of traditions, customs and ingredients. For me it is one of the ways I feel part of it all.

Before our eyes, four cooks are assembling wonderful *hiroshima-yaki* as though they were one unflagging production line. You sit there hypnotised by the impeccable coordination, seeing mountains of ingredients grow on the griddle, in a union of different consistencies and tastes that, added in the right order, bring to life a perfect combination that is hard to forget. At only 750 *yen* each, we watch our two *hiroshima-yaki* take shape, one with *udon* and the other with *sōmen*: we hear the pale noodles sizzling on the hotplate, and contemplate them as they begin to change colour and as they are swamped by eggs slithering out of their shells, thin strips of pinkish bacon and a cascade of shredded kale. Under the dancing spatulas of the cooks, it all swiftly turns into a single entity. Their fluid, precise movements turn over a mixture that gradually becomes golden.

Gabry can't stop filming the artistry with which they assemble the orders in sequence, until even the very last bits on the very edge of the griddle are covered with sauce and spring onions, and served to the client on the other side. After such theatre, it is hard not to think that the miracle released by the taste of a *hiroshima-yaki* surpasses all expectations. Every mouthful leads to the pressing desire to have another and another.

"I could carry on eating this forever..." I say to Gabry whose eyes are shining with emotion after he has finished his.

"Yes, this is decidedly one of the most incredible and unforgettable dishes in Japan..."

Unforgettable, much like Hiroshima itself.

In twenty minutes the local San'yō line train takes us to the port of Miyajimaguchi, where you can catch a boat for the famous Island of Miyajima.

The small harbour where our JR line ferry moors, next to another also belonging to a private company, is very popular with Japanese and foreign tourists, being the only way to get to the island of famed Itsukushima-jinja Shrine. At the boarding area, more than anywhere I've visited up until now, you breathe in the expectation of autumn, its colours and leaves dancing in the air. The windows in the endless rows of stores are decorated with maple leaves in flaming colours, while the manholes in the street and the electricity poles have seasonal decorations and drawings.

Okinadō, a Japanese pastry shop, which attracts us precisely because of its window invaded by plastified red leaves, sells one of the specialities of the island, *momiji-manjū*, puffy rice cakes shaped like maple leaves with a variety of fillings: from the classic *azuki* jam to chocolate and from custard to chestnut paste, these delicious pasties are so well-loved in Japan that they've gone beyond this area and even the region they come from. As is customary in many Japanese pastry shops, we are offered a taste of them all and we only manage to stop the shop assistant by buying some to take away with us. They are small but important things that I miss on the other side of the world, things that here are a normality I find it hard to get used to.

The shop assistants continue to smile even after saying goodbye on the doorstep, proud they'd made us try their entire delicious inventory. We too go on smiling until, turning to the jetty, we see the ferry embarking the last passengers. Three minutes from departure and, as usual, we begin to run.

And as usual, here, grinning broadly.

***

141

Itsukushima
厳島

There are places that are like water and the tides.
They invade our heart,
insinuating themselves into every corner of our soul.
Then, when they're at a distance, they gradually slide away,
in a leave-taking that is apparent even so,
where time follows a natural rhythm,
they come and go, like a wave of remembrance
grabbing shells of memories
and carrying out to sea all they meet

Ten minutes at sea separate us from *Kami* island and the tides. Ten minutes in which Japan is also the blue immensity that has cropped the edges of the solitary land, and that worms its way between the mountains creating islands where spirits dwell.

Looking out from the deck of the ferry, with the salt spray sticking to our hair, I see smooth crests throwing themselves at it and a carpet of sparkles every time a cloud lets the early afternoon sun through. I see the rows of floating oyster rafts, as they were hundreds of years ago, when Japan was the land of fish before it became the land of rice.

"Over here! We're nearly at the island!"

Gabry calls me to the port side to admire Itsukushima-jinja Shrine's majestic red *torii*, the island's icon called by the same name, rising out of the shimmering sea. And all of a sudden, in the light chased by photographers from all over the globe, with the forest-clad mountains in the background, the gate of the gods appears like a tiny warrior with orange legs immersed in the blue. High tide, which is now devouring its foundations, makes it difficult to believe in the magic for which this place is famous the world over. I think back to when we organised the trip, how focussed we were on the websites that projected the movements of tides on Miyajima Island, above all consulting those used by local fishermen, which report the forecast for tide peaks on several days of the year. In the month of October, a maximum decrease in the tide was forecast in the late afternoon, which for us translated into the hope of being able to walk almost as far as the *torii* before the last ferry back, sooner than booking into an expensive hotel for a night on the island.

Once we disembarked, it was easy to see how this place is constantly besieged by crowds of tourists careering down Omotesandō-shōtengai shopping street to stroll among the souvenir shops; and local deer now dependent on human food.

"I remember Nara quite well, both for the chaos and for the starving deer..."

We're not keen on tourist haunts, where storekeepers and restaurant owners are often temporary, attracted by easy money, or where contact with the west from which we want to take a break is often perceptible in the scant sensitivity and education of the foreigners, in scarce respect for the rules and culture of the Japanese people.

Plastic bags abandoned by visitors are strewn on the ground, and the exaggerated clamour of people who don't realise they are in a sacred place are sufficient for us to hotfoot it for the seafront in the direction of the *torii*, still immersed in the high tide. The steps down to the invisible beach are still impassable, but around the centre of the red and black shrine, the beach is slowly emerging, as if liberated from the enchantment that has held it prisoner in the boggy swamp the water leaves behind. I watch incredulous as small sand dunes steeped in water emerge from the sea floor.

"I find it hard to believe that in a while it will all be dry."

It is too soon for the magic to be fully accomplished, so meanwhile we decide to explore the historical area behind the shrine.

At the top of a steep stairway, the brilliant red pagoda of Toyokuni-jinja Shrine dominates the landscape, five floors of wonder, nearly ninety feet high, and although closed to the public, still posing for photographs like a model before taking the runway. In front of it is the imposing Senjōkaku pavilion, literally 'hall of a thousand tatami mats', in which you can enjoy the amazing sight of the structure rising from the ground housing 857 *tatami* and offering an excellent view of the sea. The suggestive maze of supporting wooden pilasters seems to create a temple below the temple.

We enter the tangle of delightful lanes nearby, and wander down Machiya-dōri, a shopping street full of small stores that are a lot more typical than those of Omotesandō-shōtengai, and find a series of charming two-storey houses linked by long garlands of paper bolts of lightning. Here, between one lane and another, we come across Sakamoto-kashiho, a confectioner's celebrating autumn, with a large window onto the street displaying the workshop inside. The pastry machine is running and making its magic, pouring mixture into the moulds and cooking pancake leaves that are swiftly turned out by the pastry cooks who go on to stuff them with filling. Once entered, we are welcomed by the sweet smell of newly baked *momiji-manjū* and the sweetness of a girl who invites us to sit at the guests' table, where they serve a free green tea and *momiji-manjū* straight out of the oven.

We smile at the sign to one of the panoramic spots on Miyajima Island, 'cable car ten minutes' walk, seven if you run a little bit' (written for us?). The cable car makes its way up through the forest, transporting visitors with consummate ease to Shishiiwa-tenbōdai Observatory, at the top of Mount Mi-sen; an appealing alternative to the forty-minute shin up a steep gradient.

"I don't believe I can do it!" says Gabry staring wide-eyed at the start of the footpath, where it had already become exaggeratedly steep. However, when we opt for the comfortable ride suspended above the foliage, the unexpected cost of almost 20 Euros a head put us off any attempt to go for the summit. Consolation for the ruthless decision arrives in no time in the form of a rugged path leading to Momijidani-kōen Park, a wooded area known for the spectacular autumnal colours of its many acers.

The high point of autumn colouring is forecast for mid-November but the palette of a thousand shades as greens turn to orange, then from pink to hot red, are barely held back as the leaves get ready for the *momiji-gari*, the upcoming 'leaf hunt'.

We walk the flank of the hill, which in a fortnight will be ablaze with reds, taking the opposite direction to the river that runs alongside the main path. The limpid water hops and frolics over countless obstacles, winding round and smashing into smooth rocks and enormous curved boulders, in a splintering and recomposing of red and orange reflections. Overhung as it is by maples, touching each other from either side of the river to create a tunnel that will soon - in my imagination and in reality - share the colours of the Itsukushima sunset.

Red and white. Light and shade. Beneath the shrine's long portico, between one pillar and another, the two sacred colours permeating the wood fight between light and shadow: a perpetual battle the eyes find it hard to adjust to. The result of this long-standing clash is dim light asking for silence, between solitary lanterns and the whispering sea as it slides out from under the feet of the shrine, to reveal its faded 'Japan red' foundations.

Exactly in line with the centre of the shrine, the *torii* rises out of the sea, surrounded by its aura of magic. As in all shrines, at Itsukushima-jinja there is a small shop selling good luck charms that are particularly nicely made here. We invest in a few for protection and good luck for the future.

"Well, in Itsukushima, given the importance and size of the shrine, they should have a greater effect, shouldn't they?" jokes Gabry as he buys an amulet for good health.

We contemplate the sea and its gate for the *Kami* on the *takabutai* 「高舞台」, the raised area of a shrine facing outwards in the direction of the *torii*, inhabited by two large *komainu* 「狛犬」, the lion-dogs guarding sacred places. At certain times of the year, this platform is used for performances of the traditional dance, *bugaku*[88] 「舞楽」, where men and waves become one in this world of water and divinity. To the west of the shrine, this dialogue has different roots. Small Buddhist temples, such as Daigan-ji and Gomadō Hall, are dotted about in another area populated by souvenir and food stores that attract visitors along the less busy hillside of the coast. We don't venture further because we've turned our attention to the sea, the level of which reminds

---

[88] Music and costumed dances with traditional masks narrating events of Japanese folklore. Once they were performed exclusively for nobles and the imperial Japanese court, but in the mid twentieth century they were opened to the general public too

us of the reason for our trip.

At Itsukushima-jinja Shrine, high and low tide are magical in different ways. When the tide is out you can walk under the *Kami's* gate, according to tradition a ritual that brings good fortune, and throw a coin up onto one of the *torii's* planks. With high tide the sight of the gate reflected in the sea sticks in the memory, and you can visit it in one of the rowing boats captained by a Japanese sailor wearing a straw hat.

The beach emerges slowly now, advancing towards the sea as we advance towards the *torii*, bringing with us the emotion of humans about to step over into another world. We laugh as we become aware that the low tides during summer are easier than those in autumn, when the sand dries more slowly, leaving endless puddles in which to sink; puddles that, as daylight fails, disguise their depth, tricking the more tenacious adventurers as they wander onto the newly uncovered seabed. Hop, skip and jumping towards the gate might mean you don't find the way back, while the beach is constantly changing, spitting up water and then re-absorbing it, gradually expanding it seems to come into being in front of our eyes, pulsating with reflections of the first lamps. In this bog of water and sand, the damp embraces everything, passing like a knife straight through several layers of clothing and enveloping the bones. We feel we're walking through a dense wall of water suspended in the air, the vanished sea that's left behind its inexorable presence: the warning that the place belongs to the sea and its spirits, and lends itself to man only for a short while.

As we experience this, an azure sunset, to which a photograph couldn't do justice, swathes the *torii*, suddenly lit up by powerful spotlights that turn it vermilion. We put on all our extra clothes and I'm forced to wrap my forehead in

Itsukushima-jinja 厳島神社

Itsukushima-jinja Shrine was built in 600 C.E. on Itsukushima Island, most commonly known by the name of Miyajima or 'Shrine
Island', in the bay of Hiroshima. The shrine became a UNESCO heritage site in 1996, besides having one of the three most beautiful
vistas in Japan, with the Bay of Matsushima and the panorama
from Amanohashidate.
The structure of the shrine was designed to create the illusion that
it was floating on water, according to the idea of fusion between
nature and architecture in the Heian period, and is made up of 17
Buddhist and Shinto buildings: in the central part is Honden, the
main shrine, from which protrudes Haraiden, the purification room,
overlooking the sea with a takabutai (2) platform for bugaku
dances; along suggestive red and white corridors is the west zone
with the Nō platform (4), and in the east zone, Marōdo-jinja (3),
the main minor shrine.
Ōtorii (5), literally the 'Great Torii', 52 feet high and weighing over
60 tons, is built out of camphor wood from trees over 600 years
old, its pillars are not embedded in the seabed but resting on the
rocky surface and regularly maintained. The specialness of the
place is due to its transformation with the changing tides: at high
tide, boat rides allow you to admire the shrine reflected in the sea
and to travel round the torii immersed in water; at low tide the
shrine's dense network of stilts becomes visible and you can reach
the torii by walking across the beach.
There are numerous other points of interest: once you have disembarked at the port, following the coastal road you cross a large
stone torii (1) watched over by a pair of komainu guardians; then
walking alongside Itsukushima-jinja Shrine you reach the steps
leading to Toyokuni-jinja Shrine (8), made up of a five-storey
pagoda and Senjōkaku pavilion, with a view of the sea; if you visit
in spring, in April you can't help but notice the area of cherry trees
in flower around Kōmyō-in Temple (13); while if you go there in
autumn, taking Momiji-bashi Bridge (9), the nature walk through
Momijidani-kōen Park is the perfect place to admire the foliage
colouring from the end of October onwards. Along the path is Shi-
nomiya-jinja Shrine (12) and the panoramic Akai-bashi Bridge
(10), before reaching the cable car station (11) to take you up

to Shishiiwa-tenbōdai Observatory.

Finally, on the west side of Itsukushima-jinja Shrine is a complex of buildings (6) seldom visited by tourists, including Daigan-ji Temple, Goma-dō Hall, Tahō-tō Pagoda and the remote Kiyomori-jinja Shrine (7) along the beach.

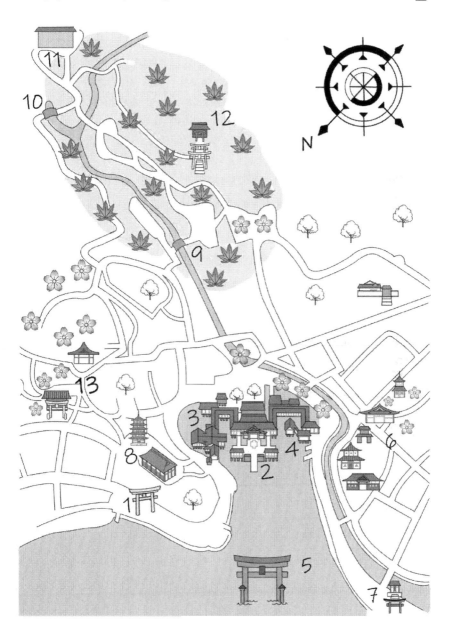

Gabry's scarf, warding off the nascent headache brought on by the damp. While the crowd on the expanding beach increases, some brave the cold water to wade over to the *torii*. The shrine behind us sits in a warm light, dissolving the shadows of its portico and mirroring itself fully in the sodden sand below. The spirit show seems endless.

Night falls and the vast gate becomes a fluorescent shape against the freezing sky while a twin *torii* stretches out at its feet, increasingly vivid as the sea steals the water away. Despite our commitment, the cold and damp are too intense and around 6pm we realise that we are not up to spending another forty minutes here, the time necessary to wait until the tide is low enough to walk under the gate.

"It's all right, fifteen yards from the gate are more than acceptable next to a trip ruined by flu!"

We leave a beach full of photographers, and children jumping from one puddle to the next, all keen to walk under the gods' gate, to attempt to ask for goodwill and protection.

The ferry leaves just as we are craving the warmth of being inside, desperate for warm air, which in the cold months is on full power under the seats in boats, trains and buses. Behind us, we leave the island's autumn: the arrival of the gods' fire on the dark inland sea.

We are heavy with damp and exhaustion when we are welcomed at the zen entrance to the historic restaurant Katsudon Nomura and into the warmth of a small, traditional dining room, a haven of safety on the way to our hotel in Okayama. A bowl of *demi-katsudon* 「デミカツ丼」, the dish whose origins are from that very place, and a portion of *miso* soup warm us with traditional flavours, served in surroundings that finally catapult us into the cosy, quiet Japan we love so deeply.

I've caught a chill and am physically drained, but with something else in my soul that I can't explain. Perhaps it is the presence of the *Kami*, disruptive and overpowering in the place created by man to get a little closer to the spirits. Under the heavy covers I still can't warm up, I wonder if they had listened to me at the great *torii*, if they recognised my dedication and pardoned my failure. If, even in the absence of a coin, they might grant my wish: to bring me a little closer to the world and life that I feel mine.

I hug Gabry, who is already asleep, prey to bodily exhaustion too. Added to which is the suffering of the mind, that all too often comes back to hurt him even now, something that, to my great sorrow, I can't yet soothe.

We need time to heal. From the past, from a life that was but that we can't see how it could be. Time, as they say, heals all...

But what if the thing we are in need of is a place?

Travel Notes

The grim story of Hiroshima is known the world over, but despite the bomb razing it to the ground on 6 August 1945 killing 260,000 people and wounding more than 160,000, in a short time it regained vitality thanks to the tenacious spirit of the Japanese.
Situated on the Seto-naikai Inland Sea, on western Honshū and accessible by shinkansen, it was proclaimed 'World Peace Centre' in 1949, becoming the symbol for denuclearization with Heiwa Kinen-kōen Park and its Peace Memorial Museum.
A lively city, it has numerous points of interest: from dark 'Carp Castle', and fantastic evening light shows; Shukkei-en Garden, and the banks of River Kyōbashi-gawa; Mitaki-dera Temple, known for its splendid autumnal gardens, red Tahō-tō Pagoda and three nearby waterfalls.

Day Trip:
* ⁂ Travel to Hiroshima and visit Shukkei-en Garden
* ⁂ Visit the Atomic Bomb Dome and Heiwa Kinen-kōen Park
* ⁂ Walk around Hondōri-shōtengai shopping arcade and taste hiroshima-yaki
* ⁂ Take the local train to Miyajimaguchi port and the ferry for Miyajima Island
* ⁂ Stroll along Omotesandō-shōtengai shopping street
* ⁂ Visit Itsukushima-jinja Shrine at high tide
* ⁂ Explore the area of Toyokuni-jinja Shrine, Senjōkaku pavilion and Machiya-dōri Street
* ⁂ Explore Momijidani-kōen Park
* ⁂ Walk to the famous torii lit-up in the evening at low tide
* ⁂ Return to Okayama

Typical Products and Souvenirs:
* ⁂ Hiroshima-yaki, okonomiyaki from Hiroshima
* ⁂ Hiroshima and Onomichi rāmen
* ⁂ Momiji-manjū, sweet pastries with various fillings
* ⁂ Shakushi, small rice ladle
* ⁂ Kaki, inland sea oysters

Himeji
姫路

Happening upon a pink-ribboned train,
we then encounter a vast white castle
with wings spread out over the city of Himeji.
We explore its dark wood, smelling of the past,
and move on into the gardens,
where carp and maple are dressed in matching shades.
Dismissing the popular bustling places,
we are beset by the euphoria of an autumnal festival
where colours, men and gods meet in fierce battle.
Seeking repose from so many marvels is like
trying to keep a lighthouse dry in the ocean,
they sweep in from every direction,
with the relentless force of the waves

The sun bathes the fired clay feathers of the 'Black Crow', standing proud and svelte guard over the city of Okayama. Today more than yesterday it watches over a cloud of leafage on the turn, approaching the long-awaited explosion of colours that is the Japanese autumn.

The tiredness resulting from our day trip to the sacred island ensnares us under the covers longer than intended, while I fight off a worsening sore throat that promptly taken medicine is finding it hard to placate. After an arduous breakfast, we drag ourselves to the station in a taxi so as to conserve as much energy as possible. We feel like the walking dead as we totter to the comfort and safety of our train, in this unusual country that always finds a way to

153

overwhelm, to swallow up in its whirl of life that knows no lawful rest other than the silence and calm of its modes of transport.

I remember when, during my solo trip a year ago, one August afternoon in Tōkyō I felt unwell. Tiredness and perhaps more the fragile time I was going through in those months, urged me to take refuge in one of the many stores opposite Akihabara station. *Manga*, action figures, collector gadgets and *otaku*[89] 「おたく」, concentrated by the thousand in these several-storey buildings that are a toing and froing of people, including kids, at all hours. To find a bit of peace from that unstoppable vitality, I appropriate a bench on the top floor of the building, a floor that is usually used for vending machines, the WC and occasionally the odd little-frequented shop. However, where I thought I'd find rest, I was hit by a continual stream of life that fascinated me, with which I fell in love and with which I got back what I'd lost: the strength and desire to get up again, and walk on. Because, in that space, among a few vending machines and benches, there was very little, and yet there was everything. It's that incomprehensible flow that doesn't find peace here in Japan, the country where every place, even the most discreet, hidden and out of the way, belongs to the Japanese and their indefatigable need to exist. And the most distinctive example are the anonymous, isolated lanes in small towns and villages, where in the dark of the evening vending machines shine out, stopovers to quench your thirst slipped in where you'd least expect them. In the country where neither time nor space are ever wasted, life flows like a boundless torrent.

---

[89] Japanese term to describe nerds who are particularly obsessed with computers, anime and manga, often to the detriment of their ability to socialize

I'm looking forward to peace and quiet as the *shinkansen* draws alongside our platform, with the easy comfort that you take for granted, disregarding the limitless energy this nation deploys everywhere, even designing out-of-the-ordinary trains, where there's no room for a nap or not being part of it all during the journey. So it is that a themed *shinkansen,* the first to cross our path, stops in front of us and plucks us out of the fatigue left over from the day before, for a journey that will be anything but relaxing. The aggressive, futuristic design of the high-speed train is now decked out in shocking pink with masses of sweet Hello Kitty logos invading the metal work and making us smile.

"Phew, at this point all we need is the *Evangelion*[90] train!" comments Gabry laughing and hiding his liking for a train that is as girly as it is original. On board, lilac seats alternate with dotted doors, Hello Kitty and other far-fetched designs. In that blaze of little pink and white cats, once again getting some rest is unthinkable. The map shows us the first entirely thematic coach, and gripped by the euphoria the Japanese feel for these things, I find myself a little girl again, in an amusement park, while I juggle between photos of the most famous cat in Japan, a gadget store and the hostess dressed in pink who is giving us a free booklet.

Everything glides by; everything becomes the desire for life in these places, with no room for tiredness or moodiness. Thirty minutes of unexpected energy and, without being the slightest bit refreshed, we are now under the Himeji sun.

Immense even at a distance, the 'White Heron' stretches out its wings at the end of the city's main street, which runs from the station to the high points in the valley's backdrop.

---

[90] Manga from the nineties set in a futuristic Tōkyō, internationally famous thanks to the profound storyline and action scenes in the relative anime

From here, unlike the prouder and more composed Black Crow of Okayama, it looks as if it is about to glide over the houses, in all the whiteness of its high walls.

In the city of the most famous castle in Japan, the day is clearer and warmer than usual and we decide to go to the large tourist office at the station to find out how to get to the main attraction while saving ourselves a half hour walk. Still more important is to know how to get to the south of the city where Nada-no-Kenka Matsuri takes place, and from the number of brochures and maps we suddenly find ourselves holding, we realise that this local festival isn't perhaps so little known after all.

We join the coming and going of the taxis heading between the station and castle, and in the blink of an eye we are beneath the snowy fortress. At the main entrance, beyond the moat flanking the wide avenue, the fortress looms with pale grace on massive walls that don't weigh down its sinuous architecture, on the contrary, seeming to thrust it upwards. Imposing but light as a bird, it rises up like the guard of a time that was and is magically still here.

The combined ticket, including the garden of Kōko-en, allows access to the castle through the large cherry and plum park, pink and white nest on which the Heron perches in spring, and providing views that tour the world.

"I don't feel at all well..." Gabry is paying the price of the damp we succumbed to last night, and suffering shakes and stomach-ache, he has to find a bench to sit down. He asks me to go on alone, and explore the places he remembers from his previous trip. I want to stay with him but can't because time, so precious here, is slipping away like water along bamboo canes in a *shishi-odoshi*.

So, I go alone to the castle with its black floors and white walls. I walk barefoot beside one of the side-walls, whose darkness is broken by windows with wooden grates, once essential for the archers defending the place and today providing unique viewpoints of the main building.

The visit itinerary of this wing offers exhibitions of samurai armour and arms, rooms set up with explanations of the castle's history and displays of the materials that made the structure as beautiful as it is indestructible: the black tiles in the particular Himeji style, the large stones in the walls and the building techniques used.

Coming out of the dim light of the complex's lateral wing, I head for a wall of light that obliges me to half-close my eyes. The milk white walls of the main fortress rise up right in front of me and from here the White Heron is visible in all its impetus, heading into the sky.

From the large square outside the main entrance, I turn to look at what the castle sees, and beneath me the city of Himeji stretches out towards the surrounding mountains. Before heading back into the darkness of its insides, for a moment I almost feel I could fly on its shoulders.

Once again barefoot, I move over the polished black wood. The smell of Japan, so distinctive in the castles, temples and shops: the wood of the Japanese cedar is like this country, even after a very long time it never loses its original fragrance. I walk around this immense structure with its simple interior, a far cry from the castles we are used to in the west. No opulence, nowhere you recognise daily life just large spaces for arms and soldiers, and the black wood absorbing every luminous ray. It's the first time I've been swallowed by a Japanese castle, and yet I feel I clearly perceive the past that shaped its history. One of constant danger from fire that could burn the entire fortress to the ground; one of soldiers carrying arms, in the confusion of an attack, running up and down the narrow wooden stairs

Himeji-jō 姫路城

Himeji-jō Castle, which became the first UNESCO heritage site in Japan in 1993, is considered one of the most beautiful castles in the country, alongside the black castles of Matsumoto and Kumamoto. Built in 1300 and later enlarged with ramparts and splendid gardens, this is the only powerful fortress in Japan to have survived frequent fires, earthquakes and bombings.

Embraced by its moats and sitting on a spectacular plateau in the heart of the city, the white castle is freely accessible through Ōtemon Gate (1) leading to San-no-maru (2), the third circle of walls where you find a great number of sakura and the peony garden, Botan-en (3), which flowers from mid-April.

Continuing through Hishi-no-mon Gate (4) you reach the paying area Ni-no-maru (5), the second circle of walls, and Nishi-no-maru Tei-en Garden (6), also full of sakura. The ramparts around the green area can be visited and contain explanations, photos and curiosities about the castle and its history. Access to visit the walls, rigorously in bare feet, starts at Wa-no-yagura Tower (7) and ends at Keshō-yagura Tower (8), one of the private residences belonging to Princess Sen, an important figure from the Edo period to whom the city is closely tied.

Then, following an intricate series of paths and gates, the final line of defence for possible invaders, you reach Bizen-maru (9), the inner circle of walls, and Daitenshu (10), the castle's main building: 150 feet high, with 7 floors offering panoramic views of the city. Besides its distinctive bright white colour, from which comes the name "White Heron" (Shirasagi-jō in Japanese), two other famous features are the stone foundations and the finely worked roof tiles stamped with the dynasty's coat of arms. Due to the astonishing Japanese anti-seismic techniques with which it was built, this building even survived the terrible Hanshin earthquake of 1995 that gravely damaged the city. To give you an idea of the central castle's resistance, it is said that the bottle of sake on the altar on the top floor remained standing throughout that disastrous event.

Finally, to the east of Ni-no-maru, is the well named Okiku-ido (11) linked to the legend of Banshū Sarayashiki, a servant who was unfairly put to death, but returns to haunt the living as a ghost.

Whereas, leaving the fortified complex, to the west of the moat is
Kōko-en Garden, where the samurai who guarded the castle used
to live. Today you can visit these nine separate white-walled landscapes, each offering a unique vista that changes with the seasons.

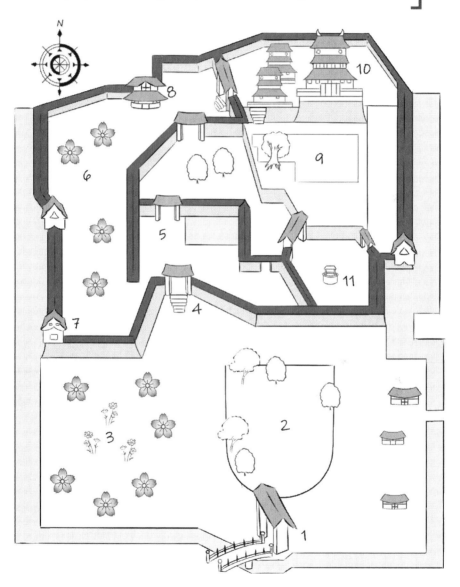

that today seem impossible to climb; one of the wise *daimyō*[91] 「大名」 devising battles and moving armies over the maps of their lands and the land of others.

On the top floor of the castle, the large windows encased by protective grids lean out over the world. Once again Himeji is an expanse of houses under the mountains of which I can now see the crests, hazy and languid. Once, from here they would have spotted the enemy and had time to prepare the castle for battle. And then the White Heron would open its wings, raining down arrows, rocks and fire. Then it was seen with respect by many.

Today nothing is as it was, and yet almost nothing has changed. The penumbra. The smell of cedar. The Heron flying over Himeji. And still today, it is hard not to admire it.

I hurry down the steps as quickly as I can, because after an hour of solitary visit I begin to feel the lack of the person to share special moments.

Last year, when I set off for Japan on my own, I often fell into this weighty state of mind. It would be particularly vivid after a moment of discovery or joy, clashing violently with the euphoria and sensation of wellbeing that follow the instantaneous happiness caught in places like these, and highlighting its sad incompleteness. In those days I lived in terror of finding the country that gave meaning to a greater part of my being would no longer offer me relief and hope, and never has a phrase felt so true as that written by Christopher J. McCandless at the end of his life.

"Happiness is only real when shared." Christopher's story is told by the journalist Jon Krakauer in his movingly intense novel 'Into the Wild', one of the books I read as a

---

[91] Feudal lords that controlled Japan during the Edo period

teenager and never managed to detach from my existence. It was on that trip that I came to fully understand those words, that I sampled the painful absence tied to the impossibility of sharing what makes us most happy.

I rush back to Gabry, the person with whom I share one of the most important things in my life, as well as all the storms that are part of it. He is pale and very weak, and as soon as we cross Sakuramon-bashi Bridge, the fortress's main entrance, he has to sit down again on a bench outside Kōko-en Garden.

I don't know if the *Kami* of Itsukushima-jinja Shrine are trying to tell us something, but I begin to think we may have annoyed them in some way...

Once again I enter alone, into a garden hemmed with white walls. I go in on tiptoes because I feel that these places, where everything is harmony and equilibrium, can feel the ugliness of our anxieties. I'm looking for answers to my malaise and to Gabry's, which I feel is not only physical. I look for a way out in a country 10,000 km away. For the umpteenth time, seeking that glimmer of happiness I long for.

On entering, I immediately find a universe of speckles: colour, light and shade. There is moss and a stone lantern beneath the first orangish maples in the garden. Kōko-en, although small enough to visit in about an hour, is divided into thirteen sectors, each of which is a garden unto itself, independent of its neighbour's character.

The first setting includes the residence of the feudal lord and large central pond, which you access by a covered walkway, suspended above the body of water, and entering thick fluorescent green fronds. At a certain point in the walk, looking out of this bridge-veranda, you witness a spectacle that cannot but heal the soul of whomever has the fortune to enjoy it: the light disintegrates on the web of acers in the arboreal vault, falling into the thick shadow in masses of luminous pieces of confetti. Irregular and fiery, they sit on the surface of a large waterfall descending in rocky steps, where the water dotted with light goes down peacefully from one level to the next, silent and without wisps, to then slide beneath the walkway itself, under the feet of the spectator. I stand enchanted in front of a view that, however artificial, is immersed in a primitive harmony of sound, light and colour penetrating every single thing.

Around the main stretch of water is a panorama of maples still untouched by autumn but which, in November, enflamed by the evening illuminations too, turns into an inimitable palette. Alas, today I have to make do with the oranges and bright yellows of the endless carp that live here and like precocious autumn leaves, flutter in the limpid water. Here you can also find Kassui-ken, the garden's *kaiseki*[92] 「懐石」 restaurant offering a marvellous view of the pond from its large windows. The place where Gabry and I should have been having lunch together and that becomes a desire in an uncertain future...

Continuing my exploration, I stumble across the teahouse garden, beautiful in its order and simplicity, and then into the wisteria canopy that in spring runs like a lilac river following the real watercourse below. In this way, the water brings together the garden's thirteen areas, passing beneath the bamboo barriers that separate them, darting over the jumps created by rocks and hollows, providing visitors with glorious walkways from which to admire the different scenery. Only in the final sections does the water suddenly disappear and harmony assume a different form, where the undisputed star is Himeji, unapproachable in its white

---

[92] Traditional cuisine made up of lots of small refined dishes

majesty.

As I leave this small paradise, Gabry is still there, lying on the bench where I had left him, now pale as the fortress and with a burning forehead. I might have to convince him that going back to the hotel is the wisest choice, were it not for the fact that he wants at all costs to go to Nada-no-Kenka Matsuri, one of the most famous *yatai* battles in Japan. The festival takes place every year on 14 and 15 October, and like most festivals, switches between sacred moments, blessings of floats and offerings at Shinto altars, and moments of action and spectacle, with dancing, parades, evening light shows, and every so often, genuine battles. On the second day people prepare for the most eagerly awaited competition, that of three *mikoshi*[93] 「神輿」 and seven *yatai* - each representing a district of the Nada area - colliding in a violent dance in which the irremediably damaged structures are gradually eliminated.

A taxi takes us to Himeji station, where we drag ourselves to the platform for the local San'yō Dentetsu line heading east towards the Hirohata arena in Shirahamaseizan-kōen Park, seat of the battles and one of the main places where it is possible to attend the festivities, as well as Matsubara Hachiman-jinja Shrine where the Shinto purification rites take place. When we get off at our stop, Mega, we are a little to the west of the park, a steep hill on the side of which are stands and terracing and where thousands of spectators gather annually. This festival is unheard of by the majority of tourists, and as we walk from the station we notice a complete absence of foreigners, only groups of excited students and local families. In the partying roads

---

[93] Portable sacred altars inside which Shinto Kami symbolically reside. Used to carry the Kami from a certain shrine around the city during the festivals as good luck, for example for a plentiful harvest

of this suburban neighbourhood, homes sit in silence, left unguarded for a few hours, dwellings that have no grilles or reinforced doors, as serene as when they are occupied. In the streets, the colours of the paper pom-poms stretching between electricity poles change from zone to zone, above the palpable atmosphere of expectation in different districts. The occasional Japanese festival-goer running late acts as our guide as they dash over crossroads, in the warren of lanes increasingly saturated with the sound of approaching drums.

Turning a corner, a group of proud combatants leave us astonished and wreathed in smiles: dressed in their team's jacket with bands around their head celebrating the typical combative Japanese spirit, instead of trousers they are wearing *sumō*[94] 「相撲」 thongs, leaving their virile and funny-looking male buttocks on show. This amusing, not to say picturesque sight anticipates the heart of the celebration, the main road leading to the arena, as usual, is dotted with coloured food stalls. In the space of a few yards, the number of people grows so much that the street is impenetrable and in the chaos everywhere around us we watch some floats still coming down the hill, followed by their snaking line of supporters and accompanied by enthusiasm and drums.

We attempt to sneak through to get as close as possible to the arena, where the space is transformed and in one or two yards explodes into packed and palpitating stands, in a whirl of pom-poms and banners around two altars of which we can only see the swaying tops: it is the dance of the two warriors, the incumbents inspecting each other before the clash. The *yatai* are already bobbing above the crowd, rising and sinking, among the electrified yells of the spectators,

---

[94] Traditional Japanese sport linked to Shintoism

bound in a single entity of districts and rivalries. A few minutes later, and suddenly each team tilts their respective wooden pole towards their own float and pushes violently against their adversary. When the impact comes, the floats seem to list dangerously from side to side, like skittles about to fall over, but the arena is so jam-packed that they stay upright, held in the grip of an uncontrollable mob.

From the confusion produced by this archaic show of force, there emerges the damaged body of a float and the bright pom-poms hanging from it, wobbling crazily over a sea of heads at every collision. The show is riveting in all its parts, all its sounds, in the primitive impetus of a battle that must be experienced to be understood and recounted. To leave that invasive euphoria and such a festive spirit isn't easy, but Gabry is notably worse and we have to get back to Okayama.

As we leave, we hear another crash behind us, and see fragments of wood and pom-poms falling off here and there, not to speak of a public in a frenzy that is as thrilling as the battle itself, in an autumn where it isn't only nature's colours that are in competition.

Approaching the station, the deserted streets give an idea of the celebration to come, the one after the cruel fight, when the teams heal the wounds of the *yatai*, putting them back together again with lighted lanterns, and the competition dissolves into lightheartedness and the smell of street food mixed with roast fish outside people's homes.

Despite trains running like clockwork, the return journey seems interminable.

Back at the hotel, when the thermometer registers a fever of 38°, I can't do other than leave Gabry asleep under the covers, and ravenous as well as disheartened, throw myself into the Okayama evening, through the streets where the car headlights are gradually stronger and everything is tinged with ice blue going navy and the black of night. I feel the previous year's solitude muscling in, when in the evening I used to wander the streets of Tōkyō with no precise goal, in search of the right direction: in the city, but above all in life itself.

Like then, I look for refuge in the feeling of calm and security that the roads of this country instil, in the relief you feel walking free of anxiety for potential danger from others. Every so often, that inherited fear would make me look over my shoulder. Then I would see a girl on a bicycle, two students heading home, a young couple and an old lady with the shopping. This is what I see when darkness falls over Okayama, when I feel safe from the real and inner spectres, in the place that I can't but call 'home'.

The grilled meat restaurant, Teppan Ku-ya, not far from the station, is the place I take refuge for a swift supper. My companions at the counter are rosy pink grilled roast beef and a portion of *takoyaki*, whose liquid batter follows the tastiness and external crispiness of the filling. Meditative and silent. Only half enjoyable.

I buy a plain *onigiri* and some fruit for Gabry at the *konbini* below the hotel, where the background music and neon sign in the semi-deserted street are the most reassuring things I could wish for just now. I'm expecting a long night by Gabry's side as his temperature has gone up again; to the extent that I am convinced the health talismans bought at Itsukushima-jinja Shrine were defective. Fortunately, watching over someone important to us in a place where we feel at home, always makes one feel that things can only improve...

As I write my diary in the heart of the night, I feel

stronger in the awareness of Japan representing for me a safe haven of serenity in the midst of a storm, the place where I can salve wounds and be certain to heal them. Perhaps Japan simply arrived in my life at the right moment, when it had to be there. When I most needed it. When something needed to be healed. When it was important to believe that everything would be all right.

Travel Notes

Himeji, situated half way between Osaka and Okayama, opposite Seto-naikai Inland Sea, is easily reached on the San'yō shinkansen line, whose station is on the main avenue leading up to the famous castle. In the north of town, Engyō-ji Temple is a beautiful Buddhist complex that is part of Saigoku Sanjūsan-sho 33 Temple Pilgrimage. Deep in the forest of Mount Shosha-zan and accessible by cable car, in this area are the famous Daikō-dō Hall, Niō-mon Gate, and Maniden Temple, built on scenic wooden columns on a hillside. Every 14 and 15 October, in the Nada area to the south of Himeji, the city's main autumn festival Nada-no-Kenka Matsuri takes place. The event involves the seven districts in the zone, whose teams are distinguishable by their coloured headbands and the bamboo decorations with pom-poms in coloured paper used in the fight. On the first day, the seven yatai and three mikoshi parade through the districts and are purified at Matsubara Hachiman-jinja Shrine. On the afternoon of the second day, in the Hirohata arena at Shirahamaseizan-kōen Park, mikoshi and yatai clash with each other to the sound of drums and crashes considered among the '100 sounds of Japan'. In the evening is the fight between the yatai finalists, all rigorously lit up.

Day Trip:
* Travel by train from Okayama to Himeji
* Visit Himeji-jō Castle
* Lunch at the Kassui-ken restaurant inside Kōko-en Garden
* Take the local train to Shirahamaseizan-kōen Park arena for Nada-no-Kenka Matsuri
* Return to Okayama

Souvenirs and Typical Products:
* Sakura kōbo sake, fermented with sakura petals
* Himeji-koma, painted wood spinning tops
* Myōchin hibashi-fūrin, wind chimes
* Himeji-hariko, washi paper products
* Hime kawa-zaiku, leather artisan goods

Okayama
岡山

Solitary and wavering steps
take me through the heart of Okayama,
city of Mediterranean flavour.
Autumn struggles to make her way in the garden,
where the light is steeped in salty air,
soft as the skin of a summer peach,
the symbol these places have made their own.
Familiar aromas and colours take me back
to the land I come from, that motherland
I would wish other in so many ways, a place of heartache
and still open wounds, but also the finer things,
family and deep affection that distance
fills with an altered intensity

Waking up with a throat that feels as though it has been pierced by a sharpened *katana*[95] 「刀」 helps to remind me how our adventure on Miyajima Island has brought unwanted blessings. And yet, after fighting his battle with flu late into the night, Gabry suddenly seems reborn, like a samurai who, getting up out of the mud on the battlefield, resumes the path of duty.

"Perhaps I should stay in bed for a bit longer, to avoid getting overtired before our visit to Takamatsu..."

I agree with him, although it means another solitary visit today, to Kōraku-en, the garden for which the city is

---

[95] Famous Japanese slightly curved sword with single, incredibly sharp blade, cross-guard and long hilt to be used with two hands

famous. Gabry, who saw it last summer, describes it as one of the most breath-taking he has ever explored, brilliant in its wide lawns seen beneath damp skies in a season now past. A season in which we were just friends, before we decided to become more than that. One in which we thought distance was enough to scrape up the broken pieces of our respective existences, having struggled to save day-to-day lives that didn't entirely belong to us, and relationships with others we had grown up with but couldn't imagine sharing a future.

As I walk along I think of that not too distant past, strange and painful, which sometimes insinuates itself in among the fissures of happiness, until relief arrives through sights, smells and tastes of places capable of mending wounds that not even time seems to be able to heal.

And then the smell of the ocean, a fragrance that sculpts the city's identity, increasing in strength near the brackish river at the bottom of the garden. I don't need to ask for directions: little Tsukimi-bashi Bridge leads naturally to Kōraku-en, guiding my steps as if I knew the place already, where you have the feeling you could never get lost.

The entrance to the park welcomes me with a rainbow of flyers about the events taking place here. Among them, the autumnal *raitsu-appu* planned for the middle of November, clearly a highly anticipated event for the whole city.

I buy a ticket that doesn't include the castle itself because I don't want to be late for my rendezvous with Gabry at Takamatsu. After a few steps Kōraku-en unfurls before your eyes and anyone expecting a confined space planted around a lantern and small lake is faced instead with an entire landscape: the hill, the large pond breaking up into lots of little streams, a newly harvested rice field, and one of tea simmering in perfect rows of green cushions.

I find it hard to take in such space, to impose a structure and a philosophy to one of the three most beautiful gardens of Japan. So I decide to begin my visit on the outer ring of paths, the one that gives me a greater chance to observe the heart of this small universe from the outside, warily seeking meaning and detail.

An example is the plum tree wood, a large army now drowsing on a compact and flawless layer of moss into which their grey roots sink with the same sweetness as a smoothed stone breaking the surface of a running rivulet. The salmon coloured canopy of leaves that has already fallen lies in rounded piles among the branching roots, making it look as though the trees are standing upside down.

A little further on, gardeners in milk white uniforms and large hats hiding their faces from the sun, work painstakingly at pulling out the slenderest of weeds, and removing one by one the leaves that disturb the equilibrium of the velvety mantle. A fascinating perfectionism that doesn't however leave much space for the unique, colourful disorder of autumn.

I reach the green tea cultivation, with its chubby lines of hedges, in expectation of spring meticulously pruned of the tender young leaves that make the fine brews for all Japan. Adjacent is the newly tilled rice field, where flowery tufts weighed down with golden grains are hung out before being threshed.

Looking over the crops and the rest of the garden is the little hill, the vantage point of every Japanese garden, and here offering a 360° panorama of Kōraku-en. The rocks sticking out of the gentle crest help the climb, among the hypnotic undulating bushes of pittosporum running up to the peak. From the top I contemplate the garden, an enchanting oasis in autumn too, where sinuous green lawns are interwoven with ivory gravel paths, waterways and moss. Not far off, like a fearless guardian, in the background rises the fortress of the Black Crow.

From the teahouse, flanking the pebbly canal, I reach the aviaries of Japanese cranes, one of the garden's most famous attractions. It's the first time I've seen them in the flesh, with their elegant silhouette rather than the angular shapes of *origami*[96] 「折り紙」. Although they are protected from extinction by captivity, in this vast aviary they don't seem as beautiful and unreachable as in their natural free habitat, light and fragile as the paper shapes portraying them. I don't like seeing them in this metal cage, which consumes the spirit with which they are shown in paintings all over Japan, and soon I end my visit, passing an autumn lotus pond in a sorry state and a wood of ancient trees where the crows, as the signs advise, enjoy playing with passersby by dropping acorns and pebbles on them from above.

I leave Kōraku-en alive with colour that, imprisoning summer memories, has hardly prepared for an autumn with only a few red acers. Although later dressed in lights in the cool of the evening, when in the large central pond, a garden within the garden lights up and everything seems even more limitless than it was before.

So many reflections accompany me on my lone walk to the castle, at the time of day when the sun is higher and the mild air spiced with a saltiness that is almost Mediterranean. Of a sudden, it provokes a wave of nostalgia for distant places, which I've felt a long way from for a while. Places that may not be home but are unconditionally family: belonging to my parents, sister, my two inseparable dogs.

---

[96] From 'ori' (to fold) and 'kami' (paper) it is an art consisting in making sculptures by folding pieces of paper

Despite the misunderstandings, and sadness of not managing to reconcile personal dreams and plans with their visions of life, right now I wish I could extract them from that setting 10,000 miles away, tear them out of the recent years of inner pain that takes the form of the roads of my city and country, of the futile arguments and the things I wish I'd never said. I'd like to remove them from a context that, like a dress that's too tight and doesn't allow you to breathe, to be a better person, and bring them here with me, so that my heart lightens a little and I can proudly show them my new self in a dress that finally fits like a glove. The one in which saying 'I love you' - so difficult elsewhere - finally becomes easy.

Maybe it is precisely this distance, sought and suffered in equal amounts, that here becomes a new tie, that succeeds in showing the beauty of affection hiding away where we feel most out of place, fragile and unappreciated.

I turn a corner and the profile of the Black Crow towers above me in all its magnificence. Once again, I must thank this country for showing me the true value of things.

It may be best to move away a bit in order to feel closer,
a little like living in the present
to reassess the past.
There are places where this happens naturally,
where a black castle all shadow and pain
turns into remarkable beauty to cherish

The black walls of Okayama-jō Castle rise like raptors against a light blue background of sky. In its presence I can admire the deep black creating a violent contrast with the white attics and lattice windows, in an excellent example of reconstruction after the destruction of the bombs in the

Second World War.

I wander around the large park near the entrance, where the stones of the ancient structure have been laid out in a circular design, and where the castle displays itself in all its majesty, an elegant, brooding gentleman it is impossible to take one's eyes off. Smaller than the castles at Himeji and Matsumoto, it succeeds in seeming as imposing as its bigger brothers, perhaps thanks to its petroleum coloured shell, and to elicit the same sensations today that it must have in the olden days, when the enemy appeared on the horizon, to behold it daring and aggressive in its crow's guise.

The area within the massive doors in the walls, which once separated the main fortress from the ancient citadel, is what remains of the protection the castle offered: I walk along the yellow lines marking out the footprints of the old buildings, remnants of a tormented past that forged a people and its values, and for this reason, would not be forgotten. It is the importance of time and the past, because what has been, for better or worse, produced what it is now.

'*A bit like life. A bit like for ourselves.*'

***

Takamatsu
高松

There are places here that seem to be drawn,
painted in reality like Japanese illustrations that
just glimpsed can pierce the heart
and throw it to the other side of the world.
Merely living in these places is enough to see
how it is the beauty of natural shapes
that moulded a culture
so distinctive and profound

The cobalt carpet of sea unfolds beneath us. I watch it puckering into bursts of froth between islets as the train hurries along, suspended on a bridge running for miles over waves and wind, weaving together these strips of land like a narrow thread in a cloth of water stained by foam. The journey over the islands of Shikoku region takes about an hour and has a unique, continually changing panorama.

The closer we get to our destination the larger the islets beneath us become, and less wild, filling up with little houses and then suddenly immense factories with smoking chimneys. Turquoise water surrounds the cliffs and then, all of a sudden, the vast, grey refinery welcomes us in the area of Japan where shrines hide in the forests and rivers are gigantic transparent roads. Two faces of a country that perhaps I love so much precisely because it is so incomprehensible.

Takamatsu is a small city on the sea to the north of the region that many wouldn't know were it not for its famous summer festival Sanuki Takamatsu Matsuri and magnificent dances. And yet, besides being able to try one of the country's tastiest dishes here, there is also another garden,

175

the cradle of one of the most significant symbols of the Rising Sun: the Japanese pine.

Gabry tells me all about the mid-summer celebrations that take place among the city streets and Chūō-kōen Park, invaded by stalls until late at night. He is still weak from the flu but his account is full of emotion, especially describing the parades of dancers, street performer, and fireworks lighting up the night alongside the lanterns hanging outside the stores.

"Of all the mid-August festivals, this is one of the most beautiful in Japan..." he tells me as we cross the park that is the festival's stage, now only inhabited by contorted pines that autumn cannot undermine.

In contrast to many tourists, I find it easy to feel the spirit of this small port city even in this season, with its empty, peaceful roads, and the salty smell mixing with that of resin and the fried food we've been so looking forward to trying.

Chikusei is the restaurant we've decided on to taste the *sanuki udon* 「讃岐うどん」, one of Japan's most popular type of *udon*, often accompanied by *tenpura* eggs here in Takamatsu. Like almost all the widespread self-service restaurants in the prefecture, this place is a little like a family-run canteen, where the smell of fried food invades the dining room, enveloping benches from which clients continually get up and down.

Two old ladies get the better of their clientele's loud chatter with their high-pitched voices, organizing the exchange of bowls at the windows of the kitchen where other ladies are busy making sure the steam coming from the pans has just the right aroma.

We are hardly through the door before a member of staff greets us: resolute and severe as a soldier, speaking a mixture of Japanese and English, she explains how the self-service system works. With no possibility of error, because it is absolutely not contemplated in the tone of her voice, we chose *udon* in hot broth accompanied by an impressively large prawn and an egg, both covered in crunchy *tenpura*, the total coming to only 400 *yen*.

Then, directly after our choice is made, thrown into the maelstrom of steam and fried cooking, we are each handed an empty bowl in which the lady pours the freshly cooked *udon* and we are accompanied over to a series of containers with illustrated instructions: dip the *udon* in a large pot of boiling water for approximately 40 seconds until fully cooked; add hot broth and then your chosen condiments: spring onions, *tenpura*, ginger, seaweed and lemon.

In the middle of this organised commotion we manage to find a relatively secluded spot where we peacefully enjoy the marvellous dish we have just created: the subtlety of the broth, the smooth consistency of the thick *udon*, the crispiness of the Japanese *tenpura* dipped in the viscous yolk that escapes as you bite into the egg, the great big crunchy and indescribably sweet prawn.

Of a sudden in the minuscule space of a bowl the *sanuki udon* turns into an explosion of taste and consistency, exactly as Takamatsu would go from being an oft ignored city to a place of hidden treasures: before we can even admire the magnificent pines and coloured dances, we find its pearly *udon* and crunchy gold improve the simplest of dishes.

At the north entrance to Ritsurin-kōen we are welcomed by different *bonsai*[97] 「盆栽」 pines kept in small coloured pots.

---

[97] Trees kept miniature inside small pots for many years. A complex art, in that as the plant grows it is encouraged to take on the desired shape and dimensions by continual root and leaf pruning.

Sanuki udon 讃岐うどん

The udon, unlike the sōmen originating in China, are a thicker type of noodles native to Japan whose thickness depends on which region they come from. Made of soft wheat flour, water and salt, they are served in hot and cold soups, accompanied by ingredients like vegetables, fish, tenpura, tōfu, chāshū and so on.

The name 'sanuki udon' comes from the ancient region of Sanuki where they were created over 1200 years ago, today Kagawa Prefecture of which Takamatsu is the largest city.

With their typical thick, tubular shape, it is the most famous among the three tastiest types of udon in Japan, alongside kishimen udon from Nagoya, with the flattened shape that looks like fat 'fettuccini', and inaniwa udon from Akita, thinner and light in colour.

In the whole prefecture, there are over 700 restaurants specializing in this type of udon in different variants. Of which the famous kametama udon is served with soy or fish-based soup topped with raw egg. Many of these restaurants are collected in the city of Takamatsu, the region's capital, and adopt the self-service formula where once the client has received their bowl of steaming noodles, they can finish cooking it in special pans, choosing the consistency they prefer and additional ingredients.

This treat, excellence of the Kagawa Prefecture which has the highest per capita consumption of udon, can be had all year: in the summer cold dishes are very popular, like the zaru and bukkake versions, in winter the noodles tend to be eaten in steaming soups made of miso, soy or curry, as in the kitsune and karē versions. Tasting sanuki udon is a real culinary journey that allows you to immerse yourself in the gastronomic culture of Kagawa and to discover why this delicacy is so loved by locals and visitors from all over the world and their consumption grows every summer in conjunction with the arrival of tourists, also eager to attend the celebrations of the Sanuki Takamatsu Matsuri.

The culture of udon is so deep-rooted that 'udon day' was established on July 2nd, during which this traditional Kagawa noodle is celebrated and promoted throughout the country.

Future descendants that, despite their dimensions, have already received years of care. Just now they are like newborns in a garden where thousands of *kuromatsu*[98] 「黒松」 and *akamatsu*[99] 「赤松」 have seen generations, transforming themselves into the symbol of a country where nature is safeguarded over time, shaped by man to enhance the order of its form and the beauty of its natural disorder. I don't know what to expect from this garden, but even after a few steps along the waterside, I am spellbound by the army of conifers that, with the eagerness of Narcissus gazing at his reflection, twist and stretch across the surface of the water, touching it lightly here and there and drawing over it the shadow of sinuous branches.

Around Shōkō Shōrei-kan, a large white and wood oriental style building, tall pines meander upwards and, exactly as in Japanese drawings, wear their foliage at several levels like brushstrokes of green clouds neatly overlaid around the black branches. I think of how much dedication has been needed by generations of expert gardeners to shape these trees, giving them an appearance that, though artificial, seems natural.

The same applies to the magnificent Tsurukame-matsu, the 'Crane Tortoise Pine', one of the oldest in the complex, along the path to the northern lake of the garden, Hok-ko. It is enveloped on the great mass beneath, sculpted by hands and time as though it were made of rock, described as a crane with wings outstretched taking off with the bark of a tortoise.

Teahouses flank the hilly confines of the garden, a high

---

[98] Japanese black pine, the country's most common pine cultivar and particularly resistant, characterized by dark grey bark and hard, dark needles

[99] Japanese red pine, cultivar with red-brown bark and soft, thin needles, a slender trunk; more delicate than the black pine

wood promontory that acts as a backdrop for the Okedoi-no-taki Falls, origin of Ritsurin-kōen's system of waterways. In this area, the streams are populated by the rounded leaves of water lilies on which tortoises and frogs languish lazily. In autumn these leaves become so thin that they resemble patches of tempera melted on the surface, drops of a thousand shades of green in a picture whose highest expression is a little bright red bridge, among the pines bowed down over the river.

So, after not even an hour's visit I find myself walking through a garden that has literally enraptured my sight and heart. Whichever way I turn, I am besieged by vistas of unimaginable beauty, where armies of dwarf pines, exhausted beneath the weight of their flattened foliage, bend in on themselves, like a layered cake whose different layers melt and collapse one on the next. Some of them look like cumulus green clouds, stratified rather like a typhoon collecting on the horizon.

Then you only have to walk beneath them to witness a spectacle that is yet more majestic: storms of branches swirling underneath the needle caps, black bolts of lightning branching out again and again, trembling against the white of the sky to become slenderer and slenderer, exploding in emerald tufts at their extremities.

I move through this world of bark and leaves, trying to immortalise a wonderland that seems exactly like that created by the Japanese brushes of the great artists. Under the vault of branches where the wood appears fluid as it runs through an infinite network of curves and offshoots, I don't seem to be able to tell this reality apart from that of the most famous paintings of Hokusai or Hiroshige.

And all of a sudden, in a universe where I would happily stay stuck, part of the identity of Japan clearly manifests itself: I take in the shapes and beauty that inspired these men, that shaped a people, that created a culture so closely tied to nature; I take in the grace of the Japanese gestures and movements, of yesterday and today; I take in the sinuosity with which their brushes move on paper and I understand the necessary and intimate correlation with writing, the symbols and shapes of nature; I understand the curves and perspectives of Japanese architecture, the lines and bases that are religious representations as in the arts of fighting. Everything is a derivation of nature, of these fluid and unapproachable shapes. A people born and raised in this type of nature could not but seize its traits - the marvel of it all - to then absorb it and make it anew, identical to itself. Every tree writhing in the dance of trunks and branches in this garden is an ancestor of it. And still today is its absolute representation.

I float along in this world like a pine over water, like Neagari Goyō-matsu, the centuries-old pine that was once a *bonsai* emerging from the sea of white gravel waving its edges, silent in the milky garden of the Kikugetsu-tei Teahouse: there it is rippling through the concentric circles around the mass of its roots, in perfect rings around a ball of wood diving not into water but into stone. In the same way, the large wooden posts that hold up the airborne branches unsettle that perfectly raked stone sea with a continual movement in its immobility. Only a line of flat stepping stones make it fordable, over to the entrance of the house, where you catch a glimpse of the *tatami* through the sliding doors opening onto the garden. I gaze at the bed of gravel falling into the water of Lake Nan-ko in which the ancient pine is mirrored, light as though it has never been, and I contemplate the lake in which pods of earth emerge, the sister islands Ten'nyo-to and Fū-sho, duplicating the colours of the acers covering

181

them, from bright green to the tints of a yellow-ochre, salmon and coral pink sunset, all melted onto the liquid surface.

We reach an area of higher ground and, hungry for more marvels, we walk around the lake coming across another small islet of bushes pruned into heart shapes with a perfection of which only the Japanese can be capable. I feel tenderness as I admire the shapes, so out of context in this place and in a country where feelings are so hidden, so discreet. And yet, every so often, sweetness is suddenly overflowing when we least expect it, or hiding pretty much everywhere, dressed in *kawaii*[100] 「可愛い」, without us realising it. As in the drawings on the street signs, or in the underground, on instructions or important notices, where sweet, infantile images are used to explain serious things. It is the tenderness and the enduring link with childhood, with the love for beautiful things that are a part of it, which this nation maintains and makes manifest.

I give Gabry a wry grin as we photograph ourselves in front of some azaleas. I didn't expect him to want to take a photo like this. Rather like the Japanese, he often appears cold and distant, behind a protective wall. But his eyes are full of tenderness; you can see he wants to go back to loving and being loved. I know this won't be the photo to dissipate the veil of sadness hanging over him; doubts about the future that is no longer the past, that he was used to. But the tenderness around us, all this love set free by the beauty of nature's shapes, does good to our inner selves.

In the end, we arrive at the view where the garden shows off all the beauty it possesses: from the panoramic high ground of Hirai-hō Hill, where we admire the umpteenth

---

[100] Japanese term used to indicate objects and people expressing tenderness or sweetness; something adorable in its childlike silliness

painting of this trip, perhaps the finest so far, in a garden where colour and shape seem surreal. Featuring in the vista is Engetsu-kyō Bridge lying long over the emerald lake while below it a straw-hatted rower in a wooden canoe cuts through the water. The boat glides along slowly, disappearing behind islets that from here look like golden buttons, dotted with acers, pines and heart–shaped trees. From above we can also see the stretches of low pines tiptoeing like a continuous floor of clouds to the edge of the water. And finally there are the gardeners atop their ladders, silently touching each sprig, adjusting and trimming it so that the grey bark turns in unimaginable curves: one sprig at a time. I watch them as they create trees that are Japan, just as Michelangelo created the Sistine ceiling. For the garden of Takamatsu with its pines is no more or less than a Japanese Sistine Chapel.

On the way to Fuyō-hō Hill, from which we spot again the great Lake Hok-ko, we pass more pines and a red bridge before reaching another small shop hidden among the trees. In the garden there are various stores selling souvenirs, wrapped confectionary or freshly cooked *dango*. Inside their old, patched wooden shells, in the constant half-light between the shelves, time seems to have stopped. They are tired places, where the décor and proprietors have grown old, the thin glass of the windows yellowed, the sliding doors rusty. Now more solitary and deserted than ever, I wonder how these places have survived the years; the meagre number of clients rising only during the summer festivals: the *dango* displayed a while before being sold. They smell of something lost but at the same time found, wells of nostalgia you easily come across here in Japan. On the corner of the umpteenth restaurant there is a tiny shop that immediately attracts my attention. Outside, on a rickety

183

wooden table, sit a dozen black pine *bonsai*, transplanted into tiny second hand pots.

I go closer, sensing the aura of melancholy pervading the tiny store, embellished with marvellous tree miniatures displaying the same beauty as the garden's giants. To buy a *bonsai* and do it in Japan is without doubt as desirable as it is hard to do. My eyes fall on one of the smaller plants, whose price is paltry compared to what we are used to.

"Do you think... we could take it with us?"

Gabry gives me the look I was expecting: since we're only half way through the trip and we'll be moving around the whole time, with our luggage in tow, and we don't even know if a Japanese plant species is allowed on the plane home, I expect him to come to the same conclusion I've reached myself.

"I think we should take it. We can call her Ciccioletta, our 'little one', and we'll nurture her ourselves, fostering her just as we do our own affection."

For a second I am caught unawares. And then, there is that feeling of confusion in which a tiny instant of happiness insinuates itself. A heartbeat projecting its loveliness into an uncertain future, bestowing on it that sweet nuance of certitude to make the present a little less hard, a little more acceptable. In silence, I watch as the lady wraps Ciccioletta in newspaper, and gaze at that slight, slender plant as though it were the most precious thing in the world. There's no time to worry about how we'll manage to carry her around Japan with us, or the danger of having to give her up at the airport, before the unkempt little pine with its few tentative branches is already in a bag dangling from my hand.

We rustle up a few more memories of this incredible place at the souvenir shop near the east exit, because sometimes we feel the lack of something a bit less if we have material objects to remember it by. In this place hiding infinite treasures, I'm thrilled to admire the delicacy of Sanuki Kagari Temari, coloured balls made of woven cotton or silk thread that children all over Japan loved to play with during the Heian period and that today are for the most part used as decorations, with increasingly complex designs and motifs. And then the Sanuki lanterns, typically elongated and made in thin coloured *washi* paper, invading temples and sanctuaries of all Japan.

Among the souvenirs and packets of *udon*, I deceive myself that I'm taking away the magic I found beneath the pines of Takamatsu, gazing at the hearts in the autumnal lake, and Gabry's smile as he looks fondly at Ciccioletta. But that's not how it is, and right away a taxi, a train and another taxi take us to Okayama, shortening the gap between places that are in fact a long way from each other, alongside time that never slows down. Someday there will be an airplane; these memories in our luggage. Perhaps Ciccioletta. Inexorably, the happiness stays here, stuck in these places, in the serpenting branches of the pines.

That night I cry under the covers. Weeping for the happiness that will no longer be and hasn't yet been.

I cry after Gabry dumped on me the stinging hurt inside his heart. A few words to make me understand he isn't happy - although we're here, we're together – and I yearn for tomorrow as I cry for a past that won't go away and a future than won't come. I cry for a Japan that I don't have, but that I desperately want.

I cry for that fleeting happiness that once again, already far from the pines that are Japan, I don't know where to look for nor how to build.

Travel Notes

The city of Takamatsu is located on the north-east coast of Shikoku, reached from Okayama on the JR Seto-Ōhashi train line that crosses the inland sea on the Great Seto-ōhashi Bridge.
Known for its sanuki udon and the summer festival, it is also famous for the largest pine garden in the country, with over a thousand varieties grown for centuries in different ways. Not surprisingly, the city's name means literally 'tall pine'.
Besides the scenic branches of its conifers, Ritsurin-kōen Garden, dating back to the 1600s, offers views such as that of Lake Nanko where still today you can go on relaxing trips in the traditional boats of the feudal lords. What is more, the city produces the highest number of pine bonsais in Japan, with dozens of specialised garden centres and highly skilled gardeners.
Sanuki Takamatsu Matsuri, from 12 to 14 August, is one of the 4 large Shikoku festivals, with distinctive dances and an hour long pyrotechnic show called Dondon Takamatsu on the evening of 13 August at the city's port.
Finally, from the port of Takamatsu small ferries leave daily for the smaller islands, such as Shōdoshima with its olive trees, and Naoshima with museums and contemporary art.

Day Trip:
* ❋ Morning visit to Kōraku-en Garden and the black castle
* ❋ Take train from Okayama to Takamatsu
* ❋ Try sanuki udon at a do-it-yourself restaurant
* ❋ Visit Ritsurin-kōen Garden
* ❋ Hunt for local souvenirs in Marugamemachi-shōtengai shopping arcade
* ❋ Return to Okayama

Typical Products and Souvenirs:
* ❋ Kuromatsu and Akamatsu pine bonsais
* ❋ Box of sanuki udon with sauces

* ❋ Sanuki kagari-temari, decorative thread balls
* ❋ Sanuki-chōchin, hand painted lanterns
* ❋ Aji-seki, local stone used for craftsmanship

Niihama
新居浜

In the city that knows no foreigners,
from daybreak to nightfall we plunge into the colours
and sounds of its autumn welcome,
in a feast bursting the river banks
and overrunning the rice fields.
Over it shines the same sun,
bathing in gold the float dragons as they do battle.
There is a life that flows humbly in these places,
without time tarnishing traditions, the belonging,
the expectancy of a moment
that has always and will always bring
the simplest and most vital elation we can enjoy

An empty container.

I wake up with the feeling of lightness you get after crying, when you've let go of a great deal more than tears. I lie there, teetering between the incredible desire to run away from that persistent moment in my life, and the impelling need to find an anchor to keep me here in Japan forever.

Immobile under the covers I wait for Gabry to hug me. I want him more than anything. And finally the embrace comes, in the silent incredulity still weighing over the room from the evening before. He reassures me, saying that the wretchedness he'd hurled at me has nothing to do with me or the road we are trying to build together. But I don't want to talk about it. I simply want to forget last night, what was said, what was thought and not said. Because more than anything I want this trip to be a rebirth, when I finally take my life in hand and decide how to be happy.

Once again we are heading for Shikoku, and once more travelling over the sea, which seems a quieter blue today, under the white clouds.

Niihama is a city to the east of Takamatsu, along the island's central coast, rarely frequented by Japanese tourism and practically not at all by western. All the same, when we arrive at the station in the late morning, we discover yet another rough diamond hidden in the secret mine of the Rising Sun, where it is not enough to cast your gaze on the gems that stand out, you also need to know how to look beneath the rock to find the more precious stones.

I feel a true traveller and not a tourist as, not far from the station platform, I find myself walking beneath the decorations of the October Niihama Taiko Matsuri, intoxicated by the wonder of my first visit to an unknown place as I take in its tradition and identity. The next step, as Takayama has just shown me, is to be a part of it.

As we stand at a loss in front of an information poster, a local girl spontaneously comes up to help us: she understands very little English, and after several attempts at explaining and answering our questions, she takes us to the nearby information centre. Because in Japan someone in need of help cannot be left to get on with it, even if you can't help them yourself.

So, from my first trips, I gradually got used to shopkeepers leaving their counters unmanned to accompany you to where you need to go, to the old gentleman leading you onto your bus, kindly asking the driver to let you know when the bus reaches your stop, of the mother and child who, seeing you worried after missing a train, come up to ask '*Daijōbu?*'[101]. A nation considered enclosed in its traditions, knows how to be unexpectedly and extremely welcoming to the foreigner. The roots of this concern for your neighbour might be traced to the society based on collectivism rather than individualism, to the story of a people isolated from the world for centuries and in which there is still the strong necessity to help one another, to respect your neighbour and behave to them as you would want them to behave to you. Our perception of the other, as though their needs are our own, expands the idea that making people happy makes us happy too, that being honest and generous pays in equal honesty and altruism, completely invalidating protagonism and the glorification of the individual widespread in the west, the continual pursuit of satisfaction of our own needs before anything else can get in the way.

Moreover, the Japanese notion of community is even more heightened in small communities, far from the great urban centres, in the countryside and villages where next to the sense of belonging is that of hospitality. And here, in the small city where there are no English signs and where contact with foreign tourism is minimal, a young girl takes us under her wing and helps us find the information we are after, the festival programme and the times and locations of the various events. Hers was a simple gesture, but one of enormous importance to us.

The current time of day and the difficulty of moving between the city's festival zones on limited public transport, convinces us to take a taxi that in a quarter of an hour reaches the mouth of River Kokuryō-gawa. On the opposite bank of the river, we can see the tall, golden festival floats, differing from those of Takayama and Himeji in their

---

[101] Question expressing interest and concern, rather like 'Everything ok?'

magnificent roofs of coloured fabric. Right here, on the wharf of the wide and placid river, is the morning competition of Kasenjiki-kōen Park, one of the more than 30 events programmed for the four days of celebration that shake Niihama in this season.

During the competition, 15 of the 50 *taikodai*[102] 「太鼓台」 compete with each other to the sound of songs, whistling and rocking until about midday, surrounded by a cordon of stalls and an enormous crowd of merry makers.

We ask the driver to set us down before we reach the bridge, taken up by the emotion of the spectacle made even more suggestive seen from afar: hundreds of people flock along the opposite bank, wandering between the floats as if the river had overflowed and taken on human form. The old, the young and the very young seem prey to a strange magic, in a euphoria in which they move as one towards the meeting place. As soon as we join the adoring crowd, two floats appear from nearby roads in their golden, garish dress, take over the road and begin to float along the sea of festival-goers.

As at our previous festival, during Niihama Taiko Matsuri the teams display their rivalry as much as they can by means of uniforms, banners and flags in the colour of their faction. But here what really makes the difference is the power and excitement with which the teams vocally express themselves in choirs of encouragement, whistles and the frenetic hoisting of each float. Fifteen-foot towers glide along in front of us, temporarily resting on two huge wheels and pushed by rows of men by means of four large wooden

---

[102] Enormous festival floats exquisitely decorated in fine cloths portraying scenes from folklore, inside which is a large taiko drum that provides the team's rhythm with its deep sound. They are fifteen feet high and can weigh as much as 3 tons, so moving them is very demanding

poles that emerge from the structure. During the competition these massive poles serve to lift the structure off the ground, in a formidable show of strength and coordination by each team. At the top of every *taikodai*, around a dome of finely decorated cloth are four men and the hanging coloured pom-poms, vast funny-looking versions of those used to tie back the curtains at home or to decorate furniture handles. Another four men stand at the fluctuating base of the tower, waving handkerchiefs in the team colour and loudly blowing their whistles. On their heads are the classic match strips, making their faces warlike and romantic. It is they who animate the parade, directing and encouraging the crowd with zeal, and chanting the rhythmic shout '*Sorya! sorya!*'[103] to spur on their team.

As at Takayama, inside the float is the pulsing heart of the great *taiko*, whose percussion beats time for the march and the team's chanting. The insistent rhythm of the songs, the jolting movements of the floats, the springing stance of the men standing on them and stretching towards the excited crowd, and the deep, regular sound of the drums are a joy and produce an explosion of life that you can't but be gripped by.

So, I find myself smiling as I skip up and down attempting to take a video to the sound of the whistling. I look around me and realise everyone else is smiling too; fathers stroll along with their children on their shoulders, pointing out the floats and magnificent images decorating their sides. It is a day everyone - adults and kids alike - experiences the joy of being together, unconditionally linked to their traditions, relating to something belonging to their ancestors that will one day belong to their own descendants. It is a day of

---

[103] 'Sorya' is a cry of incitement the Japanese use before activities requiring physical strength, for example lifting a heavy weight or sprinting in a race

celebration here in Niihama, and yet another for Japan. Here, in the country where every day of the year recalls something, where seasons are contemplated and revered for their beauty, where every moment is treated as a gift.

Because in its flow, life is so fine and precious that it must surely be celebrated.

Entranced, I walk among the floats, now side by side on the riverbank, hunkered down on their long wooden poles. The team members are having a rest in the floats' shade, young and middle aged men in jackets the colour of the pom-poms and fabrics decorating the float.

The walls of the towers look like massive sheets of gilded metal with dragons, warriors, animals and temples racing across the surface. However, closer to, one can make out the ruse of the padded cloth perfectly simulating the consistency and shine of gold. The images in relief are made with such precision and wealth of detail that they seem animated: the long red whiskers of a dragon in flight seem to protrude from the image, the armour of a samurai reflecting the thickness of its scales; the white eye of a devil sticking out globular, shiny and mapped with bloody red veins. They are true works of art that would hold their own next to sculptures made of valuable materials.

The children climb all over the parked floats, while some of the teams head for the centre of the field to line up for the start of the competition. I join Gabry to watch the first part of the real show, a sort of dance in which adversaries present themselves to the public and look each other over prior to the afternoon competition, held in another part of the city. Just like Takayama, we are incorporated in a timeless enthusiasm, although here the atmosphere is considerably more genuine, the parade less opulent and showy, more traditional and removed from any form of touristic onset.

Niihama Taiko Matsuri is not well known among foreign visitors, and brought to our senses by the rhythm possessing us we notice we are the only non-Japanese in the whole park, and probably the city. This would explain the amazed, curious and amused expressions directed at us by many of those present. We feel ourselves at the centre of attention and every time we pass a child, they stare at us in open-mouthed astonishment.

On my previous trips I never experienced being 'other', or feeling I was the odd one out in a vast crowd. The sensation made me reflect of how they would lead us to better comprehend a people cut off for so long and only opening up to the new, the other, in the last few decades: an opening up in some respects necessary and positive, in others dangerous.

In cities like Tōkyō, by now westernisation is advancing at an incessant pace and doesn't only affect the impudence and frenzy with which the west introduces its consumerism and global attitudes. It also affects the fragility with which new generations in the large cities, more distanced from the deeper Japanese traditions and culture of the countryside, approach this change. Increasingly they seem to endure rather than assimilate it, in a country where the survival of traditions has always resided in the ability to assimilate the different while keeping their own roots alive. Fortunately, cities like Niihama remind us how, in many areas, Japan is still new to this change.

An old gentleman with his hands folded behind his back smiles at us with a nod of the head and seems pleased to see us so enthusiastically enjoying the parade, proud perhaps that his city and festival are appreciated by a foreigner. We almost walk on tiptoe amidst the Japanese, who glance at us, proud of their day, as we try to show as much respect as possible for the local festivity, being careful when we take photos and where we go. It is respect we feel to our hosts, and is almost always repaid with welcome and an invitation to join them.

The queues at the food stalls are slowly building up, and we quickly join the ordered serpentine lines before the wait becomes unfeasible. Gabry takes up position in front of a *karāge*[104] 「唐揚げ」 stall, from where we see large cups overflowing with golden pieces of fried chicken appear. Whereas I wait patiently to buy a special rice *onigiri* wrapped in a piece of grilled bacon, one of the culinary peculiarities it is easy to run into at local festivals.

We picnic on the riverbank, a slight distance from the sea of festival-goers meandering excitedly between the food stalls and resting floats. Here, in front of a group of children playing bare feet on the pebbles in the shallows, the river performs its magic, exactly as it did on that day at Shirakawa-gō: concerns and worries glide swiftly away, with the lightness of the paper boats that have unexpectedly appeared on the water, chasing each other to the yelps of joy from the children whose hands they have escaped.

"It's like a scene embracing the world's serenity, don't you think?"

I look at the parents watching over their children, and smile at those who roll up their trousers so they don't get wet as they play, while others hold the smaller kids' hands as they clumsily try to pile up the round stones they've fished out here and there. I'd like time to stand still so I can savour the sight of happiness for longer and at the same time I wish it would accelerate, so that I am at the moment

---

[104] Cooking technique, generally involving chicken, rolled in flour and potato starch and deep fried, very common street food at festivals. The same technique can be used with other foods

when I can take part. I'd love to see my child teetering among the pebbles too, I'd like to hold them by the hand as they enjoy the essential simplicity of feast days like this one.

I wonder if that tenderness might one day be mine too. If I will manage to live with such serenity and see my child play, learning the meaning of life with innocence and ingenuity.

It is early afternoon when the formation of floats disperses into so many pilgrimages via the city's shrines through the narrow internal streets of Niihama.

After the pause, 15 *taikodai* meet up near Takihama JR station for the main contest, *kakikurabe*[105] 「かきくらべ」, programmed from 4:30 to 6:30pm. We decide to join two of them in their march to the Hachiman-jinja Shrine, where two teams take a pause. We realise it is an hour's walk only because we go with them. Along with a small group of people we cross the outskirts of Niihama, walking along roads that cut through the countryside.

We exchange smiles with others accompanying the float to its destination, as though holding hands along the way. From time to time the floats seem to thank their escorts with sudden explosions of exuberant chanting that break the quiet of the Japanese countryside. Our pilgrimage through the newly ploughed rice fields, splendid wrinkled sheets of dark soil dotted with yellow sprigs, around which the shadows of dislodged mud spars with the reflections in the water pooled in the furrows; bright blue puddles like the early afternoon sky shining on them. In this parcelled cloth-like land there is sometimes a late field where, among the thin and still-green rice leaves, coppery stems are now bending

---

[105] Taikodai competition consisting of a test of strength where the teams must lift their float highest and for as long as possible

195

to the ground beneath the weight of the full grains. Leaning out on the edge of the street I pick a cornstalk and dig for the rough rice inside. It is the first time in my life that I do something so banal but in daily reality, so rare. I feel contact with the beginning of things, with something of which we've lost the perception, in a world where what counts is only the end product. Now it is only a yellowish grain, but tomorrow it will be the white grain that has accompanied the history of an entire populace, becoming a single entity. I stare fascinated at the dark bundles enveloping them, and quite simply find it one of the most beautiful things I've ever seen.

The floats are resting in the shade of the trees at Ha-chiman-jinja Shrine and the teams refuelling with *onigiri* e *bentō* that a local person or family member has bought at the nearby *konbini*. We decide to go on and head for Takihama station.

When we finally reach Heiwa-dōri Street, after several miles on foot, we are tired but also ready for what is to come. The wide two-lane avenue has been closed to traffic for the event and is now colourful with food stands and a small stage set up for the jury of the contest.

"This is serious!" exclaims Gabry, while I, perennially on the hunt for culinary street specialities to spoil my stomach, am on the point of buying a strip of fried pastry coated with garlic and cheese.

Before long the street begins to fill with people, and the stage fills too, while scrupulous policemen begin their dance of arms and luminous rods to direct the flow of spectators away from the areas where the floats are on display.

When the hordes are already thronging the pavements, we hear the whistles and *taiko* come closer. The floats, emerging from side streets, begin to form a line, waiting to

Niihama Taiko Matsuri 新居浜太鼓祭

Niihama Taiko Matsuri has a thousand year history and is today considered one of the three best festivals on Shikoku, alongside the summer celebrations: Yosakoi Matsuri in Kochi and Awa Odori at Tokushima. Like most autumn festivals, it is based on a Shinto omen for a good rice harvest and is held over three days in mid-October.

The protagonists of the event are 50 enormous taikodai, one for each neighbourhood of the city, floats more than 15 foot high that weigh more than 3 tons, each containing a large taiko drum.

The floats parade through the city, jauntily covered in futon-jime, covered in fine woven gold cloth with fabric appliqués suggestively sewn into designs of folklore and Japanese myths.

The teams make up around 150 men, known as kakifu, of which four, standing on the structure, direct all the others through gestures and whistling sounds. Coordination is fundamental during the kakikurabe, the most eagerly awaited moment of the celebration: the wheels are taken off and the team starts lifting their taikodai as high as possible and for as long as possible in a climax of cheering and chanting to the beat of the drums and waving handkerchiefs. Due to this extreme demonstration of physical strength, the festival is also known by the name of Otoko Matsuri, the festival of the men.

Besides the kakikurabe, over the three days of festivities, there are more than 30 events from morning to night, including performances and parades, held in about 9 different zones in the city. In some areas the festival goes on until late at night, when the floats are hung with lanterns and lights making the nocturnal parades very beautiful. The whole event is accompanied by stalls selling food and souvenirs. On alternate years, 8 floats are paraded on the sea to carry out a propiatory fishing rite, or funamiyuki. It may happen that two rival teams wage such violent war that one or both are destroyed, although the practice has been made illegal.

During Taiko Matsuri, Ōshima Aki Matsuri at Ōshima Shrine is also famous. The main event of this festival is the nighttime parade, held each second Saturday of October, you can see typical Danjiri floats, aka 'Yomiya', gliding by lit up by lanterns.

197

access the main road for their own performance. Their enormous wooden wheels are substituted by lighter mobile supports so that the teams can lift the heavy structures in the incredible show-down to come.

We stand near the cross-roads to have a good view of the tower and the jury's stage at the same time. On the stage a graceful Japanese lady is presenting each team and float to the public. In a ringing voice sounding very much like the audio recordings in train stations and on tv, she introduces the first *taikodai* and gives the go ahead for the competition.

With astonishing force, seen in their red and straining faces, the team members make their way to the centre of the crossroads, lift the tower and begin to perform the raising and lowering that is the dance, or *kakikurabe*, accompanied by whistling, drumming and the now familiar popular chanting directed by the four men at the foot of the tower. The float jolts on the team's shoulders, the pom-poms jigger wildly and the four men seem possessed by a divinity, every time they nearly fall off but manage to absorb the violent rocking by bending their knees and adapting to sudden, disordered movements. Whistling as loud as they can to urge on their companions beneath them, willing them to push the tower higher and to keep it raised as long as they can, for several interminable minutes the team hold out to the rhythm, encouraged by the public and the presenter's praise. It is she who asks the crowd to acclaim the best teams in the contest, whilst the jury assesses the focus and coordination with which the float is lifted off the ground.

We are glued to the spectacle for ages, witnessing several 'coups de théâtre': a murmur of fear and the crowd holding its breath when one of the teams succumbs to the weight of its tower, nearly upturning the entire *taikodai* into the street. Then the men with their whistles jump down, thrown off balance by their teammates below, and hurriedly help them lift the drooping side of the heavy structure back up to regain balance.

"*Daijōbu?*" asks the presenter worriedly, who then can't but support the probable losers by asking the public to applaud the team for its tenacity. In silence the group recomposes itself, and with equal composure moves next to the floats that have already performed. No one shows any disappointment in word or gesture, only an extreme grace in the expressions of those accepting defeat.

The World Cup in Russia comes to mind, where Japan brushed against historical qualification in the quarter-finals when it lost to Belgium. There were tears from some of the players at the end of the match, an unusual way for the Japanese to show their emotions, and something that struck me deeply. But the world, being unaware of the mores of such a different culture didn't seem to notice, although it was amazed by what happened next, when the team left their changing room immaculate, in fact cleaner than it had been before: and a piece of paper was found on the table bearing the words 'Thank you' translated into Russian.

It is now five in the afternoon and the sun is inundating the road with a warmer colour, mingling the tones of autumn to create a light that is unique in the world. Everything turns into a warm golden shade, the floats shine more than ever: the colours of their drapery and pom-poms standing out and the shadows stretching over the still excited throng waiting for the last teams.

We wiggle our way through to the station where the small mobile shrine to Ōtarachihime-jinja has been set up, with purple drapery and proud priests encircling it. The evening performance of this *mikoshi* is scheduled for around

7pm, but we decide to go back to Niihama's central station for the final evening event involving the floats.

So just as the evening damp begins to prod at the skin, we leave the contest and take refuge in the small, old waiting room at Takihama station.

Sitting opposite us is an old couple. I observe their accumulated years and how they show in their oriental faces. Like the ancient trees that have lived through different eras, it feels as though I am reading in their skin the work in the fields, bringing up children, difficulties encountered on their way through life. The deep, crumpled furrows are in contrast with the clean, ironed clothes they are wearing, best clothes so humble that they are light years from the clothes we would usually wear for special occasions. I imagine them put away carefully in cupboards, their preciousness tied to the occasion, to the special moment.

"Sometimes I really think I want to drop everything and live in this simplicity, where being attached to fewer things makes them all the more precious. I'd like to get to their age and feel the importance of dressing differently for a special day, the importance of living it next to my husband, in the same spirit as the first time. Then to return home and be happy to have experienced that day for perhaps the 61st time, without thinking of whether or not they'll be a 62nd, and stowing away the clothes with the same love as all the other times. Waking up the next day to go back to working in the field, side by side with my life's companion. It seems so little, and yet I think that's all that's needed to be happy."

Gabry doesn't reply, he sits in silence, just as the old couple are, leaning against each other. In their best clothes for the day of festivity that is always the same.

The train for Niihama central station is packed with travellers from the celebrations in other areas of the city and the destination is the nocturnal parade of floats. When the doors open and the passengers disperse towards the various station exits, we are at a loss to identify one to follow to the next festival location.

So I ask a policeman, and as a result we find ourselves in the local Head of Police's car, driven directly to Nagata-dōri Street, near the Maruyoshi shopping centre. Despite numerous offers of help during our trips, this surpasses every experience so far. What's more, on this occasion we have encountered a bobby immensely grateful to have the chance to speak English with us: with great pride he tells us about the language course he had taken so as to be of help to the rare tourists visiting Niihama, and with a tenderness and genuineness that I didn't think could exist any more, he asks us if his English is of a good standard. I marvelled at his desire to feel useful, the humility with which the self is cultivated for others, the amiable fear of never being good enough to help your neighbour and the pride in being able to.

Aspects of a nation that strike and move me, which are for me the symptom of a deep esteem, of a continual search for the answer that not even anthropology can provide. *'Why here and not elsewhere?'*

We get out of the black car feeling like VIPs, make our bows and say thank you while feeling it cannot possibly suffice. Before reversing and returning to work, the policeman, whose name we don't even know, hesitates a moment, smiles and wishes us a good trip.

It is nearly 7pm and this new neighbourhood is getting ready for the nighttime performance during which, in the damp evening shadows of Niihama, eight illuminated *taikodai* will process down Nagata-dōri Street as far as the central station.

In the square in front of the shopping centre two floats are ready for the parade. Clustered around them the teams are relaxing, eating tempting street food from the small number of stalls on this stretch of road.

With nightfall, the lights on the two towers gains fullness: unlike the floats in Takayama, submerged by masses of small lights, the Niihama floats are decked out with a few large lanterns on their higher levels; from below some beams light up the high tower, creating a *raitsu-appu* effect that brings out every bas-relief, almost pulling them off the fabric to let them roam the chiaroscuro of the night. Dragons, devils and warriors acquire an unprecedented savagery and beauty as they squirm spiritedly, gnashing their teeth through the light and shade.

A little further on, the food stalls also begin to light up their tents, as the road slowly fills with people and the children's balloons proliferate above our heads, floating over the smell of fried food spreading through the air.

Just as the cool evening air is finding its way through your clothes, the first drums ring out and the floats begin their slow descent along the road. Beneath the stars the teams appear exhausted, tired out by the excitements of the day. Even the rhythmic chant of the whistles is slower now, more delicate and broken by long pauses, the sound of the *taiko* dominating the rest. They roll slowly along on their great wheels, while the beams of light from below hit them like blades, awaking and energising mythological creatures, samurais and fortresses.

Suddenly the first team brings their float to a halt, the men at the long poles begin to shake them to make the towers shudder. Their voices become louder, climbing into the dark sky. This is the signal for the *taiko* hidden in that box of spirits and warriors. The drum changes rhythm and the four men, still standing on the float, unleash a new dance of whistles and movements. The parade is on the move again but the night is no longer the same: red, yellow and white hankies whip the air, the now fluorescent pom-poms shake in the dark, bouncing up and down like the lanterns hanging next to them, like the coloured fabrics covering the top of the tower, pushing into the darkness.

From below, the road is a torchlight procession of rocking floats, of whistling to bring the crowd into line, and drumbeats creating the regal stride that makes the night majestic and solemn.

I never want to leave the show, I'd like to waft to the rhythm like the floats, lose myself in that thick tangle of darkness, light and sound, among people who, one mid-October night, have come together once more to accompany the teams in their last steadfast march of the day. But I find time here is ruthless, more so than the golden dragons of Niihama on this moonless night. I walk away, leaving all their excited elegance and magic, and yet again I feel my heart ache, shrinking smaller and smaller, as I resist the temptation to turn back.

I think of that life running on relentlessly, all those autumns bubbling over with celebrations. Last week it was Takayama, then Himeji and today Niihama. Quite soon, like a shiver running over the whole island on fire, there will be other *matsuri* in honour of autumn and its spirits. There'll be yet another night of festivities, in a season that elsewhere is associated with sadness and the end, while here it is an emanation of energetic life, in this incredible return to wonderment at nature.

We make our way to the station, a far cry from the drums,

now without the good fortune of a lift just when the legs really feel they need it. Nonetheless, soon after I appreciate it because we find ourselves wandering through unknown sleepy Niihama. We are swallowed by a new world, in deserted lanes of utter quiet, where the darkness is deepened by the glow of little lights above the wooden doors of houses, small corners of moss, stone and maple that rise up in front of terraced dwellings.

The houses, emptied by the street parties, are dark, unattended and silent as they await their owners. Someone has left their windows open, while someone else's bag of shopping sits in the bicycle basket parked outside the front door. There is joy, freedom and a sense of belonging. But then there is the distress and difficulty of accepting a world so different and far from our own. When the silence becomes so great that I begin to feel afraid I press against Gabry, as I would on the other side of the world.

'Not here.'

I repeat it to myself in an attempt to convince myself that here I am finally safe. Then, out of the darkness, a girl appears. She is entirely alone, her face lit up by the blue light of the screen of her mobile. She doesn't give us a second glance and goes on her way without a moment's thought for who she might meet in these lonely streets. I wonder again and again what it means to live without the constant awareness of danger, of evil visited on you by others, of always looking over your shoulder. How much easier and more lighthearted must daily life be for these people? What can it be like to trust others, to take it for granted they will not want to do you harm?

Around the final corner, the station sits wrapped in a halo of neon. Once again there's no time to marvel at it, before you are sitting serenely, on their feast day, of their autumn, as I'm already on the tracks running to Okayama.

"Feel like an *onigiri*?" asks Gabry on this our last evening at Okayama.

Like Niihama, I could never forget a day like this, in another city that will occupy an important place in my heart. A city smelling of the sea, that of closeness a long way off, that of joys and discoveries, but also of sickness and painful words I would rather not have had to hear. The city in which, in a few days, I feel as if I've spent a lifetime.

Tomorrow is one of farewell, and the absurd thing is that you never get used to it, because every place you visit welcomes you as if it would never let you go.

Time glides by, like the towns, station after station. And in this search for the right place, the permanent happy home, I cling on to the joy of a new beginning, so strong in these places.

Tomorrow, far from Okayama, this joy will bring relief to yet another regretful farewell.

Travel Notes

Niihama, small city on the northern coast of Shikoku and on the JR Yosan railway line, grew from a small farming village in the 1600s to an industrial centre on the Seto-naikai Inland Sea, due to the copper mines of Besshi, now open to visitors. The city attracts thousands of Japanese visitors during the autumn festival season, but also offers fantastic excursions into the surrounding mountains and around the mining area. At the end of July, River Kokuryō-gawa is the setting for Niihama Nōryō Hanabi Taikai, one of the largest firework displays in Shikoku, with over 8,000 fireworks, featuring the pyrotechnic show known as the Niagara, which is 440 yards wide. In conjunction with Niihama Taiko Matsuri, the nearby city of Saijō hosts the Saijō Matsuri, a festival with about 150 floats: taikodai, mikoshi and danjiri, as well as finely decorated minor floats made of wood. The event includes four festivals that take place between 14 and 17 October at the shrines of Kamo-jinja, Iwaoka-jinja, Isono-jinja and Iizumi-jinja. During the much-anticipated kawairi, some danjiri gather on the banks of River Kamo-gawa and enter the water with their lanterns, creating a spectacular cordon of light on the surface.

Day Trip:
* Travel by train from Okayama to Niihama
* See float display at Kasenjiki-kōen Park, along River Kokuryō-gawa (10:00am–12pm)
* Eat at festival food stalls
* Travel to Takihama station for kakikurabe contest (4:30pm–6:30pm)
* Join the evening parade of lit floats along Nagata-dōri Street, near Maruyoshi shopping centre (7:00pm–8:30pm)
* Return to Okayama

Typical Products and Souvenirs:
* Niihama-garasu, glasses made of local green glass

* Fuguzaku, puffer fish served in ponzu sauce
* Shichifuku-imo, 'ghost' sweet potato
* Zanki, deep fried boned chicken, like karāge
* Local citrus sweets and liqueurs

206

Beppu
別府

In a country where colour and reality
combine like yin and yang,
the sight of Beppu is a perpetual embrace of
water and fire, paradise and inferno.
I relish a world of indivisible contrasts,
tho' I might not understand it
I see it lessens imperfections.
Finding what does us good
is the first step towards the right life for us

An alarm ringing tired and hopeful; the 7:40 train; the cabbie clumsily pushing our heavy luggage into his black taxi, the conviction that our next trip to Japan will certainly be accompanied by fewer bags.

On the journey to Beppu we change at Kokura to catch a local train where, in a rite shared with other passengers, we turn all the seats to face the new direction of travel, towards Ōita. I had forgotten this peculiarity on Japanese trains; where you can turn your seat round when the train changes direction, just as I had forgotten that all the passengers spontaneously get up to turn the seats, not just their own, but all the seats in the carriage.

It is late morning when we reach our *ryokan*[106] 「旅館」 in Beppu, and at the entrance, on the gravel path, my enthusiasm is such that I worry I might even wipe out the

---

[106] Traditional Japanese hotel, very common in hot spring resorts

marvellous wooden construction before us. Yamada Bessō is an antique style *ryokan* not far from the railway station, a timeless jewel and economically accessible. The pebble courtyard leads under the large wooden portico, where there are benches to welcome visitors so they can remove their shoes before entering the house.

The owners are two delightful ladies who, as we watch wide-eyed, effortlessly pick up our heavy bags, avoiding scratching the floor made fragile by the passing of years. They show us into the visitors' living room, to the sound of creaking wood that is part of everything, entering a place where I could happily spend the rest of my days. In the centre of the room is a heavy round table set with two china teacups, each with a linen napkin, bathed by the light from the hexagonal window, and a view into a garden full of early autumn acers and puffs of pine. Under the windowsill sits an old bookcase bulging with books whose covers are visibly veiled with dust and time. A few *origami* storks wade in the filtered light from the thin panes of the window. To complete the picture are some wicker baskets and a coffee machine that looks like a prop from a retro movie.

Enthralled by the harmony of the room, I find myself sitting with a steaming cup of green tea and a little china plate on which, following tradition, is a slice of lemon jelly. I remember the taste of this candy, taken with Japanese tea to soften the bitterness and, despite the citrus notes, for me comparable to how I imagine the taste of wood in the olden days.

From a heavy drawer we are invited to choose two *yukata* each, of whichever design appeals. We take them with us as one of the ladies leads us down through the belly of the *ryokan*, along narrow passageways that seem to whisper at every step. Small bamboo lanterns hang on the white walls edged in black wood and sliding rice paper doors. But even the glassed corridors enclose small cloisters, beautiful troves with tiny rectangles of garden are decorated with grey stone vases, acers and smoothed stones, on one of which lies a smiling frog.

We reach our bedroom, one of the few with a bathroom en suite, as old *ryokan* often have shared bathrooms. In the enormous room, with Gabry's surname in pride of place on the door, followed by the honorary *sama*[107] 「様」, two large *futon* with downy duvets lie unrolled on the *tatami* next to the tea table and the usual floor cushions.

The wooden veranda, typical of *ryokan*, rather than looking out over the garden, has a protective wooden wall for privacy from the external *rotenburo*: in the absence of a view over maples and stone paths, it is the sound of hot spring water running into a hidden pool that melts the body and mind into the surrounding atmosphere.

Impatient to dissolve in that universe ourselves, just before leaving the *ryokan* to visit the city, we write our names on the blackboard at the entrance: at 6:30pm we'll be the ones immersed in hot spring water, rocks, steam and the autumn moon.

Beppu is the city of smoking manholes. Known throughout Japan for its natural therapeutic spas with particular, clearly distinguished features, it attracts tourists local and foreign, young and old.

The seven different *jigoku*[108] 「地獄」, yearly visited by hundreds of thousands from all over the world are an example, although this city's hot spring network is vast and

---

[107] Honorary title used in sign of respect to clients, other people and even gods

[108] 'Inferno' in Japanese

most of all used for therapeutic purposes. In fact, the wide expanse covered by Beppu's inhabited centre, unlike most smaller hot spring towns in Japan, is perfused by spring waters and an advanced system for moving boiling steam around, also used for heating in the colder months. These elements have made Beppu among the most fashionable hot spring destinations, transforming it into a steaming minestrone of attractions and wellness centres. And it is walking among the small houses, old *ryokan* and exaggerated spa skyscrapers that you come across the puffs of white vapour creeping out of manholes, or the wells used to cook *jigoku-mushi*[109] 「地獄蒸し」 food that some enterprising people have transformed into small street food activities. Even today, despite the mild weather, we see the odd tongue of steam rising from the rounded manholes even in the coastal neighbourhood.

From the variety of restaurants, you realise that Beppu, squashed between the sea and bubbling green mountains, doesn't only serve the specialities cooked in hot spring steam, but also others tied to local fishing traditions. And in the city where the sea and mild temperatures have always coexisted, we want to try the renowned prawn *tenpura* which is rumoured to be exquisite hereabouts.

Toyotsune is a nondescript two-floor restaurant not far from the port, but the *tenpura* have their place in the hearts of many review-writing tourists and locals. After a short wait at the entrance, we are shown to a small table and given a Japanese menu showing a few typical dishes including the speciality *donburi*, which are placed before us soon afterwards: two large bowls of white rice, on which sits a golden hat of ingredients abundantly overflowing the bowl. Just

---

[109] Method of cooking food in hot vapours issuing from hot springs running through towns and adding flavour to the food

like a wrapped present, ensnared in a fried crust lighter than the clouds, you can just see the orange of the pumpkin and carrots and the brilliant pinky-orange of the disproportionately large prawns lying on top. A few ingredients accompanied by the familiar smell of *miso* soup, yet another surprise beneath the black cover conserving aroma and warmth. It is a different selection of tastes, mixing sea and tradition, which for a moment seems a long way from the vaporous whisps and smell of sulphurous eggs, almost as though Beppu possesses two distinct identities.

But here in Japan, water and fire are united in an embrace that makes one think of yin and yang: indissoluble and primitive. On the island of warmth, one cannot exist without the other, much as paradise can't exist without hell. And, funnily enough, we leave this paradise of taste and gilded clouds on a sea of rice to visit one of the most famously infernal hells of Japan.

The taxi takes us to our destination in about 15 minutes, saving us a long climb up to the city's high ground. But once we reach the Umijigokumae bus stop, the panorama over the roofs of Beppu looks like a place of white smoke rising from roofs of a thousand shapes and colours, until brusquely interrupted by the sapphire ocean.

Impatiently, we plough through the confines of the ticket offices encompassing the area of the first five *jigoku*, four of which are accessible on a cumulative pass. Rather like the entrance to an amusement park for children, some people queue up to collect the first stamp of the itinerary, under the gaze of cute devils on the information and welcome signs. Everything is turned into play in this country, and an attraction of this sort lends itself particularly well to eliciting laughter from adults and young alike, faced with hot springs, each with their own mascot of a devil.

Before reaching the famous spring of Umi Jigoku, the hell of the sea, the paths snake through the park towards a large stretch of water where, in the opaque colours of hot water, they melt those of the aquatic plants and vegetation around. The rounded leaves of the water lilies make up a puzzle of buttons in green, yellow, orange and purple, dotted here and there with flowers that seem to rise out of the water on tip toes in their pink fringed tutus. Everywhere about, the woody area with its flaming acers and an army of curved shrubs pour even more colour into the water.

The hells of Beppu can be likened to a paradise of colour. We realise this when we reach Umi Jigoku, hidden beneath the powerful clouds of overbearing vapours.

Between one white plume and another, a stretch of boiling water appears; its glassy blue recalling the water of tropical atolls. Besides the endless steam, the pool is the victim of an unexpected crowd of tourists laying siege to the complex. We find it hard to get close to the pool itself until, at the side of nearby souvenir shop, we find a half-hidden flight of steps up to its terrace. From here there is a magnificent aerial view of the turquoise pool and the slender fiery red *torii* chasing each other into the woods beyond. The colours are vivid, contrasting and lit by the heat assuming the milky white form that, every now and again, hits us even at a distance. The background noise is the whistle of vapour prancing about on the surface, accompanied by the vague, continuous gurgle of the fire untiringly making Japan the twitchiest land in the world.

In search of silence and shelter from the horde of tourists at Oniishibōzu Jigoku, we head for the boiling mud hell. To get there, we stumble across a universe of pools where the subsoil plays with minerals and pressure, bringing into being

Jigoku-meguri 地獄巡り

One of the most famous attractions of Beppu is the tour of the Hells of Beppu, or jigoku-meguri, seven hot springs, unsuitable for bathing, but with unique natural features. Of these, five are in the Kannawa area, accessible by bus from Beppu JR station, while the other two are located in the Shibaseki district, about 10-15 minutes by bus from the former.

The first is Umi Jigoku, hell of the sea, with its distinctive continually bubbling cobalt blue water, in clear contrast to the tunnel of red towers leading to Hakuryū Inari-jingū Shrine behind it. There is also a large store selling souvenirs, body care and thermal mud products.

Further on we find Oniishibōzu Jigoku, a series of grey mud ponds whose bubbles bring to mind the bald heads of the Buddhist monks from which the name comes, and Kamado Jigoku, the cooker hell, which welcomes visitors with the statue of a devil looking as goofy as it is malicious. At this last there are springs of completely different aspect and colour and you can taste refreshments cooked in the hot spring vapours, jigoku-mushi, for example boiled eggs, puddings and corncobs.

Again in the Kannawa district is Oniyama Jigoku, a complex in which the hot springs alternate with enclosures for animals such as flamingos, capybara, hippos, elephants and crocodiles; and Shiraike Jigoku, white pond hell, which has a small aquarium and an enormous hot pond so cloudy it seems white.

Moving into the Shibaseki area there is Chinoike Jigoku, the bloody pond, named after its great red pool, standing out against the surrounding luxuriant vegetation.

And finally, Tatsumaki Jigoku, a unique attraction thanks to its geyser of boiling water that erupts from the caldera beneath every 30 minutes. There is also a small amphitheatre from which to watch the natural show and a store selling themed souvenirs and hot spring beauty products.

The cumulative pass, costing approximately 2100 yen (about 18 Euros) gives you access to all the hells apart from Oniyama Jigoku, which is not recommended because of the animals kept in captivity.

springs that, at a distance of a few dozen yards, are astonishingly different from each other: a coppery red pool surrounded by tropical plants; another full of grey and black stones through which a glowing steam filters; another for paddling, beset by flocks of Chinese tourists. But the true attraction of this *jigoku* are the multiple pools of grey mud, where the great blisters bubbling up from below create large white concentric discs on the sludgy surface. In that slow burble, which brings to mind minestrone soup coming to the boil, I notice patterns appearing: so many Saturns and their pure-white rings. Whilst Gabry stays true to the widespread and less romantic interpretation of the bubbles as the bald heads of Buddhist monks, from which it takes its hellish name.

Five minutes' walk away from the first complex, is Oniyama Jigoku, the entrance to which has an extra cost because of the various animals inside, mainly crocodiles. We steer well clear and go back to Kamado Jigoku, the hell welcoming visitors with a funny statue of a red devil cooking its victims in a boiling cauldron. Three pools are close to one another and look like distinctive splashes of paint on an artist's palette. You go from a pool where the flamboyant blue makes you think of a tropical sea cave to a pool that seems to be full of moulded clay, to one in the bright orange of squeezed carrot juice.

Nearby, is the refreshment area, you can try numerous foods cooked in the hot springs, such as eggs, corn on the cob and... puddings! In Japan the pudding tradition is well loved: famous in *manga*, in *anime*[110] 「アニメ」 and in TV series, they are extensively available in *konbini*, supermarkets and in small shops where they are homemade.

---

[110] Japanese cartoons with their own distinctive style, usually taken from manga comics

Puddings that, alongside eggs, can be cooked in volcanic waters and are often served as typical foods at the hot springs. Lovers of the Japanese creamy custard pudding, with its strong taste of milk, we let ourselves be tempted by curiosity and end up with a glass jar bearing the Japanese *onsen* icons. Hard to imagine, but the sulphurous aftertaste gives these sweet puddings a special something.

The final hell in this part of the city, Shiraike Jigoku, is located a little further south. Known for its minuscule warm water fish aquarium, it consists in a single large pool of a blue so cloudy it almost resembles milk.

As Beppu descends towards the sea, we encounter kiosks using the steam from under the ground to cook food. They are little stone wells, sometimes protected by a wooden and bamboo roof, at others laid out with benches and tables on which to put the puddings or eggs. The latter are cooked inside nets tied to bamboo sticks and suspended into the well where the boiling vapours cook them in no time. It isn't only the tourists who stop to buy these traditional snacks, but also old ladies and mothers who buy a package of hot spring boiled eggs, considered good for all the family.

At the Kannawa bus stop, we are lucky enough to get the last seats on a coach already full of tourists. From guides on the web, the last *jigoku* should be less than two miles away, but the windy, very narrow road through the wooded hills around Beppu, slows down the trip to such an extent that I find myself squashed between passengers for half an hour.

The Chinoike Jigoku complex is quite out of the way with respect to the previous springs, but the greater distance from the centre of Beppu is compensated by the landscape: high, sinuous hills contain and watch over the hot springs dressed in lush forest, places where you perceive the sea lurking through the exotic palms that every so often stick out powerfully from among the tall firs.

The large lava coloured pool of this *jigoku* strikes us as a ruby stuck on the emerald garment of the surrounding woods, but it doesn't detain us as long as the smaller complex, Tatsumaki Jigoku. Here, exactly like the bus before, we find a large souvenir shop exploding with tourists of all nationalities busy buying pretty *onsen* towels, products for the skin made of mud from the springs of Beppu and statuettes of funny devils from the seven hells.

All of a sudden, the assistants usher us into the small amphitheatre with flights of steps and seats for visitors. At precise 30 minute intervals, the *jigoku* geyser erupts in steam and boiling water reaching a height of ten feet. And like everything here in Japan, this natural phenomenon is also 'decked out' as an attraction to generate amazement and expectancy: the arena, the minute panel explaining the phenomenon, in fact the whole scene is managed in the smallest detail. Often the purpose of such perfectionism and care in places to visit isn't even tied to increasing the actual revenue, given the nominal entry charge. As usual, it is the desire to offer as fine an experience as possible, the beautiful memory associated with a place visited, whether the person returns or not. Japan's is a society that mollycoddles and can't help but offer what is beautiful. So a small geyser leaves us on the edge of our seats, the turquoise water gradually filling with vapour, gurgling through the rocks until it is turned into a liquid column ten feet high, noisily puffing in its protective cavern, to the equally loud amazement of the spectators. Even simplicity becomes performance.

But Japan isn't always only beauty. We are reminded of this by the long, tiring walk to Kamegawa station: a succession of rundown buildings, some of which, unoccupied, are what remains of Beppu's tourism boom of hotels and spas destroyed by the current economic crisis and the abandonment of small residential areas. Here and there, the odd inhabitant remains in the image of neglect and poverty that's hard to reconcile with the serenity, to some extent jocular, put forward to visitors or englobed in the life in large wellness clusters such as Tōkyō and Ōsaka.

Here lies the importance of being travellers as opposed to tourists. Because to travel wanting to know and not only see, helps us to really discover a place, to know its essence, identity, beauty and ugliness. I reflect thinking of all the aspects that are gradually gathered as you get to know something or someone. The suicides, the abandon of the countryside, disorientation of youth, and bullying.

"Nowhere's perfect. You need to know if it works for you, with all its defects."

I think of the place I'm running from. Of the sense of oppression that I experience when I'm in the city where I live. Of the sense of impotence I feel in wanting to rescue it. The traffic, the delinquency, the lack of respect for rules or for our neighbour. Sometimes the anger turns into sorrow, at the thought that surviving is not the same as living.

"I heard the Japanese government is financing various initiatives to revive rural centres, to promote local tourism and try to stop the young fleeing to the cities, resulting in all this," says Gabry pointing at the umpteenth warehouse full of farming tools and washing lines.

"It would be nice if they managed to develop these places like the countryside. Only if you travel to areas like these do you realise how incredible they are, how real Japan is here."

I think of my trips. On the first I spent two whole weeks in Tōkyō, boundlessly enchanted by Japan, with no perception of its real beauty. I think of the later trips, of this one with Gabry. And I'm not sure how I can live without being able to explore the hidden and rural corners of this country. The desire to share and perhaps reveal them, before time obliterates their beauty. It occurs to me that among my possible *ikigai*[111] 「生き甲斐」, this very thing may figure...

The growing tourism, seen in the immense, cement hotel buildings, long queues at the city's attractions and the animated noise in the streets has shown us a different side of the city, which has little to do with the traditional *onsen* resort. We hurry away from the modern face of Beppu, back to our *ryokan*. To the silence of the corridors lit by lamps decorated with autumn leaves, the smell of aged wood and its creak under our slippers as we walk to the hot spring outside the complex, the *rotenburo*. The soft cotton of the *yukata* is pampering and keeps out the cool of the evening. Light and perfumed it seems to become one with our bare skin as we cross the outdoor pathway where darkness is drawing in. We close the sliding door of the *onsen* behind us and for a second light and warm air caress our cheeks.

In front of us, beneath the incessant sound of dripping water, is a stone and pebble pool surrounded by the vegetation of a Japanese garden insinuating itself into every available space between the pool and the high dark wooden walls, separating us from the rest of the world and its indiscreet eyes.

We both undress in silence, Gabry because it's his first experience of an *onsen,* and me, having immersed myself in one only a year earlier, because I'm hoping to wash away a life not my own.

---

[111] Japanese concept translatable as 'life aim', or the activity that makes us happy, that we do well, that brings added value to the community and that can be remunerated

I remember the long night in the private pool of a *ryokan* in Hakone. The words flowing from the girl I met during the trip; the one who taught me how to pray to the *Kami*. Two different lives tied to the same shade, the same light. That night we stayed talking until the early morning, sitting on the edge of the pool, naked in body and soul beside the steam coming off the hot water. Casualties of the power the *onsen* can wield. We laughed and cried about our lives, our big little problems. A few days later we went our own ways, perhaps for ever. She on her tours and dreams. Me with my life falling apart and my dreams. That night, I'm certain, something happened in that solitary pool, where the spirits eavesdropped our words lost in the steam, where the warm water undid some knots and washed others away. So many words and anxieties slipped away, were melted in the warmth and left there, relieving me of tears and past troubles. Immediately afterwards, in the darkness and solitude of my room, I felt more exhausted than I ever have in all my life, but a part of me had been emptied of everything by the hot water and was finally free to greet the desire to be re-born.

The music of the water in a hot spring is impossible to describe, running down bamboo canes to shatter through bunches of dry branches laid out in front of us, and from there, dripping uninterruptedly onto the surface of the pool. The whole place is impregnated with this sound, alienating as the surrounding area where every element seems to have been prepared to help body and mind free itself from the world. When Gabry and I shake off our *yukata*, the cool air hits our bodies, unused to the sensation of the evening on our naked skin. The pale lights of the *rotenburo*, the colour and smell of the bamboo, the tinkling sounds mingling, the warm stone beneath our feet. Everything leads us towards a series of ritual actions that are almost spontaneous, and natural in this cosy universe. Sitting on our small wooden stools, we wash away impurities in the little showers. As instructed, we scrub ourselves so the body is thoroughly clean before enjoying the benefits of the *onsen*, even if this one is private. It is a form of respect and a way of washing away the dirt before cleansing oneself of fatigue and worries. On the edge of the pool, we use the *hinoki-oke*[112] 「桧桶」 to pour hot water over ourselves, acclimatising our bodies to the pool's temperature. Not one word rises into the dark night sky, only the swish of water on stone, its constant dripping, and the chirping of a cricket in the moonlight.

Then, very slowly, we descend the first stone steps, beginning our gradual immersion into the hot water. The sensation of warmth healing what was destroyed is as strong as in the past. Warmth assaults the body, taking your breath away, until you stop fighting it and let yourself fall into what becomes an embrace, a deep healing of whatever suddenly feels the need. It might be the body, it might be the mind. For a precise time period everything seems to stop, the body floats in water that doesn't seem that hot, the eyes close to listen to the world, or stay open to gaze at the moon and the colours of the small acer at the edge of the pool.

For a time you feel light-headed, as the *onsen*'s embrace folds around your limbs. Then you feel the sudden need to get away from the hot steam, all of a sudden become incandescent, as clarified by the precise, comic Japanese instructions hanging near the pool. It takes a certain amount of time to empty oneself of everything.

---

[112] Hinoki wood tub used in the kitchen for the rice to rest after cooking and in onsen to throw water over yourself when washing or to acclimatize the body to the hot temperature of the pool. Made of highly perfumed wood

So we sit on one of the rocks protruding over the water to allow our bodies to cool down in the evening. Gabry folds me in a hug, and together we look for stars in the square of dark sky hanging over the pool. No stars, just the autumn moon, precious and pale as anything. The harvest moon here in Japan is the most beautiful of the year, exactly like the instant I am living. Of a happiness about to flourish.

We sit there until the cool of the night finds its way to our skin, and then we reach for refuge in our *yukata*. Our bodies are now light as silk and the benefit of the hot spring water is revealed in the sensation of relief and relaxation that has overcome us.

We sway through the dim light of the *ryokan* as far as our room, and immediately flop onto the futons, now immersed in the warm covers, the salts still on our skin, in the serenity the *onsen* has brought us and the love that can unite two people.

Another minuscule part of me feels better, cleansed of something that was hurting. A little like then.

Once again, tonight I ask myself if it isn't here that I could mend my life, where I can go back to shining like the mid-October moon.

Travel Notes

Beppu is situated on the northeast coast of Kyūshū, the south-ernmost of the four main islands of Japan, and can easily be reached by the JR Nippō line crossing the east coast.

It is famous for being 'onsen city', having the highest number of hot springs in Japan (around 2,200) and for having 7 of the 10 types of mineral waters on earth, used as curative spas, tourist attrac-tions, as in the 'Seven Hells of Beppu', and in catering.

Beppu offers marvellous rotenburo with different types of water, old or panoramic onsen, mud and sand baths along the coast, as well as a historic Sekishō herb onsen, Kannawa Mushi-yu. Besides the hot springs and the panoramic cable car, there are several theme parks, the zoological garden and the Umitamago aquarium. In the restaurants, Beppu reimen are very popular, cold rāmen with Korean noodles, dango-jiru, flat noodles in vegetable soup, and the famous jigoku-mushi, food cooked in the steam of the hot springs near the restaurants in the Kannawa and Kamado Jigoku areas.

Day Trip:
* ✳ Travel by train from Okayama to Beppu
* ✳ Check-in at one of the city's many ryokan
* ✳ Lunch on tenpura or local fish sashimi, or jigoku-mushi at the restaurants in Kannawa district
* ✳ Visit the hells in Kannawa district
* ✳ Try hot spring boiled eggs or puddings at Kamado Jigoku
* ✳ Travel by bus to the hells in Shibaseki district
* ✳ Sup on Beppu reimen
* ✳ Spend the evening relaxing in the onsen at your ryokan

Typical Products and Souvenirs:
* ✳ Pomelo and Kabosu, seasonal citrus fruits sold in the hells
* ✳ Dango-jiru, thick 'fettuccini' in vegetable soup
* ✳ Products for the body based on thermal mud from the hells
* ✳ Jigoku-mushi, food cooked in steam from hot springs
* ✳ Beppu reimen, cold noodles in soup

Beppu
別府

I hear notes that can't be written.
The drops of warm water on the surface of the rotenburo,
a world apart, jealously guarded by wooden panels.
A world where steam melts anxious thoughts,
where light unravels the knots of the heart,
where water mends our soul

Early morning, and the light I've now learned to know filters through the gaps in the curtains from the veranda. In the Land of the Rising Sun dawn has a different consistency, and at six in the morning the patina of light settles on the world with the same vitality as the light at midday.

We slide out of our feathered refuge slightly unwillingly, but we mustn't be late for our meeting with the traditional Japanese breakfast. Dressed in my *yukata* as though wearing a uniform, I follow Gabry to the large room where the *tatami* is arranged with lots of small tables and soft cushions on which to hunker down. My cold has got worse and, stuffed with medicine, I'm in a confusional state, leaving little room for the enthusiasm the event deserves. Morning light is flooding in, at just the right strength for our sleep laden eyes. The rays come through a large glass window looking out onto the *ryokan*'s Japanese garden, a universe of acers and black pines, immaculately pruned by expert gardeners, to then touch on and light up the rice paper sliding doors dividing up the room.

Leaving our slippers at the door, we sit down in the

silence of a room as yet all to ourselves. A girl whispers good morning, while another is already laying out more than a dozen dishes as if composing a picture of different colours and aromas. The classic eggs with half cooked yokes, slices of fish in silvery scales, an enormous pan of rice and the unfailing miso soup in its usual covered pot. I recognise a lotus root and that delicious sweetish seaweed marinated in soy, but many of the contents of the little plates remained pretty much unknown. The rich breakfast is accompanied by *genmaicha* 「玄米茶」, an infusion of green tea and toasted rice grains with a very particular taste.

The calmness, silence and ritual of the Japanese breakfast seizes and nourishes body and soul. For indeed, the first meal of the day is the moment to start looking after our body, compared in eastern philosophy to the beautiful image of a temple. Feeding it with the right quantity of healthy foods, we cultivate a physical wellbeing that can't exclude the spiritual. And for the latter there is also the relaxing environment in which silence is warmed in the sun, bathing the *tatami*, linking to life in the nearby pool and lighting up the leaves of autumnal maples.

Breakfast. In Japan it's all that's needed to come into contact with the essential and primordial feelings that seem to fill the existence more than an entire life of material wealth would be able to do.

We could have spent the morning immersed in the hot sands of Beppu-kaihin Sunayu, in the thermal baths of the historic Takegawara Onsen or inside the smoking pools of Kitahama Onsen, hot springs overlooking the ocean. Or we could have gone to Ichinoide Kaikan, a small family run *onsen* with turquoise pools nestled in vegetation, where you can try dishes cooked by the owners themselves. But with my cold and great need for rest, we must make do with a gentle stroll in Beppu-kōen Park, a green area in the city centre that, apart from some beds of pink flowers, is relatively anonymous.

Some shopping at the little station cheers me up, most of all after the unchecked purchase of delightful, stylish Japanese ceramics that we find at half price in a tiny slip of a store run by a kind lady. A little further on, Bungo Chaya, a modest restaurant wedged into the box of a station at Beppu, hiding behind a window invaded by amazing reproductions of food - standing out among which is *dango-jiru* 「団子汁」, a clear broth of vegetables, mushrooms, chicken and large, thick, irregular noodles.

We sit down in the restaurant that appears to have aged with its owner, an senior gentleman from whom we request the only dish, humble in ingredients rather like the place itself. And yet, as ever, appearances really don't count in this country. Often the most mouth watering dishes are found in uninviting, dark or rickety places you wouldn't give a second glance. You have to study the menu, the owner, the clientele and, finally, be guided by your sixth sense. The gentleman serves the food himself: a typical dish from Ōita, a speciality that seems to have become rare nowadays even in these parts, perhaps because tourism has led to more and more sophisticated dishes to attract visitors and make money, putting aside recipes simpler in aspect and origin. However, even at the first taste, the bowl of cloudy broth, bobbing with the bright oranges and greens of the vegetables, seems to me to have a truly refined taste, where the delicacy of the combination is thick with the richness of the single vegetables, marinated chicken and chubby noodles that all go down to warm the stomach.

Pleasure. It's what I experience sip after sip, noodle after noodle, despite my cold, which seems to have disappeared all of a sudden. When my bowl is empty, I feel as though I've just tasted a part of autumn, embellished with the simplicity of a soup and its vegetables.

***

Fukuoka
福岡

*What wonder and excitement there is
to making a connection.
As much for people as for places.
At Fukuoka it is the swirling of the scent
issuing from the river, pervading the streets
and insinuating itself into the nocturnal neon.
It's the image of heat emanating
from the stands lined up along the bank,
sparkling and ephemeral like the moment they give us.
It is the simple love oozing from each rāmen,
and the smile of people sharing the conviviality of a meal,
that for centuries has created connections.
Where the link is made, we are finally at home*

The early afternoon train for Kokura gives us the chance to admire golden rice paddies, rare in this period of October when the harvest has usually come and gone. They look like strips of yellow cloth faded by the sun, messily darned here and there by dwellings, like solitary but identical pins: a lead blue roof reclining on four white walls.

We're on the *shinkansen* bound for Hakata, the old name

for Fukuoka, and still today tied to its past of port hub, and the city known throughout the nation for its culinary tradition: besides the myriad of dishes you can try in the equally numerous restaurants and bars, *rāmen* enthusiasts from all over the world coming to the city to enjoy the famous Hakata Rāmen, commonly known as *tonkotsu rāmen*, originally from the city and prepared with the best pork soup in Japan.

What is more, thanks to its strategic position, the city doesn't miss the opportunity to fuse traditions and ingredients from other parts of Asia, transforming tastes and creating new ones, and experimenting with dishes that today have become the identity of the city itself.

In its warm streets, after the torments of the rainy season that annually affects this region, the modern, vibrant Shin-Hakata station welcomes us, and the smell of cooking spreading through the air awakens in me the desire to explore these places to discover their identity and essence. As always, it is an instinct, a sixth sense that ignites as you step out of the station in a city: it is as if in a few minutes the smells, colours and people sketch the connection that will be instilled between oneself and the as yet unexplored place.

In Hakata it is damp after hours of rain, the uncertain afternoon light breaks through the trees into the wide avenues, dappling the wet leaves and trunks, reviving the colours to make them as vivid as the neon lights and shop signs that stand out in the gloaming. There's a continual hustle and bustle of young people, well-dressed men and women stopping to look in the windows of the many designer clothes stores, sophisticated and elegant bars and vast shopping centres of the area. The atmosphere is heavy with the scent and loud voices of women on mobile phones, in sleeveless tailleurs and elegant high heels, in a city that seems to sit in a warm bubble of dampness, a climate that seems to have nothing in common with the other cities, in a now autumnal October.

So Fukuoka suddenly appears alive, throbbing, torn between the desire not to appear less than the other big cities and their modernity, and that of raising awareness of its historical-culinary place in the world, setting itself up as the nerve centre of Japanese cuisine while maintaining all its ancient virtues. And the city is indeed distinguished by its tradition. You can sense it in the determination to keep its historical name, used to refer to the area's typical *rāmen*. You can tell as you walk down its streets where the restaurant signs are always eye-catching and original and the advertising posters display bowls of *rāmen* as though they were the last word in fashionable cars. You can feel it in the presence of the notorious *yatai*, the mobile kitchens going round the city in groups, restaurants the size of a stand, open late into the night.

Food seems to be its obsession, a cult to propagate in all its forms, the aroma of which impregnates the city.

And then there's the sea, the other unmistakeable smell drifting through the streets. It is the brackishness of the Sea of Japan, always more of an ocean, on which Fukuoka sits and stretches out its limbs and curves, the roads embracing the sea's mild humidity. Several salty rivers comb through the city, creating islands and peninsulas that Fukuoka has made its own, banks on which sit *yatai* and restaurants, where shopping centres crop up and from where tourist boats leave, and along which the briny breeze stabs at the array of skyscrapers and homes lit up by neon, to then mingle with the smell of cooking between one street and the next.

From the station, surmounted by the immense structure of the Hakata City JR prevailing over everything like the supreme ruler of shopping malls, we pass Gion-machi District to get to a branch of River Naka-gawa. In this area, the city offers a myriad views down grey tiled alleys, here and there inhabited by road construction sites with bright green plastified fences and yellow and white cones lined up with great precision. Arranged with the same care, are the rows of pastel-coloured bicycles outside restaurants and little stores pursuing each other down the small lanes. Each of the premises welcomes passersby with a folding sign sitting on the ground, large coloured *noren*, often illegible signs written in *hiragana*[113] 「ひらがな」 reflected in the puddles of recent rain. Unfortunately, we don't have time to throw ourselves into the maze of intriguing and evocative alleys ensnaring the area around Kushida-jinja Shrine, one of the districts in which there'll be a large lantern installation for tomorrow's festival.

We reach the river in late afternoon, when the ruffled surface of the wide water course blends with the colours of sunset: the cool blue of the sky and the lurid pink of the clouds melt into the water along with the luminous cubes of the buildings, whose windows are made up in twilight orange. The odd jumpy and palpitating neon sign peeps out from the skyscrapers and in the distance at the port, pointy red and white Hakata Tower rises in imitation of Tōkyō Tower. A spectacle you can't tire of, that rapidly transforms with the night, as we gradually approach 6pm. From that moment the coloured artificial lights gain the upper hand over the pitch black of the river, that turns in the magic mirror of Fukuoka's nocturnal profile. This is the time when the city undergoes the most wonderful metamorphosis.

---

[113] Syllabic, phonetic lettering system native to Japan, used for all words not written in kanji or not of foreign origin, for which katakana is used. It is distinctive for its soft, rounded shapes

The smell of the rain threatens our search for the perfect *yatai*, muddling with aromas that, now more than ever, inundate the city. Some drops of rain fall on our map, blurring the red circles we had drawn around the best places in tourist reviews. But once we arrive at the tiny group of *yatai* on the corner of Kokutai-dōri, the large road where some of the best street kitchens should be, we realize that the setting doesn't do justice to these ingenious makeshift restaurants.

So Fukuoka teaches me one of its secrets: to eat in a *yatai* is magical, and to choose which *yatai* to rely on mustn't be premeditated, but has to be based on the moment, on the sensations you experience in situ, a little like the choice of a personal *kimono*. From among the many, you choose the one whose food, signage colours and cooks strike you the most, then wait for your first mouthful to see if you've got it right. Furthermore, this is exactly the spirit of the *yatai*, to seize the moment, enjoy the now, perhaps with friends or maybe with colleagues on the way home from work, possibly in the snow when the stalls are covered in nylon cloth so that the plastified walls trap the warmth of the stoves and the laughter of customers.

The *yatai* shines in the late afternoon and evening of Fukuoka, but not at other times. In the evening there it is, and the next day, as if by magic, the place is empty, at least until sunset. So this city, the last to keep alive the restaurant cart tradition, becomes the emblem for Japanese instant pleasure that must be grasped before it goes, of continual stopping and starting again, of a cycle of beginning and end that recalls the seasons, or that of cherry blossom so loved by the Japanese. We sit at one rather than another on the basis of the company of the moment, the desire of the moment and the necessity of the moment.

That's why they are here, to welcome people's moments,

their time, gliding by, continually rushing between duty and pleasure. Of course there's no lack of 'habitués', customers loyal to a certain mobile kitchen who can't do without the company of the proprietors, their beer, their *oden*. Because every *yatai* has its personality, and although the type of dishes served is more or less similar, there is great variety between one stand and the next in terms of taste. For instance, the same *tonkotsu rāmen* are prepared by every stall in a different way. What's more, the city is famous for the incredible variety of degrees when it comes to cooking of noodles, with about seven different levels of doneness, and there are *yatai*, as in the Nagahama area, known for serving Nagahama Rāmen with a very thin *men*[114] 「麺」 native of that district. Which is why we might be drawn to one *yatai* rather than another, but what's for sure is that one evening is never the same as the next.

Back at River Naka-gawa, Gabry leads me to where his memory recalls numerous *yatai* in a much more special context. They appear suddenly on Nakagawa-dōri Street, near Canal City shopping centre, whose large mass we can make out in a rainbow blaze of lights. At Haruyoshi-bashi Bridge a spectacular luminous strip of *yatai* appear along the river, many of which are already prey to early customers. From here a multitude of lanterns and lights clings to the slender structure of the kiosks, making them shine out in the night and on the wet road. Improvised kitchens accommodating large pans from which the cooks lift encrusted lids letting a cloud of steam and spices billow out into the air. Near fiery hotplates on which succulent skewers grill, next to kegs of beer for the customers. The now opaque plastified curtains

---

[114] Generic term that indicates the long Japanese noodle, mainly the one created by hand from the rāmen-ya. It is very thick, uneven and rough, unlike the very thin sōmen and soba or the large udon

Yatai 屋台

Today, the term yatai is associated with the typical stands set up during Japanese festivals, heaped with delicious street food such as okonomiyaki, takoyaki, taiyaki and all sorts of desserts. In reality, in the 1800s and first half of the 1900s, food stalls were much more common all year round, different in aspect and used as genuine mobile rāmen and stew restaurants.

The traditional yatai structure consists of a wooden cart with two wheels, inside which are all the kitchen utensils, stools and ingredients needed to prepare the food.

Every day from early afternoon, the hikiya, or yatai owners, wheel their mobile kitchens to a predetermined space to begin setting up their provisory restaurant, which stays open until late evening.

The number of customers per yatai is limited, but their rapid turnover makes them accessible to a large number of habitual patrons or customers on their way home from work.

The evening passes among beer, rāmen, oden, motsunabe, yakitori, teppanyaki and tenpura. There are also others specializing in cocktails, western and Okinawa food.

Stringent regulations and hygiene norms before the Tōkyō Olympics in 1964 brought about a decline in mobile restaurants. Today, besides the last yatai left in the city of Kumamoto, Fukuoka is the only city in Japan in which the yatai culture survives, by looking to the future, thanks to the possibility of inheriting licences and every so often, buying new ones.

In the city of the yatai, you find them in various areas, in particular in the Tenjin area, in the Nagahama district, along the streets of Watanabe-dōri and Shōwa-dōri, and finally along River Naka-gawa in the Nakasu red light district.

The yatai are frequented by tourists mainly in spring and summer, when the evening temperature makes it enjoyable to be outside for a quick meal in company, but the more typical atmosphere is in autumn and winter, when walls of wood or vinyl sheets are used against the cold, turning the stands into boxes of happy chatting with the aroma of hot soups.

are closed around the sides of the kiosks to provide protection for customers in the colder months. I can imagine them in the Japanese winter, bent over on the tiny stools eating in their bulky overcoats, crowding together as close as possible to the counter and hot stoves, the curtains pulled against their backs in an attempt to retain the warmth of the small space.

As we walk along the bank, I look closely at these marvellous structures, condensing into a space the soul of a city, and perhaps a whole country: I feel more and more drawn to them, and particularly when I come across one that hasn't been opened up and looks like a cruddy old bench, boxed in with panels in motley materials, at a glance resembling a pile of debris ready to be thrown on the rubbish heap. Soon afterwards, as if by magic, it is a kiosk like any other, a minuscule kitchen, containing a counter and a few seats, handwritten menu and large red lanterns hanging from the corners of the roof.

I watch the spell come into being in the rows of *yatai* along the dark river, each with its distinctive character. Some are newly and colourfully decorated, others must have looked about the same for at least 50 years. Several men in suits sit noisily eating noodles, while we clock the bowls served to them in order to work out which might be our best bet. As the *yatai* are mobile street carts and we know not to expect great attention to hygiene, we try to avoid the excessively worn out stands and those serving culinary specialties from Hakata that we've decided not to taste this evening: next to the classic *oden* are the well-known and publicized Hakata omelettes stuffed with *mentaiko*, of which we still have vivid and unpleasant memories from the *korokke* in Kanazawa; *yakitori*[115] 「焼き鳥」 cooked in the Hakata manner to make them crunchy outside and juicy within, much appreciated by the locals; typically Japanese *gyōza*[116] 「餃子」 fried in a pan or grilled on a hotplate; and finally fried *rāmen*, another of this city's culinary experiments.

After only twenty minutes of indecision among these little factories of untried tastes, the thick, cloudy *tonkotsu rāmen* served by Hide-chan captures our attention. As soon as we take over two newly vacated stools, the owners welcome us with a profusion of bowing, and it's with emotion that we find ourselves in a group of Japanese people laughing and relaxing in front of a beer at the end of the working day. *Yatai*, like *izakaya*, are places where welcome and fellowship reign, the story of an evening or a lifetime; places where, regardless of nationality, it is easy to be drawn into conversation with a customer launching themselves into a disastrous English to make their interlocutor feel at ease.

In the small space of a *yatai* a family is created, we are welcomed and feel part of the group. The cooks smile at us, proud to have foreigners at their counter, and we, a bit bewildered but overcome with genuine happiness, order the longed-for white *rāmen* with pork broth, accompanied by four large skewers of chicken and succulent local beef, cooked on the boiling hotplate.

Hakata broth incorporates all the characteristics of a white pork *rāmen*, thick, rich and tasty, and yet at the same time refined and appetizing, never heavy, so that every

---

[115] Skewers of chicken cooked on hotplate or grill, another typical street food at festivals and often served in the izakaya alongside the beer

[116] Japanese version of Chinese jiaozi dumplings, the main difference being the rich flavour of garlic and thinner pastry. Often stuffed with minced meat, cabbage, spring onions and garlic. In Japan the common cooking method is in a frying pan

spoonful seems to usher in the next. That perfect balance explodes in the palate and then in the body, reinvigorated by a frisson of delight and warmth that protects it from the impending damp of the evening.

We hardly seem to have tasted it before the geometric black and white design on the bottom of the bowl shows its face. It strikes us that we are eating too fast, but next to us the customers have been replaced twice during our meal. Moreover, the *yatai* are this too: little islands for a quick snack, a place to stop for a rapid pause of joy in a frenetic daily life. Because, in the end, the Japanese always find a moment for food, for a bowl of *rāmen*. Whether it's standing at one of the minuscule *rāmen-ya*[117] 「ラーメン屋」 at the station between one train and the next or at the *yatai* on the roadside, a *rāmen* is something this nation cannot do without, like pasta for an Italian.

I reflect on how cuisine and the importance of a meal are aspects that define a people's identity, the care that goes into choosing the ingredients, the importance of preparation and taste, the significance given to the moment when you sit down to eat your own dish. The preparation of a meal is perhaps one of the few times when true individualism is forgotten, where sharing in all its forms becomes genuine: we share what we have prepared, we share the moment, we share the joy of eating something good. Teaching about local ingredients and cooking begins at school, where children go on trips to orchards and farms, and take on the challenge of actual cooking lessons. It continues at home, where the efforts and care shown towards food and its presentation are handed down with pride from generation to generation. At home, time and effort are put into making

---

[117] Restaurants specialized in rāmen

the *bentō*, true works of art that children often prepare with their mother, or in making the evening meal for those coming home from work.

Disappointed to have to abandon the experience of immersion so soon, we leave our stools to other customers and go for a wander along the river. Further on, unexpectedly, we again come across that magic of light and colour in hundreds of rounded, red lanterns hanging along the bank, following the profile of the river up to the night market held at the little park, Seiryū-kōen. Here, a series of bright red tents contain people selling artisan objects and clothes, alternating with stalls selling beer, street food and confectionary. Some stalls are empty until the next day, when the lantern festival will light up the city's evening strolls. There are picnic tables where Japan's young sit in front of beers, busy expressing all the merriness that comes with youth and alcohol, which for someone from Japan, always seems too much.

A band, carbon copy of those Korean pop groups where they have the faces of angels and hair perfectly set, entertaining the public with heart-breaking songs typical of the *dorama*[118] 「ドラマ」.

"I feel like I'm in a Japanese tv series!" I exclaim, unable to divert my attention from the guitarist and his highly melodramatic song. Along the bank, other young people sit beside the river with their sandwiches and drinks: their smiling, carefree faces glowing red from the lanterns and echoed in the beds of cosmos on the banks, making them more beautiful than by day.

At the end of the walk there is a small footbridge arching over a secondary canal and opening the way to Canal City, of which we grasp the name by gazing at pillars immersed

---

[118] Japanese tv drama series broadcast in daily or seasonal episodes

in endless fountains swimming into the belly of the building. Initially it looks to me like yet another flashy attempt at making a mega Japanese shopping centre seem original and interesting, places not daring to fail the vision that Japan has of the consumerist and self-important west. But by carrying on into the inner courtyard the building reveals itself in all its poetic wonder, in more than eight undulating terraced floors from which plants cascade towards the fountains beneath. The fountains, with lighting effects and jets of water, are sinuous canals moving between the pilasters and windows of the different buildings that make up Canal City, merging with the setting and turning the shopping centre into a Botticelli Venus just risen from the waves. Rainbow lights, that bleach the water of the fountains, are reflected in all the surfaces of the courtyard on the ground floor, where the sweet crêpe store is still serving numerous customers. Many families are enjoying the last show of water jets, lights and music at the central fountain, others wander beneath a roof of resplendent Halloween pumpkins. And I think of Tōkyō, whose shop windows are full of pumpkins and bats as it prepares for the hordes of masked youths invading the ever bustling Takeshita-dōri Street at Harajuku, or the trendy neighbourhood of Shibuya.

We leave Canal City, strangely fascinated by its architecture and colourfulness, by the way it stands out with the elegant serenity of its fountains and lights, deciding to come back for it the next day. It's odd, when it happens, to feel inexplicably drawn to a place you come across by chance. It happens with Tōkyō. Because hating cities and loving nature and the wild certainly wouldn't predict the overflowing love that I would feel as I set foot there. I had fled London and New York, and I desperately needed to escape Rome, but from the day I took the monorail to enter the belly of Tōkyō like the strips of ocean, I wanted to belong there forever.

Near Hakata station life palpitates through streets lit up as if it were day. Avoiding night clubs, restaurants and the throngs who, freed from their daily duties, are ready for an evening in company, shopping and having fun, we enjoy the mild air that makes this autumn even more surreal, and the crowds more tolerable. Then, near the ticket barrier for the JR line, the nocturnal vibrancy becomes truly chaotic for the first time. The continual, orderly to-and-fro of the Japanese inside the station seems to have been turned upside down. We are stranded near the panels showing train times, where a sea of heads gazes upwards, staring at the electronic screens of *shinkansen* alternating with local trains.

We attempt to cut a path through to our platform, disconcerted by the absence of inspectors. The reason fairly soon becomes clear: little red letters appear on the screens: more than one *shinkansen*, including the one we had planned to catch home, is delayed by more than two hours. For a long time, I stand there suspended in a confusional state, when certainty suddenly vanishes. In Japan a train that is more than ten seconds late is extremely rare, and when it happens public apologies are usually made to passengers. For longer delays there would be public apologies on television. However, 120 minutes delay on more than one line means something serious and 2011 comes to mind, when the earthquake and the tsunami that hit the north of Japan brought the country's unstoppable railway to a halt. As then, it was the Japanese television channel NHK that broke the news of an accident on the high speed train line.

So we experience how, in a system that always works impeccably, according to precise rules, a disruption of any sort is hard to deal with. It isn't a question of the rules or people adopting perfect behaviour in the case of earthquakes and typhoons, it concerns the difficulty of stepping outside the schemes and rules to cope with a last minute emergency, of endeavouring to find an alternative solution that doesn't appear in a manual. It's weird to see railway staff unable to give guidance, wandering around with their instruction manuals, bewildered, even leaving their checkpoints unmanned. And equally strange to see extra-long queues of travellers next to the platforms of delayed trains, patiently and impassively waiting for something to change, for the train to arrive sooner or later, whether it's in an hour or several. They've already factored in that this evening they will be late home and it doesn't remotely worry them. It's a kind of zen patience they have been brought up with from birth and to which is added the unquestionable certainty that everything will be resolved, that the system safeguarding them will make everything return to normal. A blind faith in the country's civil system requiring no alternative solutions. There's a world of difference between us and them: we charge around frantically from one platform to the next trying to find another train to get us out of this situation; while they, with the calm and composure that distinguishes them, stand immobile as they wait for everything to get back to normal. We come from worlds and realities that are quite different, and consequently learn to live in different ways. Perhaps due to an elasticity we inherited from a distant reality, after evaluating other possibilities, in the end we find a solution in the form of a local train for Beppu.

Once on board I can't help feeling tenderness for a people like an eternal infant trusting to the care of their society; and reflecting on the awareness of dynamism and the spirit of resolution that marks the west, deriving from the extreme need to adapt to an existence where problems and the necessity for solutions are part of everyday life.

The *yukata* slips off like silk and crumples onto the rocks warmed by steam from the *rotenburo*. I sit on the little wooden stool to purify myself of all that I've accumulated during the day, not least worries and sweat. I see my skin become rugged from the cool caress of the night, and then relax and give itself up to the bite of the hot water. I lean my head on one of the stones on the edge of the pool and close my eyes.

The chaos of the universe melts into the dripping sound of water. When I open them again the universe has changed, but is just as marvellous.

An unexpected route, taking longer to arrive. The life I'm living is somewhat like today's return journey. Everything slides away beneath this sky, everything dissipates between the sheen of the stars and the steam.

Perhaps, very slowly, I am beginning to understand. However, much life's unforeseen setbacks bring delays, deviations and sorrows, nothing matters if in the end I can come back here to enjoy the most beautiful moon I've ever seen.

Travel Notes

Fukuoka, or Hakata in honour of its past as a port city, is the biggest city in Kyūshū, still today a hub of exchange with South Korea
and a well developed metropolitan area thanks to its many railway
lines. It is famous throughout Japan for its culinary tradition and
the geniality of its inhabitants, as well as the heterogeneity of its
neighbourhoods.
In the area stretching from Hakata station to the port, futuristic
shopping centres emerge, the Hakataza theatre, Rakusui-en, the
merchant's garden, and one of the three most ancient Sumiyoshi-
jinja, sailors' shrines.
Level with the original shopping centre, Canal City, the Tenjin and
Nakasu areas on the other hand, are fashion and leisure districts,
with shopping streets (including Nishi-dōri and the lanes in the
zone of Daimyō and Imaizumi), a discreet red light district and
Naka-gawa River, fascinating at night with its neon lights. You can
take tourist trips on ferries along the river, a suggestive supper on
a traditional Japanese boat, a yakatabune, or a walk among the
various bars and yatai that enliven and bring character to the river
bank.
Further south, the Yanagibashi Rengō-ichiba Market, offers myriad
fresh vegetables and freshly caught fishes.

Day Trip:
  * Traditional breakfast at your ryokan
  * Relax in some of the city's hot springs
  * Lunch on Dango-jiru
  * Travel by train from Beppu to Fukuoka
  * Explore the districts of Tenjin and Nakasu
  * Eat supper at one of the yatai along River Naka-gawa
  * Visit the Canal City shopping centre
  * Return to Beppu and relax in the onsen at your ryokan

Typical Products and Souvenirs:
  * Hakata rāmen, the original tonkotsu style
    rāmen
  * Mentaiko tamagoyaki, omelette with mentaiko
  * Street food from yatai

Fukuoka
福岡

We often chase happiness without really knowing what it is.
Until we reach moments that overwhelm us,
in the marvel of the tears they snatch from us,
in the memory they stamp on our existence
and that become joy we treasure forever.
They are no more than instants,
and yet happiness resides in them.
Like the pearl in an oyster, it must be nurtured, cultivated,
awaited and then gathered in that instant,
and given the value it deserves.
I waited so long for this trip, feeding
it with dreams and hopes, assigning
it the value to adapt the heart.
In the same way I waited for the instant in Fukuoka
when darkness fell and beauty transfixed the eye forever.
And it really is like that,
in that very instant happiness burst in

Once again the gurgling of water running down hollowed bamboo, jangling and splashing onto the surface. I couldn't tire of these sounds; I wish they could be there every time I wake.

We wake to the calm after last night's storm: balance after chaos. Perhaps the travellers at the station were right, because sooner or later everything is destined to return to harmonious normal. In the cold light of early morning we make a last visit to the *onsen*: the air is sparkling in a different way to the evening, the steam is more delicate and the sky still has the soft nuance of dawn.

Then, after the repeated rite of packing our things, we say goodbye to the owners, who have carried our bags to the door, heedless of their increased weight. Besides Ciccioletta, there are now 4 kg of ceramics more since our arrival.

Beppu offers tourists a wide range of *onsen*, from the classical pool to those of mud and sand, to hot springs looking onto the bay, all dotted around the city. You can spend a morning touring a few of them, moving by bus or taxi between them. However, it's a bit much to do this with your luggage in tow.

As a result, needing to be rested before tonight's important event, we decide to bid a final goodbye to Beppu and take refuge in the heated carriages of the Sonic Express bound for Fukuoka. The warmth we find increasingly frequently on trains and buses, that synthetic smell of hot air resting on the impeccable fabric of the seats, brings with it the irrevocable arrival of autumn.

When we get there, Fukuoka is almost unrecognisable compared to the evening before. The morning light free of clouds and the tranquillity of having more time available, give us a new and different chance to get to know the city.

The taxi reserved for tourists plucks us out of a long queue outside the station and treats us to a short trip on which the driver, despite linguistic difficulties, is determined to keep us company by describing the streets we go down and places of culture hidden in them, including the Tōchō-ji Temple, housing one of the largest sitting statues of Buddha in Japan, as well as those of Nara and Kamakura.

Our business hotel is in the Nakasu area, the strip of land between the two branches of River Naka-gawa, just a few minutes from the *yatai*, a central zone from where you can quickly get to both the station and the port area, and a good compromise in terms of room size. And once we get here, like bees drawn to a field of daisies, we pander to the call of a place that, the previous evening, stirred our hearts and the frozen memories of our trip: Canal City.

By day, this shopping 'city' can't show off the effects of a nocturnal illumination enhancing its design and numerous fountains, but the many stores, the windows onto internal spaces and the white galleries layered like crests of a wave, attract the visitor with the same ease as pollen attracts bees. What's more, yesterday evening we intuited that it has more to it than meets the eye.

By pure chance, wandering around the place, alive with colour and people, we happen upon a flyer advertising the presence of the Rāmen Stadium, on the ninth floor of the building, an area permanently set up with a dozen restaurants where they cook different sorts of *rāmen* according to typical recipes from the various regions of Japan. The rally of *rāmen-ya* could be the sign of destiny we were waiting for, one of those that happen here, where it is important to trust our intuition. When it is important to listen to our hearts.

The stadium where the *rāmen* do battle is a large circular area with black walls and floor, against which hundreds of white lanterns stand out, hanging from the ceiling. We feel literally catapulted into one of the many suburban districts of a Japan that was and still is, that of lanterns hanging outside *izakaya* and *rāmen-ya* that in the evening light up the dark *yokochō* 「横丁」, the city's suggestive alleyways.

The scenography, although simplified, beckons us in, and we linger excitedly at the billboard listing the restaurants lined up in unison along the edge of each floor, each with its own identity, with its own secret recipe. Some also offer *yaki-gyōza*[119] 「焼餃子」, stuffed dumplings - steamed in the original China version - in Japan they began to fry them on the hotplate or in a pan, attaining perfection right here in Fukuoka, the homeland of the Japanese style *gyōza*. In the tangle of photos of bowls, soups and dumplings, with great difficulty we choose two places where we can try both, in an attempt to taste the marvels of an entire island in one go.

Honda Shōten, with a long queue at the door to recommend it, is one of the best choices we could make. At the machines outside, we pay and order our portion of garlic flavoured *tonkotsu rāmen*, never imagining the pleasure in the umpteenth bowl of our trip. At our small, secluded table, my world and happiness suddenly become straightforward, reduced to the adorable space where we sit and the bowl that is soon placed before us.

I smile and enter into a form of happiness that is suddenly mirrored in Gabry's eyes. I want to grab it and hold it there for as long as possible. I want to see it transformed into a never-ending beam. And I'd tear a bit off for the people I love and have loved in the same way. A *rāmen* is a piece of happiness: the past almost doesn't matter anymore, just the present moment. Immediately afterwards come the rich consistency and aroma of the soup, the sticks of bamboo melting in the mouth, perfectly cooked egg and the slender slices of lightly braised pork. A first taste and only delicious things remain. It's absurd to think how the cooking in these places manages to trigger a fuse, a spark of life leaving ash behind it. The innate joy and love in a dish, passed on in such a banal and direct manner to the people eating it.

---

[119] Japanese version of gyōza, fried on one side and steamed on the other. In Fukuoka they are known as tetsunabe-gyōza because typically served in a tetsunabe, the metal pan used to cook them

I try to hang on to the instant, so that the relief defining it remains in time. I do the same during the second *rāmen*, eaten next door, which cuts a poor figure next to the first, despite the delicious greens drowning in the broth. I try again when, before leaving Canal City, we meander like credulous children into the amusement arcade a few floors below: faced with an *ākēdo*[120] 「アーケード」, two *taiko* drums to play and drumsticks in hand, we are stuck there with no chance of escape, watching the musical score on the screen and hearing the rhythm of some *anime* theme tune or Japanese pop song. Pushing in yet more coins I make the moment last for as long as possible, without coming close to, let alone overtaking Gabry's score. It's the need to prolong the lightheartedness of the here and now, the sound of laughter, the serenity instilled in simple things.

What my life most lacks just now.

Beyond the solid wooden Sennen-mon Gate, in what's called the 'old city', there is a Fukuoka that goes back to being the new, old Hakata. We wander in the vicinity of Jōten-ji Temple, with its beautiful zen garden mentioned by the guide books, but we haven't time to take a look, and continue towards the Tōchō-ji Temple complex, where we find a four-storey, flame red pagoda resembling a Christmas tree covered in garlands. The courtyard is silent for a Buddhist rite. There is clear orderliness at the building's entrance, where, for a gift of 50 *yen*, we can visit the home of the giant Buddha.

I perfectly recall my trip of just a year ago when, at the stopover planned for Nara, I visited one of the oldest

---

[120] Videogame in an arcade cabinet, made up of a screen and control panel, extremely popular in amusement arcades all over the world. Works with tokens or coins

wooden temples of Japan, Tōdai-ji. An immense doorway welcomed me into the courtyard of the colossal structure, in the individuality of its aspect marked by time: the dark brown and white wood was by this time so worn and faded by bad weather it gave the place a spectral touch, making it seem more of a pirate relic than a holy Japanese building.

But it wasn't so much its singular outward appearance that stayed with me, as the moment when, having reached the top step at the entrance to the temple, my eyes focussed on the interior, going suddenly from sun reflected on white gravel to the darkness within. When my eyes adjusted to the change, I found myself in the presence of a 45-foot gilded Buddha, sitting in the centre of the room, between vast wooden columns that looked like toothpicks next to it. It took the breath away. I stood gazing at it for ages, hypnotized by the fact that, wherever I moved, the metal creature never took its eyes off me, scrutinising me, almost as though it were waiting for me to speak to it.

That day, in a life already in tumult, I managed to pass through the narrow space in one of the columns that, being the same size as the Buddha's nostril, is said to represent the prelude for a Buddhist way to enlightenment: other than children, whoever passes through is destined to reach enlightenment and happiness...

After the experience at Tōdai-ji, it's hard to be struck in the same way by the wooden Buddha of Tōchō-ji, and yet here too, the effect of the change in light revealing the colossal figure certainly doesn't leave you indifferent. The statue is indeed smaller, but the peculiarity of the eyes following you around the room remains and enthrals me while making me wary, just as it did before. We linger a bit under his probing eye, moving around and watching him as he studies us in depth, clearly reading our souls.

"Ok Buddha, all I want is to live to eighty..." says Gabry quietly, making me smile with tenderness.

"You know you can't ask the Buddha to live longer."

"Oh, no? So what can you ask then?"

I look at the Buddha, who seems to pierce me with those subtle, imperturbable eyes. I smile, innocent associate to the man who found the unfindable.

"We ask him to lead us along the path of happiness..."

The afternoon takes an age to reach the evening I've been awaiting for months. And yet, when we get to Kushida-jinja Shrine, to our great surprise the first lanterns are still dormant, although lined up on the steps to the entrance. A row of white paper oversized eggs with open tops run along the side of the steps and paths inside the complex of the shrine, covered in drawings, probably by children, full of paint and imagination. Some of the drawings are much more refined and detailed, while some are basic flowers and animals by smaller kids.

We follow the trail of lanterns as though they were Tom Thumb's breadcrumbs until we get to the shrine's central courtyard to find one of the main sets in the lantern festival. Thousands of little bags of thin coloured paper are laid out on the floor to create an enormous design that, from ground level, is impossible to understand. Curves, concentric circles and straight lines take on life through the arrangement of these crinkled cylinders of so many different colours, a spectacle so marvellous in daylight that it can't but be memorable at night, when little lights shine out through the paper veils in a rainbow of colours.

I'm feeling impatient and my emotions unbridled, quickened by the sight of an ancient ginkgo a little further on, not yet scratched by autumn's gold and nestled in its sacred cordon of lightning.

The tall *yamakasa*[121] 「山笠」 standing guard at one of the exits to the complex bids us goodbye with its cloud of dragons, warriors and gods, deftly woven into a skirmish of colour and fantasy. The float, on which there is a tower over thirty feet high, is displayed in this area all year round, protected by a permanent showcase. It really looks like a mountain of cloths and fantastical patterns amassed on top of each other, a pyramid of stories about mythical and religious characters, and even if you don't know their adventures, you become addicted to the disorienting confusion of bright colours. Although this exaggeratedly stuffed folklore gateau seems somewhat precariously balanced, today too it is one of the protagonists of the Hakata Gion Yamakasa festival, held annually in the first half of July. The most eagerly awaited moment of the festival are the races of the *kaki-yamakasa* 「舁き山笠」, the portable versions of *yamakasa*, through the city streets, sprint races that go on until late, attracting thousands of spectators from around Japan.

There is also a small plant and herb market set up in the shrine complex, and given my obsession for Japanese flora, I try to stay away: even at a distance every plant, in colour and shape of leaf and branch, strikes me as poetry from a distant country.

On every side there are altars and minor temples, each with its own architecture but all rigorously adorned with large lanterns, purplish curtains and outsize holy ropes in the most disparate tones of gold that are beginning to run through the lymph of the ancient ginkgo that lives here. As

---

[121] Literally 'mountain of decorations', the floats used at Hakata Gion Yamakasa Matsuri. In the late 1800s, with the increased use of power lines, they were divided into kaki-yamakasa, smaller floats that cross the city, and kazari-yamakasa, stationary floats forty feet tall and decorated with scenes from Japanese folklore

usual I contemplate it at some length, in the silence of its unrivalled, timeless existence, wondering how far it is from the metamorphosis that will liquefy it into a waterfall of brilliant yellow.

A pathway of red and white lanterns, as yet inanimate, takes us out of that wonderful collection of holy and traditional buildings, to the road leading to the hotel where we've decided to await the event.

There's a need for rest before dealing with emotion.

6 p.m. in Fukuoka is the glacial blue colour of an autumnal nightfall and the smell of the cold glass of the hotel window I'm leaning against. My heart is beating at an irregular rhythm. A sensation that feels familiar, reminding me of leaning my forehead against the cabin window in the plane before touching down onto the Haneda runway for the first time, many years ago. That anxiety of a first time, the slight heebie-jeebies at the idea of finding yourself face to face with the unknown, something that might disappoint, or steal your heart forever. For me, between the joy of discovery and the fear of disappointment, the latter usually prevails. And yet, that day was different. A visceral sensation was pressing on my stomach: that overwhelming sense of belonging I couldn't shake off. On no trip had I felt such harmony with the thing we call destiny. In no other moment of my existence had I had the certainty of being exactly where I should be, and going exactly where I should be going. The sensation whispering to me that all would be well, that something important was about to happen, was pressing on my stomach again now. The feeling that made me hold my breath for 20 seconds in the lift on the Tōkyō Skytree, before looking out over the indescribable, before happiness of a purity we experience only a few times in life,

engulfed me in the tidal wave of tears and sobbing.

Outside the hotel, I recognise the anticipatory sensation, the excitement and fear of the unknown. My legs are trembling as I slowly walk up the short flight of steps to one of the shrine's entrances. The blue sky is palpitating with the hope of keeping any chance of rain at bay for the evening, one of the most keenly awaited of our trip.

The first sparse, crinkled lanterns to be lit look delicate and wonderful. In the afternoon they were lovely even without their heart of light, but now they are spellbinding to say the least. I hold my breath as we walk along, as more and more are lit all the while. Carefully observing the living glows sitting on the ground sharpens my senses enough to give me the perception of darkness intensifying, at each step, at each stride towards the place I feel I need to go. My heartbeat speeds up as we reach the corner round which we can hear the murmur of the crowd in the swiftly falling darkness.

'That's where I must go.'

Gabry grabs my hand, hurrying me along. Then everything happens very quickly, in too blurry a way for the mind and heart to form thoughts and emotions. I spot the oval-shaped lanterns, focus on the barriers in this new darkness, and as I try to get my bearings my attention stumbles on the dark shapes of people. I feel the warmth of unknown bodies against my own, hear an incomprehensible mumbling noise, and see the darkness harmonising everything; and then the colours.

'This is where I must be.'

I find myself faced with hundreds of coloured lanterns, they were here a few hours ago but I seem to be seeing them for the first time. I feel my heart break its rhythm for a fraction of a second, and I'm left wondering if it had ever really beaten before. The set is there before me, immense, unreachable, brilliant in the night, unintelligible, like anything too beautiful to be described. The emotion is the same as before, something I could recognise after a thousand lives.

'This is where I must exist.'

The tears course over my sobbing smile as I lose perception of reality, such that I don't realise how we've got to the little open terrace from which I'm gazing at a shimmering, sparkling expanse. From here, the cluster of vibrant, trembling colour becomes a painting of sunflowers and cherry blossom. From here happiness takes on a shape, colour and memory.

These last two years, I realise how in life almost nothing is certain and defined: there's job insecurity, relationship insecurity, a future of which it's impossible to know where and how. In such uncertainty, what is more important than the occasional moment of happiness? Precious instants we don't know will come again and so we must grasp the beauty of the present to our heart, and carry it with us, like an anchor in a vague and flustered existence. Moments when the power of what is incredible about living gives us the strength to take on any storm. And this evening the lanterns of Fukuoka emanate a light that, from the other side of the ocean, is my lighthouse to reach this far, always and anyway. Whatever the height of wave I'll find myself swimming through in between.

We look closely at the city map with highlighted routes indicating where they hold the lantern scenes, and at a small stand near the shrine find all the remaining information needed for the festival. Then, to my great joy, we discover that near the main lantern scenes you can have your form stamped: and once you've collected four stamps, you receive the gift of a special book on the festival.

I'm surprised to find that Gabry joins me in wanting to cross from one side of the city to the other to win a prize worth the beauty of a memory. He too is motivated to take on the challenge, and begins to plan the ideal route to take in all possible sets and complete the full collection of stamps by 10:30pm, the time the festival ends and the last lanterns give over to the dark of night.

Our lantern chase through the roads of Fukuoka becomes an excuse to lose ourselves in the city streets, among people from here. From romantic couples strolling hand in hand to sweet young families wandering among the smaller lanes, in the shade of streets divested of electric light, every corner has something magical about it, suspended in time and in the colours that the lanterns suddenly reveal.

Bewitched, everyone follows the light paths, guided by the strip of luminous bags and keen for the next lanterns, curious to see the larger and smaller compositions. The air is fizzing, steeped in wonder, and in the desire to be sated with beauty, of which the Japanese are extreme enthusiasts.

We reach Tōchō-ji Temple, wrapped in darkness and completely unrecognisable. In the large courtyard we are greeted by hundreds of lanterns: sinuous lines creating huge, sophisticated designs, coiling around the bases of the trees and running like continuous brushstrokes of light across the zen garden's gravel. Designs of stars, moons and planets gleam in a universe of trembling colour. Not only lanterns, but also candles forming *kanji* and little animals on the ground, while chains of red and yellow trace fiery trails around the pagoda, as if wanting to bring alive the colours now suffocated by the night. Imperfect paper bags that, lined up close to each other, create perfect green and yellow paths, leading us to the enormous composition in the field overlooking River Mikasa-gawa.

Hakata Tōmyō 博多灯明

The lantern festival at Fukuoka, an annual event since 1994 and much loved by residents, is inspired by the traditional festivals of the 'Thousand Votive Candles', known as Sentōmyō, held at shrines and temples in the prefecture from July to September.

The most famous of these is at the Dazaifu Tenman-gū Shrine on 25 September, at the close of Jinkōshiki Matsuri, a 5-day festival with more than 900 years of history, with Kagura dances, mikoshi parades and thousands of flickering lanterns lining the main streets of Dazaifu. During Hakata Tōmyō, more than 40,000 candles inside lanterns light up not only temples, but also alleyways, historic sites, schools, parks and other points of interest, creating a fantastic atmosphere that lures tens of thousands of visitors and draws the active community into the organization of the festival itself.

The lanterns are homemade by residents out of simple bags of coloured washi paper, laid on the ground to make up designs that are different every year. A handful of sand, in which the candle is sitting, ensures the lantern's equilibrium. Many lanterns have further decorative geometric elements in cardboard, wood or bamboo, making the nocturnal city unique and suggestive due to the effect of the little flames inside the coloured paper. As a result, every year, on one October Saturday, hundreds of volunteers rush to light all the lanterns laid in their positions the day before, so that people can appreciate the play of light from 6pm until the candles burn out after about 3 hours.

The lantern installations feature in about 20-25 areas of the city including between the central JR Hakata railway station and the port, and appear every year on the official event site's map. Near some areas, generally those that have the larger decorations, there are information centres with maps and event material.

What's more, in some of them you can take part in the usual Japanese stamp gathering: when you've collected them all you are given a prize, such as bibliographic or photographic material relating to the event and those in previous years.

The routes laid out around this area have lanterns in the shape of a cone, created by simply making a pyramid roll of paper covered in hand-drawn and printed pictures. Each of them deserves a photo and some are very touching, such as one with a beautiful Japanese red lily in watercolours.

An entire wall of luminous cones marks out a small eating area, where old ladies plunge their ladles into the large pots of *rāmen*, or neatly wrap up hundreds of delightful handmade rice triangles.

I feel at home, like a figure in one of those many profound Japanese films, unknown to the west, which merit all the prizes going.

The smell of the food counters, with the clarion chatter of the children sitting at picnic tables with their families, accompany us to the small clearing around Sesshin-in Temple. Here a galaxy of ringed planets and stars anticipates the spectacle of the immense field next door: more than a thousand lanterns in the most wide-ranging colours are set up for the festival's largest drawing, which is hard to make out while walking along the luminous lines intersecting one another. I envy the drone as it flutters over our heads, moving hysterically from one part of the park to another, taking panoramic photos. As I look around, trying not to lose sight of Gabry, soon morphed into one of the many shadows sloping around in the darkness of that immense sea of sparks. We explore all we can, taking hundreds of photos that attempt to harness the bright surface, we win the most important of the stamps, and then we begin our ascent to the northern area of the city, towards the port.

Between one alley and the next, the owners of the diminutive shops there have set up stalls selling snacks and home-made foods, like the sachet of vegetables in *tenpura* we buy and devour soon afterwards in front of a lantern layout in the shape of flowers, butterflies and enchanting luminous pomegranates hung from the branches of the trees.

Hamaguchi-kōen Park is on the way to the port and gives us the umpteenth surprise for eyes and heart. Coloured lanterns in concentric, geometric patterns are englobed by cubic frames in white card, culminating in a tower of cubes with a pulsating belly of pink and red. A beautifully studied sight that we admire perched on the children's slide in the park, a secret short cut told us an old man because in Japan, beauty is there to be shared.

Some streets, bejewelled with lanterns made by the local children, lead up to an elementary school where we have our penultimate stamp applied and we enjoy the nocturnal rainbow from an upper window. However, it is when we get to Ōhama-kōen Park that happiness comes back to tickle my throat, not having an expressible form other than the tears I can feel clutching at the edges of my eyelids. The smell of the ocean, still echoing summer, reaches us with a caress from the river, alongside the melancholic words of a musician singing at the centre of a small spiral of golden lanterns.

A little further on, a wall of cubes and lanterns introduces us to the enchantment of a new composition. This time the centre of the design is a large semispherical net enclosing a nucleus of lanterns in vivacious colours, a heart of light that attracts us exactly as would an incandescent celestial body to its molten core.

I could go on forever walking round this marvel, like a satellite gone crazy. But time is rushing by and after the myriad compliments we receive at the presentation of our prize for gathering four stamps, we head off to the port with the calm and tenderness with which the first lantern flames are beginning to dwindle.

On the pier, in the direction of the metallic network of the red tower over the port of Hakata, a world is concentrated in which the edges of reality appear blurred, where a sailing ship at anchor in the dark water overlooks arrangements of candles made out of bamboo stems, hundreds of tiny cylinders of different heights making up a radiant carpet of incredible zen allure. All attention is on them, however much the glowing shopping centre Bayside Place Hakata attempts to make the night ocean sparkle with colour.

One last great design near the buildings of the International Terminal lights up some skaters sliding away over some humps in the darkness: the final secret corner of beauty, in a world fit to bursting with it.

Exhausted, we collapse into the soft seats covered with white lace of one of the many black taxis running up and down the streets of Fukuoka this evening. We leave behind us an avenue of lanterns about to succumb to the advancing night, like us to the inevitable end of another unforgettable moment.

By 10pm, when the festival is drawing to a close, the night market at Canal City is shining out in the night, warmed by the red lights of stalls that we had found closed the day before. Here, lots of people who like us have sated their gaze with the sight of the lanterns scattered across the city, are now set on sating their hunger. Stalls selling grilled meat are besieged by long queues, while the laid tables teem with beer and youthful laughter. Attracted by the smaller stalls where artisans sell homemade products, we entrust ourselves to a young girl for a plate of rice and very tasty curry. We enjoy it sitting next to other young people on the bank of River Naka-gawa, where the little hanging lanterns bring out the fuchsias and pinks of the cosmos beside the nocturnal river. As in Shirakawa-gō, it is they that light up the colours of these autumn days. From here we can see the houses and clubs wrapped in their coloured neon halos stretch over the water, turning into rapid brushstrokes trembling with a mass of colour. The lighthearted babble of Japanese youth is comforting, so far from the west where every day you have to guard against others, deceit and the desire to damage rather than respect; from the prepotence that crushes this simple state, of being young and living your dreams. There, where we live with the anxiety of having to survive, of having to watch your back, on the metro, on the bus, in a dark street at night, in daily life and at work. The anxiety of not being strong enough to get the better of the next person, of not being able to trample on them, or being able to protect those we love.

I admonish myself for always idealizing this nation too much, forcing myself to be aware of the negative and paradoxal aspects too, but however much I do, it is never enough. The weight of the reality of that other side of the world only increases.

We find a strange atmosphere in the vibrant neon streets of the red light district just before we get to our hotel. The odd furtive couple is going into a love hotel while some shy young men look hesitantly at the desk of a house of pleasure. I try to think of these situations as I would in my own country but I can't: holding Gabry by the hand, I look closely at the signs in the shape of hearts and the 'menu' displayed at the entrance, covered in photos of beautiful Japanese girls dressed as nurses or bunnies. Perhaps the past evening has so filled me with incredible emotions that I find it difficult to feel any negative ones, even faced with bizarre Japanese sexuality and its more controversial aspects. It is as though here even a brothel were despoiled of the negative malice it possesses in the west, clothed in a shroud of paradox that makes it funny, almost infantile, a far cry from the scent of violence and vulgarity felt elsewhere.

I might be exaggerating, so I try to make myself fish out happy moments that are not tied to these places. When I take my little dog Bobby in my arms, for 17 years the most important being in my life, in a few seconds the greatest loss I had ever encountered. When one night I made love with the person with whom I thought I would spend a whole existence, in the innocence of disregarding change that, in eight years, would turn us into adults.

However hard I try, I simply can't grasp other memories of true happiness than these. Too rare, now too far away.

Gazing at the sleepy roads from the window of a tiny hotel room. The shiver I feel touching the chilled glass prompts questions without answers, and makes me wonder why here those moments of happiness have so quickly become so numerous. It's almost too easy.

In bed, curled up and waiting for sleep, I feel Gabry's hand slide under my side and pull me towards the warmth of his body. Soon afterwards we make love. A love that flourishes on the night I've lived all that wonderment, explodes violently against the insecurities and difficulties that suffocate us, pulverising that painfully sharp blade of unhappiness. A love that I want to go on forever, but that only lasts a short time. A love we have here and now, tomorrow who knows?

Now is an instant that quickly becomes past, exactly like the night of lanterns at Fukuoka. Perhaps the happiness I'm searching for isn't something due, but something to win; cultivated and then enjoyed in the desperately short time it can allow us. It is something that needs attention but above all care. Care for the moments that are imperceptible instants, to find, grab, nurture and embed in our existence before they promptly vanish, overlooked by the lack of value we give them in time.

Happiness is in the care of and love for these instants. However many we want them to be.

I can feel Gabry's fingers intertwined with mine, his relaxed breathing as he sleeps. And each new day in these places, everything seems simpler to me. Becoming clearer, a little at a time.

In the end, looking more carefully, couldn't this instant be defined like that too, happiness?

Travel Notes

The four districts of Gokusho, Reisen, Ōhama and Naraya make up the 'old city' of Fukuoka, an area, between Hakata station and the city port, rich with history, artisans' stores and places of worship. The suggestive wooden gate of Hakata Sennen-mon is the start of the temple walk to around twenty points of interest, including Tōchō-ji Temple, with its red pagoda and the immense wooden Buddha, Jōten-ji Temple, famous for its zen meditation garden and Kushida-jinja Shrine, with its thousand year old ginkgo and permanently displayed forty foot kazari-yamakasa. In autumn, the evening light event Hakata Lights-up Walk makes exploration a magical experience.

After visiting the historic shops in the Kawabatadōri-shōtengai shopping arcade, it is enjoyable to spend the evening around Fukuoka's port, with its two hundred foot steel panoramic tower and the Wangan-ichiba Market entertainment area, chock-full of restaurants, onsen and local fishing products.

Day Trip:
* Relax in the onsen at your ryokan or in town
* Take the train from Beppu to Fukuoka
* Lunch at Rāmen Stadium, Canal City
* Visit the old city and Buddha of Tōchō-ji Temple
* Take a walk around Kushida-jinja Shrine and begin the hunt for stamps during the Hakata Tōmyō event
* Enjoy an evening meal at the port or along River Naka-gawa

Typical Products and Souvenirs:
* Mizutaki, chicken and vegetable nabemono
* Hakata-ningyō, unvarnished ceramic dolls
* Hakata-magemono, objects in cypress and cedar wood
* Hakata-ori, traditional handmade fabric
* Tetsunabe-gyōza, Japanese style dumplings cooked and served in tetsunabe

Kyōto
京都

It's easy to learn humility in Japan,
the chance to live a serene life with few things
to make life decent in its simplicity.
I got to know the Japan of the great metropoles,
but beyond them I've found completely different realities.
I've been given the gift of a smile from the person who lives
selling the sweets they've made in the local market,
someone who doesn't earn a lot
and is content with a little,
who loves to give away the little they possess.
Someone who nurtures wealth in their own existence

It's easy to hate time for the cruel ease with which it leaves behind the finest moments. Just as it's impossible to avoid being aware how fragile but powerful happy moments are, explosions of colour in the daily routine of existence. It seems Japan has an image for this too, in the cherry blossoms filling streets and lives with wonder for a brief instant, just sufficient not to be forgotten. To be awaited time and again.

I always want to feel the way I did yesterday evening, like cherry blossom under the rays of a first spring day: alive, caught up in an explosion of emotions, in the tears of a primordial joy which, though fleeting, is eternal.

The unforgettable hours we lived yesterday are gone, that pocket of devoured time that was just enough to make them seem they weren't sufficiently lived.

I feel melancholy on the journey to Kyōto, three hours as the *shinkansen* snakes over hills and through rice paddies that are now a lacework of mud. Here and there the first orange gashes mark the hills, the first signs of autumn, which here in Japan, is a blossoming of fire.

Kyōto welcomes us with its nostalgia for the past, accentuated by that excessive effort to accept the modern that can be seen in the central station, with its preposterous spaces and crystal blue windows. In itself, this construction, which defies the laws of modern design, is quite simply beautiful, elegant and sophisticated as a *geisha*[122] 「芸者」 strolling through the streets of Gion.

And yet, years after it was built, the city seems still not to have entirely accepted it. Far from the hustle and bustle of the old capital of Japan's futuristic station, the past gradually makes a space for itself in the first glimpses of the sinuous roofs of Tō-ji Temple, its pagoda brushing the sky of the city that for centuries has been embellishing itself with swooping tiles, dark wooden beams and red marquetry, just like the hair of the *maiko*[123] 「舞妓」 adorned with fine clips.

The place where we'll stay is snuck into a small residential street of tightly packed two storey houses, so close they can hardly breathe but each with their minuscule garden, six feet square with a contorted pine and an acer still unaware of autumn. Above us is a view of Japan made up of electric poles and power lines scoring the sky, pitched roofs of narrow blue tiles that seem worn enough to fly off at the first puff of wind. A lady is hanging out the washing on her

---

[122] Japanese entertainer, expert in the traditional Japanese performing arts of playing music, singing, dancing and making witty conversation. The geisha take part in formal parties, often to entertain wealthy clients

[123] Apprentice geisha, younger in age, wearing gaudy accessories in their hair, high wooden sandals and white make up on their face and neck

small faded balcony, behind her a sliding door made of fine glass framed by wood now faded by the sun.

A Japanese woman is waiting for us by one of the court-yard gates, she is about thirty with short hair and a shy smile. She welcomes us in good English and the typical hospitality that we always find striking. Scrolling through the web pages, this Airbnb was love at first sight; it is a fair distance from the central station and anonymous business hotels but gave us the chance to stay somewhere with traditional interiors, as guests of a Japanese couple.

However, we hardly have time to get used to it before we're off again: we drop out bags and plunge back into the traffic of a city that's a far cry from the discipline of Tōkyō and overwhelmed by its tangle of bus lines intrepidly substituting the handful of metro lines. We go along Kujō-dōri Street, sneaking into Tō-ji Temple, calm in spiritual silence, while outside commotion is all about today.

On the 21 of the month, the market stalls at Kōbō-ichi flank the temple and pagoda, offering the stream of clients, groceries, crafts, clothing and household goods of every type. We fall into line with the flow of people swaying through the labyrinth of coloured workshops that from above look like a blue, red and green carpet unfurled down the paths of the whole complex. It is a true flea market, although become more touristic over the years, and always holds surprises if you look closely. As we are only passing through we resist the temptation of taking a peek at any of the ceramic and print stalls, making just one stop at the stall of an old man selling sharp knives at discounted prices: perfectly hewn blades of a purplish silver with handles in light coloured wood on which are engraved the *kanji* of a signature; as elegant as a *katana*, despite being smaller and with different destined use. Gabry tells me how Japanese knives, considered the best in the world due to the alloys used and the incredible techniques for working the blades, can reach stratospheric prices, so that you can find blades at 3,000 to 7,000 *yen*, so those sold at this stall at Kōbō-ichi Market are an opportunity not to be missed. I feel tenderness watching his delight at the purchase, a joy mingled with present passions and future dreams, and the subtle desire for serenity affecting the soul more than these knives would.

Almost immediately we hurry away from all those moving bodies to perch at the bus stop and wait for the bus to take us to Shimogamo-jinja Shrine, the most eagerly awaited destination of the day. Here, like every bus stop in the city, there are no electronic panels to tell you when your bus will be coming. In this strange blend of ancient and modern, there are only small lights in sequence to show how close the bus is and a little yellow ribbon moving between them; a system, given the precision with which it works, in no way inferior to the modern electronic systems to be found in Tōkyō.

The coins rattle noisily into the ticket machine next to the bus driver. We pay 600 *yen* for our day pass just before getting off, after nearly an hour's travel bringing us to one of the suburbs to the north of Kyōto. There is a large wooded area called Tadasu-no-mori where, on some weekends, seasonal themed events are organised with music and activities for children, made colourful by the small stands of food and Japanese crafts of which there are many. Everything happens in the incredible setting of the forest around Shimogamo-jinja Shrine and its great vermilion *torii*.

As hardcore Japanese market-goers, it was impossible to resist this singular setting where, at somewhat unpredictable intervals tied to the seasons, the Mori-no-Tezukuri-ichi

Tō-ji 東寺 & Kōbō-ichi 弘法市

In 794 B.C.E. the capital of Japan was moved from Nara to Heiankyō (today's Kyōto) and two temples were erected to guard the southern entrance of the city, Tō-ji to the east and Sai-ji to the west (no longer in existence today). A few years later, the emperor entrusted the design of this temple to Kūkai (774 – 835), also known as Kōbō Daishi, the monk who founded the Shingon-shū Buddhist School on Mount Kōya-san after years of studying Buddhism in China. During his studies, the monk also explored Chinese advanced civil engineering and later applied this knowledge to design Tō-ji.

Inside the temple there is a paying area giving access to the garden surrounding the Lake Hyōtan-ike (1), with an imposing fuji-zakura (2), a 40-foot high cherry tree that is over 130 years old, undisputed star of the evening illuminations between mid-March and mid-April, when the sakura are in blossom. There is another evening opening period in November, when it is the maples mirrored in the water that are illuminated. Continuing southwards, you reach the complex's most famous structure, which is to say the five-floor wooden pagoda (3), at 180 feet the tallest in Japan. Whilst to the east of the pool are two more large buildings: Kon-dō (4), the main room containing a statue of the Buddha of medicine and two statues of the Bodhisattva of the sun and moon, and Kō-dō (5), the room comprising another 21 statues. Outside this area there are various structures, such as Miei-dō (6) and Hōmotsu-kan (7), respectively the ex-residence of Kūkai and the museum of the temple treasures.

Every 21 of the month the main attraction here is Kōbō-ichi Market: at the death of Kūkai, on 21 March 835, his followers decided to commemorate his death once a month on that day in a pilgrimage to Tō-ji. The surrounding shops, seeing the arrival of a stream of potential clients, began to set up their green tea stalls around the temple. With the passing of years, the number of shops has increased, transforming the commemoration into the city's largest market, with over a thousand stalls (8). Being a flea market, you can easily find very inexpensive tea services, vases and bowls made with exquisite workmanship, often by the stall owners themselves. You also find bonsai, calligraphy materials, kimono silks and other artistic works. And between purchases you can stop to re-fresh yourself at the food stalls selling takoyaki, yakisoba and cold beer.

Again at the temple of Tō-ji, on the first Sunday of the month there is a small artisans' market, Garakuta-ichi. Another two important markets in the city are the artisans' market at Hyakumanben Chion-ji Temple, every 15 of the month, and the market at the shrine of Kitano Tenman-gū, also known as Tenjin-ichi, on 25 of the month. Besides these, there are lots of other small markets going on in various zones of the city on different dates but mainly at the weekend; a unique experience to discover yet another hid-den tradition in this country.

Handcraft Market attracts crafts people and hobbyists from Kyōto and around. Perhaps it was destiny, perhaps just good luck that the market should happen to be on this Sunday, and in particular the Local stall awaits. Gabry met the young couple who work on it and their two small children on his previous trip, at another city market, where he had the good fortune to taste their biscuits, home made from delicious seasonal ingredients. Being a family business, proceeds are mainly linked to participating in the local markets and events that take place in Kyōto over the year, and we are thrilled at the idea of being their customers again.

As soon as we enter the wood, beneath the intricate archway of branches on which the moss is already taking the greenery's place, everything in the serene setting around us is an invitation to remember the simplicity and importance of small things, two aspects that the western world has managed to wrench out of its inhabitants' daily life, replacing them with consumerism and materialism. On the other side of the world people's wealth is determined by the possession of objects. People, their quality of life and personal achievements are judged on the basis of their salary, their company title, the properties they own, and how recent the models of smartphone or car they flaunt around the city. That the most recent off-road vehicle is the least suitable for intense city traffic is of secondary importance compared to appearing affluent in your neighbour's eyes. These are the objects, the cold and provisory elements used to define a person and their life. It is appearance and not substance that determines a person's identity.

I find all this profoundly sad, while the Tadasu-no-mori forest wraps us in its universe, showing me a different reality, emptying of significance what seems indispensable elsewhere and filling it with what surrounds us. All of a sudden, everything seems ascribable to the word the Japanese use to describe the image embracing the simplicity and all the complexity of life. *Komorebi*, the sunlight filtering through the leaves of trees like raindrops, beauty that passes from nature to our watching eyes, giving substance to the surrounding area and to the simplicity it holds.

And so, in a forest alive with the shouts of children, I watch the sun splintering through the roof of leaves above me, in a kaleidoscope of warm golden rays streaming through the cold iridescent greens, and the criss-cross of slender black branches energising the light filled foliage. *Komorebi* is all of this, but here at Shimogamo-jinja, it is also the light slipping into the stream running alongside the market and hitting the colourful bicycles parked on a cushion of dry leaves, lighting up the rainbow tenting of the stalls, and tingling the children's faces as they play barefoot in the stream. I can hear them laugh for pure joy, and see them carrying jars to catch insects and frogs.

Here and there on the bank, near the stalls, people are sitting on coloured groundsheets, enjoying *onigiri* made at home or bought from the food-stalls. Once again I get the feeling I may be falling into the trap of idealising these places, of glorifying a world that seems so far from the west, when, having found the map of the market around the shrine's great red *torii*, we start trawling the little shops. The sense immediately comes to the fore of the serenity tied to the essence of the lives of these people. Remote lives from the ones a tourist stumbles across in a metropolis full of men in dark jacket and white shirt, and stunning women in smart suits. Here, in the forest of *komorebi*, are other lives: family life, with children and old people, living in the extensive countryside and hilly areas on the edge of large cities, living off their rice field and artisan activities.

And so we meet a girl dreaming of visiting Rome, saving the money she earns from her handmade fabric bags, and the old lady who supplements the income from her husband's rice field by painting stones from the rivers, transforming them into cats and tortoises. And the guys from Local, who remember Gabry straight off and introduce their children, offering us biscuits to taste and from whom we buy slices of berry and pumpkin cakes. It only takes a taste to realise that the best pastry shop in town couldn't recreate the taste of a small cake produced with love in the oven at home. They smile for the photo we take of us all, in front of the table decorated with packets of biscuits waiting to be taken away by customers. They smile at life, proud to show off the stickers they've made for the packaging: a hand-written label meticulously describing ingredients and expiry dates.

Like many Japanese at the market, their life seems to revolve entirely around this place, made up of simple things and humble dreams.

Today, in the west, the simplicity of things eludes us,
time taken over what is truly important.
In a society where poverty is interior and exterior,
the essence of life is sacrificed
just to possess more, or more than others

Before coming on this trip, I found myself reading 'Le coordinate della felicità', the autobiography of Gianluca Gotto who, abandoning a western life made up of appearances, spiritual poverty, career and materialism, had begun living in Thailand like a digital nomad. What struck him most in Thailand were people's smiles. Never absent, always serene and voluntary.

In his book he reflects on the fact that he came from a rich country where people, although possessing so many things, never smiled, in fact usually appeared cross, always in competition to possess more than the next person and prevail upon them. Whereas in Thailand poor people with very few things never stopped smiling, freely offering him that little they had and always ready to help.

Seeing the two young people smile brought this paradox to mind. I think of it as they give us a packet of biscuits, for which therefore they will never be paid, and which may mean one less toy for their children. I think how possessing less leaves more space for people's inner wealth; more space for happiness and less for the unhappiness of never possessing enough.

Further on, a lady sells Gabry a small cloth notebook covered in lotus flowers in snazzy colours.

"You can use this for the good copy of the diary you're keeping of our trip," he tells me as he pays for my present.

He has never been too affected by the deeper aspects of this country, and yet now he seems to perceive this serenity in the same way. He talks about it, confiding his thoughts and concluding that perhaps true life is here and not on the other side of the world.

At another stall we buy a pendant, a delicate cherry petal in transparent wax. The lady keeping the stall, also smiling, is selling the fruits of her passion and speaks of her work proudly; she seems almost moved when we congratulate her for what she does: transforming the fragile beauty of life into jewels.

At a certain point the snake of coloured umbrellas on the woody path ends, and some families have already set up their picnics on the crunchy autumn leaves piled on the ground. We buy our lunch at a picturesque van turned into a little Mexican kitchen, drawn closer by the long queue of customers. Inside the cramped van, in a minuscule kitchen that seems better equipped than a Michelin star restaurant, a young Japanese man prepares the dishes at an incredible speed.

Soon afterwards we are sitting by the river, with a delicious plate of handmade nachos, fresh guacamole sauce from which emerge pieces of fresh cut tomato, a plate of fragrant curry rice on which lies a soft egg, and a handful of sweet pastries from Local. Around us is the chatter of picnickers, and the sound of the water slowly flowing through the dwarf reeds in the ditch, punctuated by a child's cry of enthusiasm as he catches a frog in his net.

I hold my breath, and beneath the light trickling through the leaves of the forest, I realise that in this tiny instant, collected around us is all I could possibly need in life.

Shimogamo-jinja Shrine offers a last moment of exploration before we leave the forest still at the peak of its special day, before the market closes at 4pm and the sacred silence returns. Recent restoration of the two old structures has brought out the vermilion red, in deep contrast with the white of the gravel of the clearing on which they sit. Their indefatigable presence seemingly immune to the passage of time, opposes the surrounding wood, damaged by the latest typhoon that brought down several trees, now leaning precariously against each other.

The southern path leads us to Kawai-jinja Shrine and to the intersection with Mikage-dōri, where a miniature *torii* prevents vehicle access. This beautiful pedestrian way is framed by a string of small traditional style villas, beside which moss covered rocks mark the edge of a rivulet running along the pavement. I'm delighted by the unexpected presence of the rivulet defiantly insinuating itself into the urban fabric, and watch the water jostle its way through the thick shrubberies of dwarf bamboo framing the walk. Through containment barriers built of wood and straw, the pebble bed running to the end of the walk where the rivulet disappears as suddenly as it appeared, and the umpteenth slice of unforeseen wonder dissolving into the normality of the city, just before Aoi-kōen Park.

But it is here, at the intersection of rivers Kamo-gawa and Takano-gawa, that we are again impressed by the strip of land fought over by two areas of water, a green park that provides the population of Kyōto with a place to meet in the late afternoon when the heat of the sun has weakened and relaxing here after a day's work would be particularly enjoyable.

Numerous bicycles parked along the bank project their shadows onto the grass, elongated by a jaded light that nonetheless sparkles and bedazzles on the surface of the rivers. Some children run after a ball before it falls into the lazy transparent water, others hop up and down in it happily, their feet nipped by the cold. Lots of families have laid out their picnic rugs, with dozens of containers of all shapes and sizes from which family and friends help themselves in the Japanese way of being together, displaying appreciation and gratitude for the company of others.

In this way Kyōto lives around its river like the man of the household returning home in the evening, cocooned by the domestic space and the warmth of their family after a long day of hard work. Before crossing, we inspect at the placid course of the water through the huge stones with more apprehension than the children who, care-free, jump without hesitation from one rock to the next.

By the glints of the river along which Kyōto sits,
thoughts turn to the importance of ourselves.
I listen to the water gurgle past and feel peace
that I never feel on the other side of the world.
Stripped of the superfluous, for the first time
I lack nothing: here, in simplicity,
I finally have all I need to feel alive.
To be myself at last

When we reach the other side and go up the soft bank to the road, behind us there is that domineering serenity again, beneath an autumnal sundown that kickstarts its show.

The day glides past like this, like the historical roads of Higashiyama district beneath our feet. I've only once walked down them before today, and yet I recognise the contours as though they had been stamped on my memory: the ascents and descents where the sound of *geta*[124] 「下駄」 echoes between the wooden houses; Yasaka-no-tō Pagoda at Hōkan-ji Temple sticking out high-handedly from the background like a guiding star in the neighbourhood; the souvenir and *kimono* shops, just now busy bringing in their 'rental' signs; the overpowering but invisible presence of Kiyomizu-dera Temple that sooner or later, I promise, I will come back to visit without its prison of scaffolding.

The district is getting ready for its nightly transformation, when time evaporates into a dimension of silence and lanterns, where it's hard to understand if Kyōto has really ceased to exist and change like all the other cities, crystallizing itself for ever in the beauty of a passing instant.

No time to find the *obi*[125] 「帯」 for my *yukata*, here in the

[124] Traditional wooden sandals, raised a few centimetres from the ground and held to the foot like flip flops. Typical footwear worn by geisha

[125] Intricately decorated wide belt worn round the waist over the kimono

neighbourhood where lamplight and the colours of hanging silks alternate behind the fine glass of so many shops; *kimono* and *yukata* girded by *obi* that become inseparable from the fabrics of the clothes, as though nothing could match as perfectly as what is on display.

No time to admire this parallel universe; perhaps tomorrow.

This evening the entire Higashiyama district will be like one of the amazing *wagashi* [126] 「和菓子」 sold here in Kyōto, the city possessing the perfect art: of a beauty too pure and 'recherché' to be consumed in a hurry.

The beam of the moon lets itself be swallowed by the dark night without lessening its shine, while in our room a lamp sends out the typical halo of Japanese lanterns, reaching and alighting on each separate thing: on the *tatami*, the *futon* and the interior rice paper windows.

It's about 7:30 when we are ready for our evening at the Kōdai-ji, one of the rare temples that in the month of October opens its gates for the nocturnal autumn *raitsu-appu* in the garden. Last year I had the fortune to be here at an evening opening. It was August and the sweltering heat of the day gave way to the song of crickets, the solitary roads of Gion were gilded with light from ancient lamps and, unexpectedly, the nocturnal garden of Kōdai-ji as well.

As before, Daidokoro-zaka Slope steps up to the entrance of the temple in a staging of light and colour. The vault of the trees that surrounds it lights up in the darkness, in greens and oranges so bright they seem radioactive. Ground level lighting illuminates the wide stone steps, crossing

---

[126] Small traditional Japanese confection often served with green tea, made of mochi, azuki bean paste and fruit. Enchanting miniature works of art in coloured sweet pastry with vegetable ingredients and shaped with extreme care

them like sharp incandescent blades. More floodlights are placed by the trunks, inundating the foliage with a white glow bringing depth to shadows and sculpting every single frond in the night, like a felt pen outlining the iridescent lines of a shaded background.

We find this world, where light fills the night with vivid shapes and impossible colours, is repeated inside Kōdai-ji Temple where the covered bridge of Garyō-rō, the dragon's corridor, brings to life one of the most enchanting nocturnal scenes on Garyō-chi Pond beneath. The shadows among the scales of the roof transform the bridge into the back of a dragon slipping away, skimming the water and arching up to the Tamaya building. Under its belly, the black, immobile water of the pond becomes a mirror for the explosion of colour just above.

The dozens of lights sprouting from below, in the darkness around the row of trees and shrubs on the bank, set alight every single shade of green, red, pink and orange in the interplay of leaves and branches. Some of the acers have foliage that are clusters of burning stars, a sky full of colours to be slathered on the black of the night. At the foot of the autumnal 'milky way', as if in a parallel universe, twin trees lit by the same crisp and powerful colours stretch across the pool. I gaze dumbfounded as this other reality takes shape: were it the door to another world, I wouldn't hesitate to plunge in and be gone forever.

Rows of lanterns guide us like a trail of breadcrumbs to the main building, flanking the garden and Kangetsu-dai Bridge, designed to see the moon reflected on the surface of Engetsu-chi Pond. The place is pervaded by magic that you begin to see when you get to the main building, flowing through the rice paper doors opened onto the large rocky inner garden.

There are hills and ripples of gravel brought to life by suggestive beams of artificial light, in a silent sigh of moving colour that seems to call ancestral spirits by making every element appear alive, including heavy Chokushi-mon Gate, the entrance for imperial messengers.

We continue our walk, finding ourselves in the middle of more luminous trails climbing the surrounding paths and hills. Like a procession of fireflies, they lead the way to the temple's bamboo grove, miniature equivalent of the forest of Arashiyama to the west of Kyōto. Here, before the garden bids goodnight, the polished green and turquoise spears of the bamboo stretch towards the luminescent vault to a cage of stems closing above our heads, ensnaring sight and heart with wonder.

In the late evening, the ancient district of Higashiyama displays all the nostalgic fascination of Kyōto in days gone by: it is the city described in Arthur Golden's novel, 'Memoirs of a Geisha', in the silence of the roads lit by the orange light of streetlamps, in the stores and houses with their ancient look, closed behind grid-pattern wooden doors.

At the bottom of Daidokoro-zaka Slope, along priceless Nene-no-michi Lane splashed with the sudden red of the maples, the houses sleep, wrapped in garlands of Japanese lanterns, hanging from roofs, at deserted entrances and porches and in secret alleys hiding behind.

I imagine living in one of these little wooden houses, waking up in the morning and walking to my shop, removing my shoes at the front door, sliding the door on worn wooden castors, being met by the acrid smells of camphor and cedar while the light filtering through the little windows picks out the dust particles from the hanging fabrics, on which carp and *kanji* float beneath rapid brushstrokes.

'In another life...'

The green porches lit by hexagonal lanterns on Shijō-dōri Street, prey to a constant passage of people by day, are already semi deserted and the dozens of shops selling green tea or *maccha*[127] 「抹茶」 and fabrics, in an endless chain, are swallowed in the darkness of their windows.

Although Takatsuji-dōri Street is also enveloped in silence, the window of a small pizzeria-restaurant, Goichi Piza shines out, and would go entirely unobserved were it not for the fame of its pizza and Italian dishes, loved by Japanese and Italians visiting Kyōto. The owner is a young Japanese man who spent time in Italy learning the art of the Neapolitan pizza and much more: he is famous both for his international pastas and sauces and for simple soups from Italian traditional cooking.

Finding him extremely friendly and his Italian fluent, we spend a very enjoyable evening talking about his culinary skills while we tuck into an exquisite 'Pasta Cacio e Pepe', and 'Pizza Margherita' with a thick soft base and a delicious freshly-made 'Sicilian Cannolo', as good as anything you'd find in Italy. Before we leave he offers us a glass of his home-made limoncello. A sip of the Mediterranean.

Who would ever have thought it; to eat our own traditional dishes more than 6,500 miles away...

Another black taxi with white lace trimmings takes us along the quiet streets to where we are staying. The blanched moon, striped with black electricity cables, lays a pale veil over a neighbourhood on the verge of sleep.

I slip into bed lulled by the smell of *tatami* and the creak of the wooden floor, and yet the lunar light is too bright to let me fall asleep, as it forces its way through the windows

---

[127] A powdered green tea commonly known as 'matcha', it is widely used as an ingredient for confectionary and for the tea ceremony

to turn the walls ivory. In a house that feels more familiar than it really is, I sense the peace of the places and food of today, shielded from the world and the passage of time, under a blanket of simplicity, affection and pure, essential feelings.

Here I'm learning the importance of simplicity every day, along with the sharing of beauty, of learning how to look and to grasp the important details behind the veil of appearances.

Here I'm learning to be a better person.

'Home' for me is all this, and it's here.

Travel Notes

Kyōto was the capital of Japan from 794 to 1869, the year in which Tōkyō took its place. Seat of the emperor and base of the shōgun who ruled the country for hundreds of years, the city was built to a chessboard plan around the imperial palace, in a grid of streets where it is easy to get your bearings thanks in part to the River Kamo-gawa, which splits the city in two.

As it only has two metro lines, taxis and buses are the best way to explore the city. To the north, after the bifurcation of Rivers Takano-gawa and Kamo-gawa, you find Shimogamo-jinja Shrine, an UNESCO heritage site. Also used as a place to relax for the inhabitants of Kyōto, there is the Tadasu-no-mori Forest where various handcraft markets are held, among which Mori-no-Tezukuri-ichi. The event takes place from 9am to 4pm, not on fixed dates, but announced on the official site and social networks. The market boasts more than 300 stalls selling objects made by hand. The most part of the sellers are mothers or students, amateur makers living in the Kansai area, and yet many of the products are well designed and of very high quality. Various homemade food stalls also participate in the event, selling biscuits, jams and lemonade, and there are also vans cooking pizzas and other delights.

Just south of the forest, on the east bank of the River Kamo-gawa, is Higashiyama district, famous for its numerous temples located a short walk from each other, some of which are among the most celebrated of the city. You go from Ginkaku-ji, the silver temple, to Shrines Heian-jingū and Yasaka-jinja to the gates of Gion, the ancient district of the geisha, with its characteristic narrow lanes. Heading south, you come across Kōdai-ji Temple with its impressive garden, surrounded by a grid of traditional slopes such as Ninen-zaka and Sannen-zaka, up which climb wood buildings and stores selling local crafts, souvenirs and kimono, with the Yasaka-no-tō Pagoda of Hōkan-ji Temple in the background.

The famous complex of temples, Kiyomizu-dera, is also located here: the temple overlooking the city, home of three holy waterfalls. Sanjūsangen-dō, the hall containing the 1001 statues of the goddess Kannon, marks the edge of the area of Higashiyama, from which you go on to the southeast suburb of the city, a zone often frequented by tourists due to the famous trail of red torii belonging to Fushimi Inari-taisha Shrine. Here too there are numerous temples, not least Tōfuku-ji with its amazing zen garden of rocks.

Day Trip:
* Take the train from Fukuoka to Kyōto
* Visit Kōbō-ichi Market near Tō-ji Temple
* Visit the Mori-no-Tezukuri-ichi Handcraft Market in the forest of Shimogamo-jinja Shrine
* Take a walk along River Kamo-gawa and through Higashiyama district with its temples and historic roads
* Visit Kōdai-ji Temple and its garden for the autumnal evening light show
* Eat pizza or pasta at Goichi Piza

Typical Products and Souvenirs:
* Kyō-gashi, refined and elaborate confectionary typical of Kyōto
* Uji-cha, high quality local green tea from Uji region, south of Kyōto
* Chazutsu, decorated tea containers
* Tsukemono, pickled vegetables
* Saba-zushi, mackerel sushi
* Furoshiki, fabric used as a bag in which to wrap presents, bentō and other objects
* Tenugui, fabrics for internal decoration
* Crafts at Kyōto's markets

Kyōto
京都

At a distance of more than a year, Kyōto is still the same,
the penetrating and unmistakable
smells and colours of the covered market,
fragile narrow streets smelling of the past around the temple,
the perfume of limpid water in the river,
the strong taste of tōfu, the familiar smell of rāmen
heated as customers arrive,
the lights of the massive station high-handedly reminding us
how this city is still
the second beating heart of Japan...

Open your eyes. Finding yourself precisely where you want to be. I'd love the wonder you feel gazing at thin rice paper, glowing white under the early morning rays, to be there every time I wake, like the serenity and equilibrium that come with it.

Breakfast is Local's pumpkin tart and the sound of a school bell ringing nearby. Unique, it is the very sound I heard as a child watching my favourite *anime* on tv.

Today the plan was to explore the area around the Imperial Palace of Kyōto, where at midday the departure is scheduled for the Jidai Matsuri parade, the Procession of the Ages, reaching Heian-jingū Shrine at 2:30pm. From there, on a local train, we would travel north to catch the tram for the shrine on Mount Kurama-yama, famous for its ancient cedar wood and for Kurama-no-Hi Matsuri, the festival of fire held on 22 October. However, recent storms have made

282

the area around the shrine inaccessible, so reluctantly we have to overturn our plans for the day.

Along Kujō-dōri Street, we find consolation in a Tō-ji Temple that is quite different from the day before. Immersed in the silence of the early morning and free from the hundreds of stalls and their noisy exchanges, it is revealed in its mystical aspect, as the autumn sun warms up the blue tiles and dark wood walls, delving into the shadows in the eaves of its inseparable, illustrious pagoda.

Just opposite, we drift onto one of the many city buses, to then be turned out in the labyrinth of narrow roads around Nishiki-ichiba, Kyōto's covered market. This picturesque market, animated by the frenetic swerving gait of clumsy porters weighed down by piles of large boxes of merchandise and tenacious little old ladies with their shopping bags, is a long covered way with a highly coloured glass ceiling, only interrupted when lateral ways intersect. Lurking beneath the chromatic rainbow are rows of closely-packed very disparate stores selling food and objects. Having explored the market in summer, swollen with tourists and the pungent smells of freshly-displayed foods, visiting it now on a tranquil autumn morning gives us the chance to enjoy the slightly freakish and at the same time fascinating aspect that makes it feel a little like Alice's Wonderland, where on every corner you might happen upon something extraordinary or entirely new.

Like most oriental markets, the shops lay out all their wares for the customers: whether fabrics or foodstuffs, everything is arranged so that it can be seen by potential purchasers. The variety of ingredients you can find here is incredible, maroon baby octopus, cooked and impaled on wooden skewers, monstrous dried fish, trays of pickled lotus stems, slices of *daikon* laid out like photo negatives. The strangest, most colourful things - although it is often better not to ask oneself about the method of preservation - are here in the middle of the stores' comic signs on which you see a mixture of adorable whistling octopuses and inexplicably smiling turnips.

And as if this artistic gobbledygook of local produce and products were not enough, autumn decorations abound, with phosphorescent red maple leaves and garlands of chestnuts snaking between the goods. Again at Nishiki-ichiba Market, it is easy to get stuck in the marvellous chopstick shops, among hundreds of decorated models on which you can have your name engraved and with which to accompany the most varied *hashioki* 「箸置き」, chopstick holders in the shape of *takoyaki*, leeks, *shiitake* and many other things. The frenzy of colours and smells in the market even seems to gain possession of the numerous shops selling tea caddies, knives, ceramics and fabrics in the adjoining lanes, genuine black holes for anyone passing by.

We leave the liveliness of this shopping area with difficulty to head over onto the opposite bank of River Kamogawa, the line of water that attempts to split up the disordered mingling of ancient and modern in the city by imposing organized criteria.

The beauty of the Kiyomizu district is already noticeable around the rise in the land up to Hōkan-ji Temple's pagoda, a lookout that sits proud among the low buildings of the area. At intervals on this small paved road, you find more modern buildings among the older two-floor Kyōto houses, many of which today are shops selling souvenirs, crafts and local produce. The fascination of these places also resides in the tiny, beautifully kept green spaces at the entrance, corners that look like little rainforests watered by the autumn rain. In these small ecosystems, among fern fronds emerging from grey rocks, the red leaves of the odd nandina muscle in, with no fear of the cold weather, unleashing the smell of musk that is becoming the familiar embrace of autumn with the golden fluttering of leaves in the air.

The walk uphill to the pagoda includes Kongō-ji Temple and its altar, covered in cascades of chubby balls of gaudily coloured fabrics, keepers of the prayers and desires of visitors. Equally rich in colour are the *yukata* and *kimono* worn by the Asian girls who appear from every corner of this neighbourhood: very often they are young tourists, for the most part Chinese, who hire a *kimono* at one of the many shops around to then snap a disproportionate number of selfies with the temples in the background.

At the top of Ninen-zaka Slope, access to a secondary street thronged with craft shops and sellers of delicious *korokke*, is Okutan Kiyomizu, the ideal restaurant to discover that the *tōfu*[128] 「豆腐」 you've eaten so far is a different matter from the one prepared by hand in Japan, whose cult and tradition have ancient roots. Besides offering customers homemade firm or soft *tōfu*, this is a typical restaurant in which to totally immerse oneself to fully experience this authentic dish.

Which is how we find ourselves on a little bridge above an interior garden, where inside spaces merge into little cloisters with acers and other plants. In such elegant surroundings, a clever play of natural and artificial light reaches the glass room where we are sitting.

Here, the low tables have traditional stone hotplates on which the terracotta pot sits that contains the *tōfu*, better defined as *yudōfu* 「湯豆腐」 , in that it is served hot in its

---

[128] Bean curd made from coagulating soy milk with nigari. The result can be a solid white block of varied consistency for different types of tōfu. It has a delicate taste and is used in savoury and sweet dishes, often flavoured or marinated

cooking water. In such an atmosphere, even simply eating *tōfu* becomes a deep and meditative experience, where the beauty of the table laden with different sized bowls is part of the meal itself. The colours, aromas and tastes jostle in their great variety to accompany the same dish: *tōfu* on the hotplate with *miso*, glazed with sesame and *wasabi*, or as a sweet version. Side dishes are *shiso* leaves in *tenpura*, *shiitake* mushrooms, tender slices of pumpkin and fried soy beans, bowls of rice and sweet potatoes, one of the autumnal dishes par excellence. Tastes and consistencies I'm trying now for the first time in my life, sitting on the *tatami*, in front of a pot of *tōfu* that has never been so secret and steeped in charm.

It's afternoon and we're outside Kiyomizu-dera Temple, still swaddled in scaffolding that for years has hidden its beauty. We promise ourselves we'll come back to admire its immense wooden skeleton, to stand on its deck and admire Kyōto from on high, drink the water from the Otowa-no-taki Falls with its three fountains, choosing the virtue we'd most like to have: success, longevity or wisdom.

We go in search of consolation in the neighbourhood streets, focused on finding an *obi* for my *yukata* in one of the many shops. After all, it has been more than a year since the *yukata* that 'chose me' has been without an *obi*. The tradition tied to these articles of clothing is historically rooted in Japanese custom, but also in stories and anecdotes transformed and adapted over time and geography, so that sometimes it's hard to understand whether they are simply an example of the world wanting to think of Japan as a land of myths and fascinating stories.

Among the various legends I've come across is the one about the choice of garment not being left to chance because there must be a particular chemistry between the *yukata* and

the wearer. It is precisely due to the sudden connection between the two that it is said the garment chooses the wearer
rather than the other way round. This strange and romantic
paradox shouldn't come as a surprise given the intimate relationship the Japanese have with all objects that are part of
their daily life, the care and respect with which they treat
them and the importance they hold in their lives. This out-
look isn't only influenced by Shinto religion, for which all
objects are endowed with a soul, but also by the different
manner of possessing objects in eastern and western cul-
tures. Despite the wave of westernization invading Japan in
recent decades, bringing with it unbridled consumerism to
the large urban centres, the ancient and intimate relationship with material objects remains, perhaps upheld by the
native religion.

If on the other side of the world we are used to giving
little importance to objects because we have so many and
can always have more in a short time, in more genuine Japan, heir to a past of poverty and a still humble present, the
spirit of *mottainai*[129] 「もったいない」 is still alive. Objects
are not bought on a whim but out of need, they are then
cared for and maintained for as long as possible, in part out
of necessity and in part because it is time that gives them
importance and stature. While in the west an object becomes
obsolete as soon as it is bought, here the same object has a
value that increases over time, through memories attached
to it that give it consistency, defining its existence and giving it a soul.

Going back to the choice of my *yukata*, I can't deny that it
really does seem to have gone according to the legend. I've
always thought that the *yukata* worn by a western woman

---

[129] Concept tied to re-use and lack of wastage. It derives from the expression of
disappointment used when something is thrown away that could yet be useful.

Kiyomizu-dera 清水寺

Literally 'Temple of Pure Water', this Buddhist temple owes its name to the Otowa-no-taki Falls, to the east of Kyōto, near which it is located. Founded in 780 and part of UNESCO heritage since 1994, Kiyomizu-dera Temple is famous for its forty foot balcony, the highest wooden balcony in the country, built with 139 pilasters to look out over the city.

During the Edo period there was a belief according to which if you survived jumping from such a height your wish would be granted. After more than 200 people threw themselves off it, the practice was banned. The famous balcony, restored between 2017 and 2020, offers a marvellous view over the surrounding cherries and acers, depending on the season. Moreover, thanks to strict building regulations, the city has no skyscrapers and on clear days you can enjoy a breathtaking panorama over the ancient capital in all is magnificence.

Around Hon-dō (6), the main hall, the area offers many points of interest: going through the enormous Niō-mon Gate (1), the 46 foot entrance to the complex, you find yourself at the bell of Shōrō (4) and a second entrance, Sai-mon Gate (2), leading to the 100 foot pagoda named Sanjū-no-tō (3), one of the largest three-floor pagodas in Japan; continuing to the main building you go through Todoroki-mon Gate and a tunnel open on both sides (5), with hundreds of hanging fūrin blowing in the pleasant summer wind.

To the south, visible from Hon-dō Hall's balcony, Koyasu-no-tō Pagoda (9) sticks out of its bed of green, while looking east, there are great photo opportunities of the main building from the smaller balcony of Okuno-in Temple (7). At the foot of this last is Otowa-no-taki Fall (8), from which gush the three virtuous fountains of success, longevity and wisdom.

Behind the main building is Jishu-jinja Shrine (10) dedicated to Ōkuninushi, the Kami of love. Opposite that are two rocks 60 feet apart: it is said that anyone capable of walking from one rock to the other with their eyes closed will find love.

Finally, in the north zone of the complex is a green area called Sekibutsu-gun (11) covered in dozens of jizō statuettes, while to the south is a pagoda entirely made of stone (12) and a historic shop selling pastries and green tea.

In autumn, when the maple leaves go red, numerous floodlights are arranged around the balcony, while in spring the many sakura make a walk in the area quite as moving.

What is more, every year in mid-March the Hanatōro is held, another illumination event around the area of Higashiyama.

completely loses its charm and I've never felt the need to trespass on a tradition that has nothing to do with fashion and lacks wearability in my country of origin. And yet, on that day, in a small shopping arcade in Kyōto, I was struck by a shop window full of typical fabrics and painted handkerchiefs, one of my greatest weaknesses, and decided to go in. The corner of the shop devoted to *yukata* interested me most because of the patterns on the fabrics, and in that sea of garments crushed together, I hurriedly cast an eye and pulled out five or six *yukata* decorated with maple leaves in autumnal colours. A few moments later, as I was leaving the shop and saying goodbye to the assistant, the magic happened: a final distracted glance, and my hand pulls out a *yukata* made in a different cotton from the others and in a colour white quite different to the bright shades and patterns on the others I'd seen. I look more closely, and noticing a pattern on the lower part of the garment, I ask the assistant to tell me about it, without imagining for a minute that I had found the *yukata* that once arranged correctly with the right sequence of pleats and folds, would perfectly adhere to my body.

At the mirror, the *yukata*, with its snow white background and trail of dark blue cherry blossom swept by the wind, seemed to speak to me, transforming my appearance and changing the reflection into a me I'd never seen before. Perhaps it was the feminine, sensual woman I'd imagined, or perhaps the Japanese me I'd always wanted to be.

"I believe it's yours..." said the assistant excitedly. Initially finding it hard to decipher the sensation that overcame me, I suddenly felt overwhelmed. "Yes, it really is yours..."

Decidedly, the *yukata* had chosen me. Given the originality of the fabric and design, the purchase was no small affair and I had to leave behind the *obi* that went fantastically well with it.

Since then, so many things have happened in my life and I certainly would never have imagined finding myself on a late October afternoon with Gabry, in one of the many *kimono* stores in the Kiyomizu area, hunting for a replacement for that missing *obi*. An *obi* that soon turned up, folded in its tissue paper, in a small store smelling of wood and newly-ironed fabrics. It is the contrast between the old rose highlights of the silk and the colours of my *yukata* that became the indivisible link between the two items, now inexorably belonging to each other. It can happen like that with an *obi*, opposites often being the perfect combination.

Life often brings unexpected developments, of which there and then we don't immediately see the relevance. It is time that defines it, a little as it does objects: some time later, we think back to when we bought it, at what stage of our life we were, in what state of mind, who we had by our side, and of the experience that has irremediably come between the present and the day the object came to us.

It is time that helps us understand the real value of things, even the most discreet things.

Walking the roads I've walked down in the past,
everything here has remained the same,
as if awaiting my return.
Only in the evening, behind the window
of no particular café,
do I manage to explain the knot I feel around my heart.
Time hasn't changed these places,
although it has made the things I saw then
with the eyes of an end, into a new beginning.
It isn't the eternal, immutable Kyōto that has changed,
it's me

291

An afternoon among the stores and ways of old Kyōto, and then once more on the other side of the river, in the modern districts around a galactic Kyōto Tower clad in artificial colours, and the train station in which it is reflected. This is Nishinotōin-chō District, another skein of narrow roads that when night falls explodes with the bright signs of *rāmen-ya* and *izakaya*.

Around the time of the evening meal, the roads become deserted of passersby and these venues turn into dozens of little pulsating hearts. Screened by windows, one can hear the laughter of Japanese office-men laying aside discipline and seriousness in front of a bowl of noodles and a mug of beer. The aroma of *rāmen* and *tenpura* is in the air and slips out as soon as a door is opened and the bell announces the arrival of another customer.

"*Irasshaimase!*"[130] exclaim the cooks as they dash behind the counter, repeating to perfection the sequence of movements that culminate in plating up noodles in their secret ingredient broth.

This is the time of day I like best, when in any corner of Japan, people get ready in unison to end their day of hard work, bringing satisfaction or failure. However it went, tomorrow is another day, and people share that hope with friends over a steaming bowl of *rāmen*, a pleasant 'back to square one' even if the previous hours weren't pleasurable at all. At suppertime, every *rāmen-ya* is a place to meet and the cooks do their utmost to serve the most important dish of the day well.

So, excited at the thought of tasting one of the best *rāmen* in Kyōto, we wait for two stools to be vacated in the small restaurant of Ginjō Rāmen Kubota, under the beholden eyes

---

[130] Widespread expression of welcome in Japan, said by owners at the entrance to their establishment, for example a hotel, shop or restaurant

of the cooks. Sitting at the counter we have a good view of all the activities taking place in the narrow steel kitchen where, among mountains of pans and accessories of various types, each member of staff knows exactly what to grab at which moment, with speed and coordination that has the appearance of a ritual. There are very few types of *rāmen* to choose from and we go for the speciality that has made the place famous, *tsukemen* 「つけ麺」. The noodles are strained through cold water and excess starch removed, then they are forcefully shaken in the colander over the floor to remove all the water and then be curled up in a different bowl to that containing the steaming broth. This allows the noodles to keep their consistency and avoid being over-cooked in the hot broth, besides giving the palate a delicious contrast between the two different temperatures.

Faced with two bowls recounting the most coveted pleas-ures of the human being, we are entranced by the noodles, different from any we have encountered until this moment. Long, undulating and incredibly thick, they bring to mind the homemade water-and-flour pasta from various regions in Italy. And finally the broth, thick enough to attach to the noodles in the right quantity and make every mouthful, or suction, truly unforgettable, so thick that, once you've fin-ished soaking the noodles in it, to sip the rest it has to be thinned by adding more liquid. In this game of taste and consistency, comes the egg and its yolk, guardian of the sa-cred in Japanese cooking, which explodes in the mouth, freed from the firm soft-boiled white marinated in soy.

After a meal of the sort, the contentment with which we stroll towards Kyōto station is indescribable: "This is defi-nitely one of the best *tsukemen* ever tasted in Japan."

It is now dark and Kyōto Tower continues to be vividly reflected in the enormous glass façade of central station. The tower, shining out in the dark sky, with its red and blue rings and white trunk, certainly hasn't the appeal of Tōkyō Tower, nor the elegance of Tōkyō Skytree, and yet with its alien spacecraft look it arouses the fondness of tourists, and is forgiven its modest height. Opposite, the glass shell of Kyōto station, a bit like a chocolate box, is full of different shapes of light and colour. Crossing the threshold means going into the night and leaving it behind: in the immense central concourse, where escalators interweave weightlessly as if in a painting by Picasso, you stand there blinded by the store lights and bewitched by the geometric shapes of the spaces they create; overhead, the roof is a deep vault, a steel and glass lattice arching powerfully into the sky.

In the station, anything is possible: from the underground shopping city, stretching out beneath, where you might easily find restaurants like Okonomiyaki Machiya and their unforgettable *okonomiyaki*, or the great staircase of Kyōto station, magically brought alive by thematic LED projections. I keep expecting to see red and orange leaves fluttering down the steps, bringing vibrancy to that wing of the station, but alas today maintenance scaffolding dampens the magic that usually follows the rhythm of the seasons.

After two weeks of abstinence from Italian 'espresso' coffee, we feel the need to try one of the many bars near the station. At a cafeteria belonging to the Caffè Veloce chain, we take advantage of the late evening space to sit down, when the majority of the shops have already closed their shutters. We wrest two coffees and a pastry off the waitress for the price of 800 *yen*, not repaid so much in the taste of the coffee as the atmosphere of the café.

"It's like one of those cafés writers come to work in..." I can't help saying, noticing the rows of little tables, the large windows reflecting little internal lights and from which you can watch the outside world at a spatial distance: passersby holding cell phones with their blue screens, taxis with their bright signs, *kanji* in black and red neon. Next to me a gentleman is sitting in front of an open notebook. I immediately imagine him an author who finds the refuge of that café ideal for transforming his world into words, and I wish with my whole being that his life, at that precise instant, belonged to me.

"Maybe one day it'll be you sitting here writing your book," Gabry brings me back to reality with words that ricochet through my ears, pinch my throat and go straight to my heart.

In a life, another life, I couldn't have wanted anything more than to sit in a Japanese café writing words to reach others. Recounting the beauty of life. Telling of love and pain. Narrating my road to happiness.

I reflect on how that life has slipped away, crushed under the weight of events, of reality inadvertently become mundane, and of the courage that I've often found I simply don't possess. We can assuage our soul by blaming others or unexpected events for our shortcomings. But what stops us from our realization and the pursuit of our dreams, more than lack of commitment or determination, is fear of not being good enough, of failing as we go down a road different from the crowd, or that others can easily belittle. In the moment it's hard to see how, in life, a failure that happens while we are doing something we like is a good sight milder than the brutal regret of not having tried, of surrendering to the acceptance of a life that might belong to those around us, but not to us.

After recent years, the picture of me in a Japanese café with a notebook in front of me has crystalized, a faded shadow of the life I would have wanted and didn't have. I think back to the dreams and enthusiasm of the early years at university, the detailed plans we discussed among friends and with my companion of the time. Then the beginning of the crack, the doubt about which path to take, friendships that slowly move in different directions, a worsening relationship with my parents, the void after the death of my dog, friend and brother who, in nearly 18 years, had brought out the best in me, with all my dreams and the sensitivity I so wanted to put down on paper.

And then my first trip to Japan, where I found my place in the world and the desire to escape a life that no longer seemed to be mine. Accepting the end of a relationship with a person with whom I'd shared nearly eight years of future. Surrendering to a job where I was shouted at every day for not being good enough. The fear of disappointing others and the decision to quit. The arguments about not buying a one way ticket.

'The end of it all.'

Since then I had begun to live with the cruel awareness that I possessed nothing but memories of the past. Ahead there were no dreams or plans, only nothingness, the insecurity of the person I'd been and whom all of a sudden I hated, and the desire not to feel the weight of it any more.

"You know what? Maybe you won't write here, you'll start when we get home. You could begin writing again and... write about this trip. A new beginning, no?"

Gabry takes my hand, pulling me out of the maelstrom of oppressive darkness. I look at him and realize I haven't got any answers: I don't know if I'll ever write, or if I'll get the chance to do it in a Japanese café, or if I'll stay attached to Japan for the rest of my life. But I pause on his smile, just as unsure of the future, his kind eyes wanting to help others before giving courage and strength to himself, his need to begin to hope that what we've lost or left incomplete, might still return in a different shape. I've no certainty other than the choice of a new beginning.

And whilst Gabry is next to me in a Japanese writers' café, I ask myself if that beginning doesn't depend on me.

'And if it's not already now.'

A second 'espresso' at Ogawa Coffee, beneath Kyōto Tower, to get rid of the taste of the previous one. A waiter with a dream to learn Italian and travel around Italy talking to two Italians studying Japanese with the dream of exploring Japan.

Life is a paradox and awesome at the same time. When it feels as though there's nothing left to surprise us, when you can't make out a way ahead or when there seems to be an end to dreams, it finds a new beginning to start building a new path, brick by brick.

Once at home, I hug Gabry under the covers. Once the light is out in our room it is completely dark.

"The end of another wonderful day," I hear sadness making itself heard.

"Come on, there's another tomorrow. And between Kyōto, Kōbe and Ōsaka there are bound to be surprises."

It only takes a second for the sadness to change into longing for the night to pass quickly. A little like life itself, perhaps we sometimes have to change perspective to be aware of how the end is always the reason for a new beginning.

Of how time can help us get through failure and pain, giving them the value of experience and how it can transform fear into courage, showing us that the road to happiness, unlike others, is never a blind alley.

Travel Notes

While east of River Kamo-gawa you can immerse yourself in a by-gone Kyōto, among temples and ancient neighbourhoods, the heterogeneity and vitality of the districts west of the river allow a continual leap from past to present.

Starting in the north, the splendid Kinkaku-ji Temple with its golden walls reflected in water attracts thousands of tourists, while heading south you can visit the gardens of the Imperial Palace and scenic Nijō-jō Castle. To northwest, the outskirts of Arashiyama is famous for its bamboo forest, placid River Katsura-gawa passing through, panoramic Togestu-bashi Bridge and the picturesque roads with little shops and numerous temples, such as Tenryū-ji and its striking pond and zen garden.

Also west of River Kamo-gawa, but in the direction of the city centre, there are several districts of interest: the Nishiki area, which hosts the homonymous market and disperses its customers through the nearby shopping streets Kawaramachi-dōri and Teramachi Kyōgoku-shōtengai, and the picturesque evening district of Ponto-chō, with its canal and traditional lanes on the river, are some of the most unique.

Not much further down the modern area develops around the architecturally interesting Kyōto station and panoramic tower. Near Tō-ji Temple is Kōbō-ichi market and the tallest wooden pagoda in Japan, rising to a height of almost 180 feet.

On 22 October, in the west of Kyōto, two very popular events take place: Jidai Matsuri and Kurama-no-Hi Matsuri.

Jidai Matsuri, or the Procession of the Ages, is an annual event numbered among the most important of the city, along with Aoi Matsuri and Gion Matsuri. The festival, inaugurated in 1895 with the construction of Heian-jingū Shrine, is to celebrate the anniversary of the foundation of Heian-kyō (the old name for Kyōto) in 794 with the aim of maintaining the city's importance when the capital was moved to Tōkyō in 1868. The celebration begins in the morning outside the Imperial Palace with homage paid to the miko-shi, which represent the first and last emperors to reign from the city, Kanmu and Kōmei. The costumed procession covers more than a mile, lasting 5 hours and begins at 12:00 midday, with around 2,000 participants dressed as samurai, military figures and common folk from early eras to that of Meiji. They are followed by Japanese women wearing elaborate court outfits called jūnihitoe. Finally, the mikoshi are transported from the palace to Heian-jingū Shrine to the sound of traditional gagaku music.

That evening, near the village of Kurama, there is an original fire festival inspired by the journey in 940 of the god Yuki Daimyōjin to Yuki-jinja Shrine on the slopes of Mount Kurama-yama, with the purpose of protecting the city after a series of disasters, and today considered a rite of passage for the young. The festival begins at 6pm, when, near the village, they light watch fires, kagaribi, and prepare torches of various sizes, called taimatsu. Children have small torches, while those carried by adults can weigh as much as 175 pounds. The festival continues as hundreds of torch carriers gather at San-mon Gate, then the sacred cord is cut, and the men participate in a trial of strength as they carry heavy mikoshi up the steep path of Mount Kurama-yama to the Yuki-jinja Shrine buried deep in nature. The festival ends around midnight with an enormous bonfire of torches.

Day Trip:
* Visit Nishiki-ichiba market and walk along the nearby shopping streets, Teramachi Kyōgoku-shōtengai or Kawaramachi-dōri
* Join Jidai Matsuri, beginning of the costumed procession at the Imperial Palace to Heian-jingū Shrine (12pm–2:30pm)
* Take a train north to Kurama station
* Visit Kurama-dera Temple and ancient wood
* Join Kurama-no-Hi Matsuri, the lighting of torches in the village at the foot of the mountain around 6pm

An Alternative to Festivals:
* Visit Kiyomizu-dera Temple
* Taste yudōfu and then go shopping in the Kiyomizu area
* Go out for tsukemen at Ginjo-rāmen Kubota
* Enjoy an evening stroll near Kyōto station

Typical Products and Souvenirs:
* Yudōfu, tōfu in its cooking water
* Kimono and obi around Kiyomizu-dera Temple
* Kyō-sensu and Kyō-uchiwa, Kyōto fans

Kyōto
京都

We say goodbye to Kyōto with the melancholy
that comes as we lament the days
racing past too quickly.
Perhaps to embrace this fragile passage
we plunge once more into those unchanging lanes,
sights we'll miss when we are far away,
lanes that, on tiptoe by the river, remind us
how we too can only flow
like water in our life's progress

New beginnings are always challenging. This morning, Kyōto is caressed by a gentle sun, alleviated by the autumn air, and we try to hide tiredness we can feel accumulating day by day. Breakfast with the last of Local's cakes – blueberries, fig and apple – is the best way to try.

A little later, like tortoises moving clumsily under the weight of their great shell, we proceed, dragging our shell of memories in the form of four cumbersome cases. Who knows what people think when they see us catch the bus while hauling unwieldy bags as quickly as possible... Only once we've left our mammouth burden at one of the Takkyūbin dispatch stores near Nishiki-ichiba Market, are we ready to begin exploring, convinced our next trips will be the epitome of the zen itinerary: essential bags only.

Before crossing the river, we let ourselves be swallowed up and indulged by the Gion atmosphere, that ancient quarter famous for *geisha*. Here, more than in the city's other historical districts, the main street leading to Gion Corner theatre has kept the allure of bygone Kyōto, when these lanes were filled with dozens of teahouses in which the *geisha* and *maiko* accompanied their clients to the various entertainments offered by the city.

Today, Gion has a nostalgic appearance, the tranquil two-floor *machiya*[131] 「町家」 are closed in on themselves, almost as if trying to hold the last breath of a tradition that time has worn out. Many of these traditional homes have been restructured, but the feeling I get every time I walk through this district is linked to a time gone by, where historical events didn't succeed in saving a sophisticated tradition like that of the 'métier' of the *geisha*. Gion is now overrun with tourists in hired *kimono* and by a toing and froing of taxis with the inevitable luminous heart on their roof, nonetheless emptied of its true essence, of what made it unique in the world, in its fragile beauty.

Even now, something of its distant splendour awakes in the evening hours, when the silence of the past circulates among the dim lanterns along the roads, when the windows of the upper floors light up with a secret life, when the shadows projected onto rice paper tell of tea ceremonies that still survive, of rituals where the few remaining *geisha* take part.

It is sad to witness the hunt for them in certain hours of the day, when hordes of visitors, without the smallest sense of respect for the identity and the spirit of these places, station themselves in the key roads waiting for taxis from which a *geisha* might step into the light.

On one of my travels I happened upon some *geisha* leaving a house on the neighbourhood's main street. That day,

---

[131] Traditional town houses built entirely of wood. Originating from the Heian era and successively transformed, still today they abound in Kyōto and often have shops on the ground floor

happening to notice movement behind one of the many slid-ing doors along the street, I stopped very discreetly to watch from the pavement opposite: the 'mother', the old lady who instructs the *geisha* and prepares them before each appoint-ment, was lining up four girls ready to accompany their cli-ents. From that distance, the little I managed to see was enough to give me a glimpse of the Japan of yesteryear, now gone, a secret world that could never return. I was utterly absorbed by it, sucked into that rift behind which the girls showed poise as they crossed their hands over the large *obi* of their silk *kimono*. It seemed to me that I could feel their emotion and insecurity faced with the importance of the job they would soon be doing, the teaching they would soon put into practice. Every gesture, every word, every perfor-mance, all for the client's pleasure, all fruit of a long and laborious training to make their very presence pure art. *Gei-sha* exist for this, to represent beauty in all forms, whether performing arts, gesture or conversation, and to bring joy to those with whom they share their time. Even the gentle smile of their red-painted lips encapsulates the staggering beauty desired by all, emanating from the ethereal face hid-den by white, and the neck exposed far enough to show the experience of the performing artist.

That day the fiery red smiles of the young *maiko* showed the tension of the moment, and it made them appear all the more enchanting. Then, all of a sudden, the first taxi pulls up to the door. In a fraction of a second, a phalanx of tourists crowds around the vehicle, like a wave of paparazzi bearing down on a filmstar. The silence is broken by people begin-ning to call to their partner or child at the top of their voice and point out the location of the 'coveted prey'.

I was shocked by the sight, while the old lady, opening the wooden door, shouted something that sounded like

"Please, show some respect! Please move back!" with a rapid sign of her hand she brought out two of the girls and, with unparalleled firmness, helped them into the car, protecting them from the camera flashes and excessive proximity of the tourists. A few seconds passed and the taxi with its luminous heart escaped the avid and indiscreet crowd that, not sated, began to lean through the half-open door.

When a man even tried to take a photo of the *machiya*'s interior, the old lady shouted again and shut the door. I still feel shame that the man hadn't understood the gravity of what he'd done. And I feel chagrin for the lady, who goes on protecting what is left of a world as breakable as crystal. Soon afterwards, one of the entertainers had trouble opening the door of her taxi. She smiled in discomfort, trying to catch the eye of the lady of the house while some people immediately rushed up and thrust their cameras into her face. The girl dropped her head, trying to avoid the people violating the moment, defiling her figure and what she represented. Someone present, who like me was watching from a distance, was so appalled by the sight as to cast reproaches in English. "Keep back! Show some respect!"

I'll never forget that day. Although situations of the sort don't often occur and you can easily meet *maiko* strolling calmly down the streets of Gion without undesirable tourists giving them chase, a few episodes of the sort do harm to a reality that survives with difficulty today.

Which is why Gion inevitably seems to me like a crystal that might shatter irreparably.

Once over Shijō-ōhashi Bridge we reach Ponto-chō, one of the most enchanting zones and that I like the most in the city of Kyōto. From the bridge you can turn into Kiyamachi-dōri, the street crossed by Takase-gawa Canal and that runs past myriad pubs, restaurants and *izakaya*, or you can go down the bank of River Kamo-gawa where a cycling and walking route flanks the river, beneath an array of small houses and restaurants, which at night turn into a staggeringly pretty string of lights and lanterns. From sunset, the street is a mass of lights and activity around bars and pubs, many of which are of western stamp, the assiduous coming and going of young people in a meeting place for all those tourists who might be disappointed to find a Japan devoid of discotheques and western night life. By 10pm, it's easy to bump quite safely into groups of young Koreans, Chinese and Japanese who are so tipsy they end up lying on the banks of Takase-gawa Canal; an unusual and picturesque sight.

In any case the Kiyamachi-dōri Street is a delightful corner of Ponto-chō and suppertime is the best time to enjoy the little floodlit bridges leaping from one bank to the other, under the green willow fronds, or the lights of the bars melting into the surface of the water below. Strolling around there today, early on a normal October morning, brings a new and particular atmosphere. The locals are still asleep and the lanterns hang dark from the windows overlooking the water. Some weeping willows let their branches fall right into the canal, as if trying to fish for autumn leaves that slip away, conveyed by the current. A white heron wanders silently around the canal, slowly testing the shallow water with its long legs.

Back near the bridge, keep a look out for Ponto-chō Alley, the true heart of the district, a narrow lane squashed between the row of houses on Kiyamachi-dōri Street and River Kamo-gawa. I want to show Gabry Ponto-chō Alley, because like many other visitors, this lovely little lane went unnoticed, swallowed up in the row of dwellings that, like an expert cabinet maker, carves through its particular beauty. The alley has various *izakaya*, some sophisticated restaurants and some typically Japanese pubs hidden at the top of the flight of steps in front of the two-floor houses. By day its charm is in the small details in these houses, like the characteristic walls of those curved to the ground and covered in bamboo slats, the straw curtains hanging here and there to protect the silent privacy of the homes, and stone bowls sitting by the door full of clumps of purple daisies. Whereas by night, Ponto-chō Alley is transformed into a poetic and thoroughly Japanese painting: hanging lanterns shine out in red and cream and chase each other along the ground; over doorways, silks painted in black *kanji* glow with light from behind; where there is the noise of tableware, and menus displayed on stands; tiny secondary alleyways, hidden in the shadows during the day, become amazing sights under festoons of hanging lights. When night falls, this alley is one of the places I would like to exist, where silence whispers of a cozy, vibrant life, taking on shapes and colours that once they enter your heart, never leave.

So, every time I return home, the deepest nostalgia that takes hold of me is tied to the memory of places like Ponto-chō Alley in Kyōto, like the labyrinth of lanes and spider's web of lanterns at Nakano in Tōkyō, like the village of lanterns and *izakaya* at Dekonaru-yokochō Alley in Takayama. Places that after the sun sets turn into a wonderland to stick in the heart and memory, making them hard to forget.

We move on from the area to dive into the modernity emanated by Kyōto Tower, which is only prey to the romanticism of young couples at night as they gaze at the city's carpet of lights dotted with flaming pagodas and fluorescent-roofed temples.

On floor 11F of The Cube, the shopping centre within the station now throbbing with activity and train announcements, away from the eyes of visitors passing through, is Katsukura, a restaurant that knows a thing or two about fried food. Here you can choose from different types of menu or single dishes, where the ingredients are all rigorously fried in *panko*[132] 「パン粉」. From seasonal vegetables to giant prawns, to the famous *tonkatsu*, everything in this restaurant is covered in a coating of breadcrumbs with the impossible consistency of a crunchy cloud. Katsukura also boasts numerous original sauces that go perfectly with the fried food, making it hard to resist that thick golden crust, whatever it has inside.

It is hard to resist the smell of frying that billows out of the premises, or the great bowls crowned with *panko* that go up and down inside the windows. Although further along, on floor 10F of the great staircase, lurks another compelling kingdom, Kyōto Rāmen Kōji, the 'Rāmen Road of Kyōto'. This floor is a genuine theme park dedicated to *rāmen*, where dozens of highly-coloured *rāmen-ya* line up along its black corridor, well disguised by little *izakaya* decked with lanterns and illuminated signs in a perennial artificial night. Like Rāmen Stadium in Fukuoka, venues differentiate themselves depending on the type of *rāmen* served, which varies between different prefectures. Inexorable tradition muscles in on the panels of *rāmen* photos and ticket machines with a retro look churning out orders in the heart of the station looking to the future.

In the end, although never sated by the multiple forms that soup can assume in this country, we opt for the crunchy gold of Katsukura. We wait anxiously, after a meal

---

[132] Fried and dried white breadcrumbs used for breading and crumbling foods. Incorporating more air, panko produces a light, crunchy coating

bordering on the over abundant, to get on our *shinkansen* for the half hour separating us from Shin-Kōbe and a brief rest before visiting the Nunobiki-no-taki Falls. Before Japanese cuisine unveils another of its treasures.

***

Kōbe
神戸

Like the pillars of Hercules,
the sacred waterfalls are the intangible entrance
to a city with dual identities.
By day Kōbe is the movement of titanic harbour cranes,
as untiring as the taxis shifting
businessmen to and from offices.
By night it becomes a tangle of roads
a glistening necklace of restaurants,
it becomes the aroma of a work of art
set like a precarious painting on red hot griddles

Nunobiki. A flash of nature in the heart of Kōbe, unexpected and sudden just as you exit the station, when enormous characters painted on a cement wall give directions: circa 400 yards for the falls and nearly 2.5 miles to reach the raised zone from where you can visit Nunobiki's herb gardens.

Between flights of steps and woody paths, after a first fall, Men-taki, not very convincing and mainly hidden in the undergrowth, the second fall's fine observation point means you can get close to immortalize the water's slender, ribbon-like descent from nearby, as well as the little turquoise lake

307

beneath and the variegated rock wall, which looks like a piece of scrunched tissue paper in the woods. This is On-taki, the largest of Nunobiki-no-taki's four falls and often cited in old Japanese poems. Twisting and turning as it widens, the ribbon of water recalls a piece of white fabric, and the name Nunobiki literally means 'pulled cloths'. From the On-taki pool, the twin Meoto-daki Falls launch themselves lower down in parallel water courses, and benches give visitors the opportunity to contemplate this work of art from in amidst the luxuriant mesh of surrounding nature.

Urged on by an innate explorative spirit and the need to digest the *tenpura* devoured at lunchtime, we head off along the path, shared with old ladies that seem a thousand times fitter than us. We go by the Ontaki-chaya Teahouse, perched on the slope overlooking the waterfall. This traditional little refuge offers a fixed menu of ham and eggs that, like the ladies we've just met, seems almost out of place in this context but witnesses how trekking is intrinsic to life in Kōbe, the city contested by sea and a mountainous chain behind.

Much of the city's population lives near similar trekking routes, and - an unusual phenomenon in large Japanese cities - on fine mornings many of the residents get up early to climb the hills. After a bit of exercise, they have coffee or breakfast immersed in nature before going to work, before being drawn back into the elegant modern skyscrapers that Kōbe flaunts, a little out of pride and a little in memory of its rebirth after the destruction of the devasting Hanshin earthquake in 1995.

An unexpected panoramic terrace, the first on the trail well dug into the vegetation, is the unusual profile of Kōbe I was looking for. I stand captivated by the emerald green waves of forest below on which orange canopies seem to float, sinuous waves that suddenly break off near the skyscrapers, raised like Lego constructions on the horizon. Just beyond is the ocean in commotion, inhabited by harbour cranes, lines traced by jetties, the warning flash of the lighthouse. From up here, under a sky gradually going to sunset, Kōbe looks like a layered cake that won't amalgamate.

Walking back down to the station we notice the bubble cabins of the cable cars that stretch over to the Nunobiki herb garden, where the scenic greenhouses and hanging gardens accompany the view over Kōbe from one of the highest points over the bay.

Once back down at sea level, we drift down a series of streets busy with traffic, anonymous were it not for the beautiful vases and flowerbeds everywhere, overflowing with autumnal chrysanthemums and cosmos. It is only when the neon lights of the shopping centres begin to redesign the profile of the city on the canvas of approaching evening, that Kōbe turns into an international city, elegant and essential like the many restaurants lighting up the streets. The name suffices to attract visitors from all over the world, just as the restaurants need no flashy or weird decoration to attract their clientele. If you walk through the city at suppertime it is for a very good reason.

At 5pm, slightly intimidated and emotional, we are outside Aoyama, one of the most famous restaurants in Kōbe. There are just a few tables, so you can only eat here if you've booked at least two months in advance, we and a handful of other clients are led over to a large but minimal counter with teppanyaki. In front of us, rather as if we were in a contemporary art museum, are a series of Kōbe steaks, intense pink streaked with white, of a thickness and compactness that seem unreal, and a decidedly unusual chef. It isn't clear if the chef is extremely extrovert and eccentric, or interpreting

Kōbe-gyū 神戸牛

The term wagyū generically indicates Japanese beef, in turn divided into four breeds. About 90% of the beef belongs to the dark skinned Kuroge breed, widely used in the past to work the fields.

This type of meat is identified by intense marbling, in other words a high quantity of fat tending to mix with the meat itself, rather than agglomerate at the sides as usually happens. All wagyū beef is sold with the name of the breeding region and some are particularly prized, such as the famous wagyū from Tottori and Hida.

Wagyū from the Tajima region, to the north of Kōbe in Hyōgo Prefecture, is considered 'original beef' because of its high quality and amazingly homogenous marbling, the distribution of fat inside the cuts of beef that is responsible for the characteristic, visible white striations of the slices.

The breed is also defined 'original' as its pureblood bulls are used to improve the beef in neighbouring regions, generating other selections of very high quality such as Matsusaka in Mie Prefecture, the most renowned beef in Japan after Kōbe, or the beef from Ōmi and Yonezawa, respectively produced in Shiga and Yamagata Prefectures.

Kōbe beef is a selection of wagyū deriving exclusively from the region of Tajima, and besides exceeding many qualitative standards, is then classified according to the quantity of quality steak in the carcass (from grade A, the highest, to grade C, the lowest), the quality in terms of the beef's colour and sheen, density and texture, colour, lustre and quality of fat, the steak-fat ratio etc.

Tajima beef commands a high price, above all for very high quality cuts known as 'Kōbe A5' or 'Premium wagyū', so that tourist restaurants tend to sell the more economical beef cuts.

So, in general it is best to book, well in advance, restaurants that have been active in the city for many years and have a solid reputation.

the role of a bizarre person, but our supper turns out to be full of laughter, with unexpected questions and jokes from this extraordinary individual.

For nearly 50 dollars a head, we get ready to taste about a quarter of a pound of prize Kōbe beef with sautéed vegetables and *shiitake* mushrooms. Included in the price, without a doubt, is the performance accompanying the preparation of the dish: with unequalled meticulousness, we watch the chef slice the vegetables with his Japanese knives and lay them out on the hotplate with extreme precision. The same happens with the steak, cut through as though it were butter, in perfect parallelepipeds of pure fuchsia succulence. There is mystique in the moment the steak is cooked, and finally the tasting that follows: an explosion of flavour, the cubes of steak seem to burst in the mouth and melt at minimal pressure, unleashing the fat to make them amazingly ripe and juicy, an experience to try at least once in a lifetime.

A light rain begins its pictorial work on the streets of Kōbe, where neon signs and commercial skyscrapers slather the wet tarmac. In front of the restaurant, a taxi comes to a halt, making the water under its wheels fizzle. Once inside, I see Kōbe raindrops on the car window and then on the *shinkansen* melt exactly like that first bite of steak.

Just time to skim by, to perceive its potential wonder, imagining the lights of the towers and skyscrapers gleaming like rubies and sapphires across the bay, and we are already hoping to come back.

Perhaps on our next trip, perhaps, who knows.

***

311

Ōsaka
大阪

A puzzle of colours, the hullabaloo of the crowd,
myriad smells turning into portions
messily spilled over a table.
And the street becomes the door to the universe,
mesmerizing and exhausting, a chaos of light and life.
So in this other, unexpected Japan,
the heart fills with new pieces of existence

It would be easy to loathe this drizzle, cloaking everything in its veil of wetness. But I'm fidgeting in my seat in the grip of happiness because this is the best weather you could wish for to visit celebrated Dōtonbori, Ōsaka's neon street.

In less than half an hour we are at Shin-Ōsaka station, where the metro, packed as if it were the middle of the day, takes us to Shinsaibashi. Here, a boiling coffee from Lilo Coffee keeps out the damp from the rain, while the colours light up on the bridge over Dōtonbori-gawa, a dark choppy river running straight through the hosts of fluorescent skyscrapers, a world of blue, purple, green and dazzling red walls glowing in the night, to exhaust the gaze.

Here we are near the lit up arch that says 'Dōtonbori', like the background in a Broadway musical. In a few yards we go from solitary dripping parked bicycles to a vortex of light and colour through which a crazy river of humanity moves. The rain and wet tarmac do the rest. Above us, like a mass of deep-sea jellyfish fluctuating in the pitch dark ocean, transparent umbrellas float along, glittering with colours released by the neons.

The road is like a black hole full of excessive glare sucking in the night, pulling in every shadow and tinge and turning it into blinding signs, advertising billboards and giant *kanji*. Here, electricity assumes every possible form and any type of excess appears normal: vast crabs moving their legs above *tenpura* stores, three-dimensional plates of dumplings occupying entire walls of buildings, puffer fish morphing into enormous fluttering signs. And then, under strings of red lanterns, the little *takoyaki* stalls lined up with the same maniac rhythm with which the octopus balls are continually turned inside boiling molds.

The din is deafening and between a fluorescent dragon leaping out on one side and a skyscraper with an outsize screen on the other, my body can't seem to filter the tangle of stimuli coming from every direction. Quite soon I feel the need to get away from the whirl of light and colour, and from the throng surging haphazardly from the main to secondary streets having nothing in common with the perfect, rhythmic flow of arteries in Tōkyō. Young Japanese and foreigners give a face to this city, as international as it is chaotic, generating a strange confusion between the genuine aspects of a historic city port and the less savory aspects of mingling difference.

I find Ōsaka almost too far from the Japan I love to visit, far even from Tōkyō, the city with a place in my heart, and that seems to give me an inner peace it'd be impossible to find here. Gabry seems exhausted too, perplexed by the absurd panoramic wheel of Don Quixote Dōtonbori and its fluorescent loop cabins towering above the walk along the canal.

On the train back to Kyōto, we mull over the reality we've just left behind, a place whose beauty is perhaps in the incomprehensible desire to fascinate through excess, whether with colours or the diverse. An artificial beauty that wears you out, possibly a trifle clumsy and vulgar, just another face of a country that never ceases to amaze.

In short, there are marvels to discover in Ōsaka too, only very often in the form of neon.

Back in the city of temples, the elegant lanterns giving off a golden glow. After the neon chaos, Kyōto welcomes us with its primordial nature, with the delicate chirping of crickets and the pale light of the autumn moon. Perhaps we love Japan mainly from this angle, for what makes it stay the same and how it knows how to bring out wonder without forcing its creation.

When I am here I want to go after simple beauty, as it has been for centuries, not ostentatious but hidden in details. Beauty that appears all of a sudden or manifests itself just at the right moment. A little like Mount Fuji-san in his incomparable loveliness. So often hidden, the lord of the mountains has no need to make an appearance to show how magnificent he is. Most of the time he stays half hidden, just visible through the clouds and mist. Only he decides when to show himself fully. The beauty of Mount Fuji-san is concealed, as that of Japan come to that.

Before going to sleep, all that's left is for me to pray to the *Kami* to make tomorrow one of the days when the beauty that ties me to this world decides to show its face.

Travel Notes

At 30 minutes distance from each other thanks to the Tōkaidō–San'yō shinkansen line, Kōbe and Ōsaka are two large metropolitan areas of Japan that lend themselves well to day trips from Kyōto if you have a Japan Rail Pass.

Kōbe, capital city of Hyōgo Prefecture, is located between the sea and the mountainous Rokkō chain, a position that gives the city a dual identity. The large harbour, among the first to be opened to foreign commerce along with the ports of Yokohama, Nagasaki, Hakodate and Niigata, today offers an area rich with attractions and modern architecture. At the same time Mount Rokkō–san, the highest peak of the chain, provides the city's green background and trekking opportunities to the inhabitants of Kōbe, as well as tourist attractions such as the alpine botanic garden, a carillon museum, the first golf course in Japan and Rokkō Garden Terrace, a tourist complex with restaurants, shops and panoramic spots that are particularly appreciated at sundown.

The Shin–Kōbe cable car is one of three transport services taking tourists up the southern slopes of the mountain chain from Shin–Kōbe station, passing the Nunobiki–no–taki Falls and Nunobiki's herb gardens, and offering, near the uphill station, spectacular evening views over the city.

On the slopes of the chain, the four waterfalls of Nunobiki–no–taki (On–taki, Men–taki, Meoto–daki and Tsutsumiga–daki) are considered among the most important of Japan's divine waterfalls, with Kegon–no–taki in Nikkō and Nachi–no–taki in Wakayama Prefecture. Higher up, along the excursion route, you can enjoy the panoramic view over the port of Kōbe or the Nunobiki Gohonmatsu dam, Japan's first cement gravity dam.

***

Ōsaka is the second Japanese city in terms of land area and can be reached by means of a thick network of metro lines. All the same, the JR Shin–Ōsaka shinkansen station, to the north of Ōsaka–Umeda central station, is not that close to the city's main points of interest.

One of the best times to visit Ōsaka is certainly evening, when Dōtonbori, the famous neon road running along River Dōtonbori–gawa from Dōtonbori–bashi Bridge to Nippon–bashi Bridge, turns into one of the most thrilling zones of the city. Historically theatre land, today it is famous for nightlife and entertainment in an eccentric atmosphere popular among international visitors, and the location of a series of celebrated restaurants offering a vast range of traditional and modern Japanese dishes, many of which are directly associated with the city, such as okonomiyaki, takoyaki, kushikatsu and kitsune udon. Besides the restaurants, Dōtonbori Street is also renowned for the huge number of signs to its eateries, bars and clubs. Among these, the mobile crab belonging to the restaurant Kani Dōraku and the puffer fish outside the Zuboraya restaurant, but most of all the advertising billboard that has become an icon for Ōsaka in Japan, the sign for the Glico confectionary firm with the image of a runner reaching the finish line. Originally installed in 1935, the current version (the sixth) uses LED rather than neon and was installed in October 2014. Also Ebisu Tower, the 250 foot panoramic wheel built on the facade of the shop Don Quixote Dōtonbori and decorated with a picture of Ebisu (protector of fishermen and of fortune), symbol of the area around Ebisu-bashi Bridge.

Day Trip:
- Walk around Kyōto's Gion and Ponto-chō districts
- Eat at Kyōto Rāmen Kōji in Kyōto station (floor 10F taking the great outside staircase)
- Travel by train from Kyōto to Shin-Kōbe
- Go trekking along the Nunobiki-no-taki Falls' path
- Dine on Kōbe-gyū at a well-known restaurant
- Take the train from Shin-Kōbe to Shin-Ōsaka
- Enjoy an evening stroll along Dōtonbori Street in Ōsaka
- Return to Kyōto

Typical Products and Souvenirs:
- Tanba-Tachikui-yaki, ceramics from Hyōgo Prefecture
- Kitsune udon, udon soup with fried tōfu
- Kushikatsu, skewers fried in batter
- Tonpeiyaki, cabbage and pork omelette

- Takoyaki, octopus balls in batter
- Kōbe-gyū, the famous Tajima beef

Hakone
箱根

After three weeks, here we are again,
at the incomparable sacred mountain,
no longer summer faded and yet still green,
but more imposing, embraced by its first snows,
more elusive, like the clouds that waft around it.
That great size escapes one with the same ease
beauty around us can leave us unaware.
Embedded in the vapour dancing on an autumn eve,
like the aroma of gyōza prepared by one
who can see the serenity beyond the end,
or in the splendour of the October moon
for the first time no longer ignored.
I wouldn't know how to define it otherwise,
the beauty of small things,
inundating life and
simply making it wonderful

It appears before we have the chance to prepare ourselves, as though it possessed the power to reveal itself in a precise instant of which only it is aware. Always there and yet, if it so decides, always able to assume the consistency of the clouds wrapped around it. On the *shinkansen* for Odawara, not long before Shin-Fuji station, we get a clear view of Mount Fuji-san from the left hand side of our carriage. The significance of this mountain for the Japanese is something deeper and more intimate than mere veneration. The mountain, rising above the lands of Japan from the dawn of time,

317

is considered the father perennially watching over his infant, following its every move. It seems something of a trick of fate that, according to the reading *on'yomi*[133] 「音読み」, the name 'Fuji' 「富士」 followed by the *kanji* for mountain 「山」 reads 'Fuji-san', where 'san' is misleading, identifying itself in the Japanese honorary particle of 'sir', usually added to the end of a person's name when spoken of. Moreover, Fuji-san isn't only the primordial mountain, it is the mountain that lives, breathes and has a soul, like all things lived in by the *Kami* here in Japan.

'Fuji-san.'

Later, when it is visible, in its perfectly conical shape, in the immensity of the base behind which the sun rises, we understand its identity. Breath caught by emotion, feeling tiny in the presence of divinity, the sensation of having been born of it. The majesty and reverence this mountain inspires catches us unaware, like seeing its snowy peak, dusted with that pure white of which there was no trace just a fortnight before. A white chimney slipping over the rocky walls, splitting into lots of white rivulets to form a hat to protect it from approaching autumn.

It isn't easy to photograph from the racing train: the clouds around it change continually, lapping at the central body, holding it in a bite to then free it soon afterwards; they rise to the tip attempting to englobe it, to then leave residual vapours over the crater, a white aureole crowning it god of the sky as well as the earth. The Japanese have different words for it depending on the shapes of the clouds hanging around, names that escape my memory with the speed that the mountain changes appearance. Then, with the same

---

[133] Pronunciation imported from the Chinese reading of ideograms used when a word is composed of more than one kanji. Whereas when a kanji is alone or accompanied by hiragana, the kun'yomi pronunciation native of Japan is used

rapidity it materialized, the mountain of mountains disappears behind the raised ground and walls of white nimbostratus cloud, leaving us thirsting for the chance to feast our eyes on its beauty for longer.

After about two and a half hours we reach Odawara station where we each buy a Hakone Free Pass, a two day pass giving you access to most transport and visits around Ashino-ko, in the hotspring area of Hakone. This lake, not far from Tōkyō city, offers incredible natural views and several ways to catch sight of the sovereign mountain, besides a visitable sulphur site, a well known area for hotsprings with numerous attractions and museums thereabouts.

It was here that last year I happened upon the Little Prince Museum, perhaps due to the umpteenth twist of fate, not in France but in the woods of Hakone...

Our journey to the lake begins on board the train on the popular Hakone-Tozan line, a convoy of two red old-style wagons cutting through the mountains on an old railway immersed in the woods, every so often changing direction at the small stations on the way.

The trip turns out to be a delightful experience: narrow clay-red brick tunnels look like small black holes swallowing up the rails to shoot them out into the wall of light at the end of the darkness. And every time that white wall shatters at the end of the tunnel, we find ourselves surrounded by green and orange walls bordering the pebbly bed of the tracks. Between one tunnel and the next we are suddenly suspended on a bridge between the mountains, above patches of yellow and red emerging from the emerald green of the cedars. I can hardly imagine the sight in November from this bridge, admiring an enchanted world, where the extent of tones expressible in nature becomes fuddled with the fullness of it all.

Gōra, first hotspring location near Lake Ashi-no-ko, welcomes us with its picturesque aspect from the Hakone-Tozan railway line and in limpid air smelling of late autumn, of the first hoarfrost settling on the shrubs of surrounding ridges, the first cold that evening sends crawling over the roofs of the houses. Here it feels as though the cool of autumn has reduced the number of tourists, who are few and mainly Japanese.

Not far from the station, in a small square inhabited by three small shops, Gabry leaves me lurking with the bags to carry out a special mission: to buy *gyōza* from an equally special place. When we planned these two days in Hakone, we came across the story of a *gyōza* store called Gyōza-Centre, that had become famous in and around Gōra for its incredibly good dumplings. This humble family activity was destroyed by a sudden devastating fire, after which there was nothing left of the store or their home next door, bringing an end to the tradition of the Gōra *gyōza* and employment for a dozen people.

However, before long, using social media, a small crowd funder and the deep sense of solidarity that links the Japanese, the owners managed to set up a small temporary kitchen in the neighbouring building to continue selling takeaway *gyōza* and save money to rebuild the store.

A little bit later, on one of the benches at the entrance to Hakone-Gōra-kōen Park, coloured by unusual cascades of flowers of every type, Gabry unveils the handful of steaming dumplings wrapped in takeaway aluminium.

"They're amazing! And they smell indescribable!"

Nestled among bushes of every shade of rose, life, in its sometimes painful unpredictability, seems to us incredibly beautiful in the way it strives to create a new beginning after an end. We think this as we admire twenty-one golden dumplings giving off an unforgettable aroma. Octopus, Japanese herbs, cabbage, I don't know of a smell that could fill me with greater joy, but after working our way through them in the blink of an eye, it isn't hard to reflect on the importance of small things, such as *gyōza* in an isolated spot in the mountains of Hakone, for the people who create them and those lucky enough to receive them.

A lone taxi saves us from dragging our bags for half an hour down woody bends near the little town, leading to the *ryokan* area thick in Hakone's woods. There are many premises here and for every budget, and we decided to save especially for this, to spend a night in one of the best hotspring *ryokan*.

The taxi drops us off outside a large wooden and glass building integrated as a golden light pulsating in the darkness of the surrounding wood. Barefoot, we enter the *ryokan*, immediately finding warm parquet beneath our feet, which covers the entire hall, as big as the common room in a mountain refuge, with an open fireplace in the centre, its chimney rising elegantly to the ceiling.

Our room also has the simple, linear beauty that is the purest expression of Japanese style, a personal but ample space where the *tatami*, low black lacquered table and petrol coloured cushions come together in the incredible effect of diffused lighting hidden here and there. And then the greatest luxury, through the glass wall opposite the bed, behind a semi-transparent curtain you only see when it is lit up: our own private *onsen*. An intermediary area with a shower and basin to wash before entering the hot spring, a refuge protected from the cool of autumn by dark wooden walls, bamboo matting dropping from the window open to the woods and the steam released from the marble pool embedded in the centre means the cold has no chance of taking hold.

Hakone-Tozan Tetsudō 箱根登山鉄道

The Hakone-Tozan Tetsudō Railway is the first mountain railway line in Japan, linking the Odawara shinkansen station to the hilly area of hotsprings around Lake Ashi-no-ko and bringing tourism from all over the country and in particular Tōkyō. The company routes include the railway line connecting the stations of Odawara, Hakone-Yumoto and Gōra, the funicular between Gōra and Sōunzan to travel between the various hotspring locations, and a cable car to the station at Tōgendai port.

The Hakone-Tozan Tetsudō Railway, with its retro style red train, is renowned for the panoramic stretch through the Fuji-Hakone-Izu Kokuritsu-kōen National Park, particularly suggestive mountains and forests in spring and autumn. The line was carefully planned to limit its impact on the landscape and has three hairpin turns in steeper parts. In the areas of particular interest the train takes visitors on an actual nature tour, slowing down at the most impressive spots. A particularly popular stretch is between the stations of Gōra and Hakone-Yumoto in which, towards the end of June, thousands of hydrangeas are in flower and the company runs night trains to admire the hydrangeas lit up for the occasion.

The cable car offers panoramic aerial views over the Ōwakudani Valley and sulphur vents, source of the hot springs for which Hakone is famous. On clear days, you can also have a good view Mount Fuji-san while sitting comfortably in your cabin.

Belonging to the Odakyū railway group, the Hakone-Tozan Tetsudō Railway and its lines are not included in the Japan Rail Pass. However, you can choose a tourist pass from those available at Odakyū's various stations, including Odawara. The Hakone Free Pass, valid for 2 or 3 days, is particularly useful as besides the above lines, there is unrestricted travel on the sailboats of Lake Ashi-no-ko and many bus lines in the area to reach the south side of the lake. The pass also gives you discounts in many Hakone venues, which you can check on the official site or flyers at the stations.

My emotions when faced with such an image of beauty are impossible to describe, apart from a continual skipping from one room to another.

"Gabry, look, it's so beautiful?! A private *onsen* you'd only dream of!"

At moments like this, I think of all the sacrifices made, the choices taken and experiences coped with that one way or another have inexorably brought me here, to a present, which though transient, fills my eyes and heart with joy. And I feel such enormous gratitude, even towards things that used to seem incomprehensible or unjust, that at the time I simply wished were different. The things my family said, the richness of my previous relationship, times when I would work late into the night.

Almost always there are things we don't manage to understand or accept when they happen but of which later, at another point in our existence, we can suddenly see the meaning and importance. And it doesn't matter how different our future path, how much we move away from what we were or what we've done. New paths and choices begin from where we had got to, who we had become and what we had taken on up to that moment, of good and bad, pain and happiness.

Only time can bring wisdom, the capacity to recognise the right choice even when we've made the one that's wrong or inappropriate for a present that isn't yet the future, but will inevitably, sooner or later, become it.

We stroll ten minutes' walk from our *ryokan* in the silence of the streets of Gōra, interrupted by a solitary bird whose song fills the surrounding woods. Possibly a woodpecker living among the tall cedars.

Naka-Gōra station is one of the stops on the Hakone-

Tozan funicular route that starts at Gōra railway station and terminates at Sōunzan station. The slow little train, glides up the side of the mountain, arriving at the time indicated on the timetables displayed at the stops, and with equal precision reaching Sōunzan, end of the line. From there, the cable car carries us through the mountains in the direction of the sulphur vents at Ōwakudani Valley, our destination, and then down towards Lake Ashi-no-ko.

We hurry into the glass sphere that transports us, dangling like a Christmas decoration, along the wire stretched between the peaks. From up here the world has quite different dimensions and the majestic pines whose pointed crests we couldn't see before, turn into an unspecified floor of green, giving no sense of the height of what is below. Exactly like the surface of a blue ocean that swallows light and keeps its depths secret, we fly silently over a sea of deep green in which bubbles of yellow and orange are beginning to emerge.

When the cable we are suspended from suddenly rises sharply, we find ourselves at the edge of the mountain ridge we are about to climb. The glass egg in which we are hanging doesn't accelerate at all, and yet I can't help myself clinging to Gabry and holding my breath at the sight of the void yawning beneath us.

Ōwakudani, literally 'large boiling valley', and its sulphur vents, is a perfect example of the concept of Dante's inferno: a stony, grey desert opening up in the heart of the mountain, sullied here and there by sprays of intense yellow sulphur and strewn with venomous jets of incandescent gas; on the walls of the immense mine, are stone pathways of steps, drainage channels, and cement terraces undulating over each other like folds in a fan, in a context a bit like Isengard's caverns in 'The Lord of the Rings'.

When we finally land, the smell of sulphur merges with the crisp air of over 3,300 feet up Mount Hakone-yama. We can't walk in the smoking quarry because since an eruption of vapours some years ago it has been closed to the public. So we head for the warmth of one of the typical shops found at the touristic stations along the aerial route of Hakone cable car.

The shops sell food products based on ingredients cooked in the sulphurous waters nearby and almost all the souvenirs follow the theme of black eggs, the place's mascot. Soon after, having spent 400 *yen*, I leave the main shop with my bag of 5 hard-boiled eggs with shells that are black due to being cooked in water from the local hot springs, but there are plenty of things I'd still like to try from the handful of shops. Here, as in the other station shops, they amuse themselves by mixing local ingredients, such as Ōwakudani *katsu-karē* 「カツカレー」, a rice dish with pork and curry inspired by the vulcanic scenario of Ōwakudani Valley, or chocolate in the shape of a black egg with white yolk stuffed with almond.

Before leaving the sulphur vent valley, from one of the panoramic terraces I look for that other, elusive mountain with eyes, mind and all my being's desire. The clouds on the horizon are the awareness that it won't happen, and yet the horizon ahead of us still leaves my breath caught with emotion.

The sun is going down behind the zigzagging profile of the mountains, bruising the sky with gold and pink and opening a strip between the dark earth and the mantle of navy clouds just above. It's in that gloaming strip that we can make out the languid profile of the lord of the mountains, a sinuous outline rising vast behind the other peaks into the mists of the sky.

We have no idea how high it goes nor can we really see the fullness of its cone with any precision, but exactly as in the morning, we feel a resounding sense of reverence, of unworthiness before the mountain that calls itself Fuji-san.

Night falls in the autumnal Gōra hills, and of the few family restaurants here, Tamura Ginkatsu-tei Honten, known for its delicious fried *tōfu* immersed in egg and *dashi* sauce, turns out to be closed for its day of rest. But it's just as well.

So Gabry leads me to the building where the takeaway *gyōza* are sold; it's an anonymous construction next to the one destroyed by the fire. The latter is now being rebuilt and I can see the dark scars made by the flames, like those in the heart of anyone who must have seen that most precious of things taken away: the beauty of a humble but serene life.

A gentleman welcomes us with a wide smile and invites us in from the cold to wait for our *gyōza* to be cooked, but when he realizes we'd prefer to sit out in the open his face lights up. Although speaking no English he persuades us to follow him. He wants to show us something and accompanies us a short distance towards the road. Here the light from the streetlamps is dimmer and seems to be sucked into the deep black of the woods edging the tarmac road.

The man starts pointing to the sky, smiling and nodding, leaving us bewildered at his unexplained enthusiasm. We try to make out the unknown sounds that all of sudden have lost any similarity to those we have very laboriously learned so far.

"*Tsuki!*"[134]

"Mmm, *suki?*[135] Could he be saying he likes something?"

---

[134] 'Moon' in Japanese language

[135] Term meaning 'I like it' in Japanese, similar to the verb to love and be fond of

"Maybe he likes the sky..."

We collide with the wall of linguistic incomprehensibility, all the more distressing because his eyes express such hope at our understanding. Then, all of a sudden, the dark cloud dissolves, swept away by a familiar sound that turns straight into an image.

"Ah, *tsuki*! The moon! He's showing us the moon!"

We look up and realize how, until that moment, the marvellous spectacle of the full autumn moon had inexplicably gone unnoticed to our western eyes.

This is the season in Japan for *tsukimi*, literally 'moon-viewing', a ritual tied to the tradition of the positive effect of the moon on cultivation and the general cult of beauty embodied in the observation of nature throughout the seasons. Here, the autumn moon is considered the most beautiful and luminous of the year, and to celebrate the moment when it is admired, they gather sprigs of pampas grass in flower as it has the same sliver colour of the moon itself. There are also moon-shaped seasonal foods like the delicious *dango*, spherical confectionary in rice pastry, or *tsukimi udon*, where the egg yolk is laid on the top of the *udon* soup, in imitation of the moon in the sky.

I gaze at the moon through the guilty eyes of one who hasn't realized the importance of paying attention or understood the enthusiastic expression of someone, unlike us, who can see the wonder around him. Who can find love in little things. The gentleman smiles with happy melancholy as the moon shows itself more clearly: like a pearl guarded by an oyster, we watch it leave the slender embrace of two pink clouds.

Once again, I think of how much I've been taught by this country, how many essential things I was lacking on the other side of the world, where the importance of looking at the moon seems lost forever. I wonder to myself how these people, having lost so much, still manage to gaze at the moon, finding the strength and time to appreciate it. With the same focus. The same wonder. And perhaps the answer is more banal than it might appear. The moon is still there, stunning and enchanting this autumn, while nothing and no one can stop us admiring its great beauty. It would be a shame, in this life, to miss even one look.

In our room the muted lighting enhances an evening meal of *kimuchi*[136] 「キムチ」 *gyōza* and funny black eggs. We put on the *yukata* over our naked bodies before bathing in the floodlit pool beyond the glass wall. I listen to the tap running, creating steam around the perfumed *hinoki* wood bucket on the marble edge.

The night air sneaks through the wooden screen to where it's just us and the steam, and creates a contrast with the hot water that soon becomes intoxicating. We spend quite a long time sitting side by side, immersed in those simple things that of a sudden become our whole universe: the steam, the tinkling of drops water on the surface, the light of the moon bleaching the bamboo curtain.

And we are gradually withdrawn from sadness, from the upset of our respective lives and thoughts of the future. And we make love. Pure, elusive. Simple.

Life becomes harder when we stop appreciating simple things. How can I not be grateful to the place that is showing me the importance of simplicity?

What I like to call '*the beauty of small things*'.

---

[136] Traditional Korean side dish of cabbage and turnip fermented in spices such as chili pepper, spring onion, garlic, ginger and jeotgal. Used in many soups

Travel Notes

Hakone is the most well-known and fashionable hot spring complex in the mountains around Tōkyō, reached in under two hours on a shinkansen from Shinjuku to Odawara.

The various ryokan within the area are spread between Gōra, in the valley, and Sōunzan at the top, with a large difference in altitude between the two stations that makes the funicular necessary. Located in the mountain forests, many ryokan offer traditional kaiseki catering services, while the few restaurants in the area are mainly found around the station at Gōra, a small town with a notable variety of spring waters and as a result considered the best hot spring area in the zone. Again in Gōra there is a western style park with flower gardens and greenhouses called Hakone–Gōra-kōen.

Sengokuhara, to the north of Gōra and exclusively accessible by road, is rich in tourist attractions: Hakone's highly popular open air museum, Chōkoku–no–mori Bijutsu–kan, which combines exhibiting sculptures outside and views over the valley and surrounding mountains; Hakone Shisseika–en, the botanical garden dedicated to wetlands; the Pōra Bijutsu–kan Art Museum, with avant-garde architecture where you find a large number of works by Impressionist painters, including Pablo Picasso and Yasushi Sugiyama; the Mononofu–no–sato Bijutsu–kan Museum exhibiting samurai armour from the Muromachi and Edo periods; the Venetian glass museum Garasunomori Bijutsu–kan and the themed village–museum dedicated to The Little Prince, Hoshi–no–Ōjisama.

Among the most famous onsen in the Gōra area, Kowakien Yunessun is a hot spring complex with an aquatic amusement park suitable for all ages: visitors can enjoy water slides, sake–themed hot springs, green tea, wine and coffee, the large traditional rotenburo Mori–no–yu, the ancient Rome–themed hot springs or buy local products in the Mio Mall.

The Fujiya Hotel is also in the area, the oldest and most luxurious hotel–spa of Hakone, dating from 1878. It boasts many famous guests and today tourists book well in advance to try its delicious curry rice beef.

Day Trip:
- ✵ Travel by train from Kyōto to Odawara
- ✵ Buy a Hakone Free Pass at Odawara station and take the panoramic Hakone–Tozan Tetsudō railway as far as Gōra.
- ✵ Try eating gyōza at the Gyōza Centre
- ✵ Visit Hakone–Gōra–kōen Park
- ✵ Visit the sulphur vents of Ōwakudani Valley
- ✵ Eat kaiseki cuisine at a restaurant in or around Gōra or at your own ryokan
- ✵ Relax in your ryokan's onsen

Typical Products and Souvenirs:
- ✵ Yosegi–zaiku, local mosaic style wooden artisanal items
- ✵ Odawara–shikki, local red lacquer
- ✵ Kuro–tamago, black eggs from the hot springs of Ōwakudani
- ✵ Themed souvenirs from the various museums in the Sengokuhara zone
- ✵ Wagashi from the pastry stores between Gōra and Hakone–Yumoto
- ✵ Tōfu cooked in hot spring water at the famous Tōfudokoro Hagino store, near Hakone–Yumoto station

Hakone
箱根

We appreciate beauty
when it is not given with superficiality,
but offered with parsimony,
when we can enjoy it only after being patient.
In this way its value grows the instant we experience it,
enough to want it again

A sunbeam hits the jet of running water with precision, amalgamating with it and then gently overturning into the stone pool. It's easy to imagine this small private *onsen* was designed taking that early morning sunbeam into account, with the delicacy it is captured by the tap water. As easy as immersing oneself in the deep embrace of the hot water that chases away every shiver from the autumn dawn. It's harder to leave it, to have to say goodbye to the steam, pack our bags once again, fold our *yukata* and leave them on the unmade bed. This refuge for the soul has welcomed us just one night, and yet it is as unforgettable as the moments passed here and the beauty tied to them.

The route on the funicular is the same as the day before as far as Ōwakudani Valley, where a second cable car will take us gliding over Lake Ashi-no-ko. Above, a sky of such an intense blue that you feel you could touch it doesn't prepare us for when, at the ridge of the quarry, the snowy peak of Fuji-san, painted on a canvas of sky floating on a bed of clouds pierces our gaze.

I try to capture the impact of its presence through the

lens, attempting not to lose the perfection of the detail of its snow-covered crests, elegant and more surreal than a tempera painting. The mountain keeps us glued to the window up to the moment it disappears behind a sudden tide of clouds.

"We're never really ready to admire it are we..." I say as the *Kami's* first gift of the day modifies into a memory.

The second Hakone-Tozan cable car gently drops to the lake, giving us the chance to admire from close to the geometric tips of the cedars stretching as far as the eye can see to the water surface. The call of a bird of prey suddenly echoes over the carpet of pointed green tips, and then we find we are lucky enough to have as travelling companion an observant Japanese photographer who begins to point animatedly towards the wood: like a king on a throne, an elegant eagle is perching at the top of a fir tree, near the cables, gazing proudly in the direction of the lake. As for Mount Fujisan, I embrace another fantastic, unforeseen and fleeting image that, once experienced, will last a lifetime.

The lake opens out below us like a sapphire set in the mountains, under siege from the armies of trees all around Tōgendai port, a place welcoming me with the same spirit as last year. One of the three pirate ships awaits the influx of tourists, with its fake gold trimmings and many masts wrapped in perennially furled sails. A little further on, small swan-shaped boats float at ease, waiting to carry couples of friends and lovers.

"This galleon is very nice, a bit out of place, but very nice," comments a smiling Gabry, who like me has by now learned to appreciate the Japanese nations' sense of fantasy.

Nonetheless, at the port we aren't seduced by the themed boat and its well-known panoramic tour sailing us to Hakone-machi and then Moto-Hakone, where the slender red *torii* slips out of the forest of ancient cedars to paddle in the water of the lake. Instead, at the end of the bus line, we get on the coach heading for Hakone-en station, a less tiring alternative although with less fascinating views than the panoramic route winding a mile or so along the shore. A route that, making its way through thick vegetation, unbeknownst to many visitors hides the view of Kuzuryū-jinja Shrine dedicated to the dragon god Kuzuryū and its shy *torii* lapping the water, several enchanting views of the lake and the marvellous black and white Hakuryū-jinja Shrine.

When we reach the group of stores and small attractions at Hakone-en, we are at the foot of Mount Komaga-take, one of the highest peaks in the area from which to admire Mount Fuji-san and home of Hakone Mototsumiya Shrine. The cable car, the cost of which is not included in the travel pass for the zone, is already in action, moving up and down every 20 minutes, and on the way up the puzzle of shapes and colours gradually comes clear as you near the summit. From our glass capsule, the mountain appears like a piece of cloth patched with different fabrics: lurid velvet of the closely packed conifers gives over to low, curved cushions of the red, yellow and greyish bushes, a pottage of tones that just above disperse into the bright green sea of the clumping bamboo of the mountains. I'm thrilled by the bamboo, which from above could easily be taken for an abundant, soft layer of moss, and fascinated to discover the autumnal mantle girding Japanese as opposed to western mountains. Like people belonging to different nations, they appear in a progressive change of apparel as we go up in altitude, but in totally different styles.

On the peak, the ugly cement station building swallowing up the cable car jars in the breathtaking beauty of the view over the lake beneath us. But soon, in the excitement

Fuji-Hakone-Izu Kokuritsu-kōen
富士箱根伊豆国立公園

Fuji-Hakone-Izu Kokuritsu-kōen, one of the first four national parks instituted in Japan and today the most visited in the country thanks to its nearness to Tōkyō, is a collection of tourist sites dotted around the region, among which Mount Fuji-san and its five surrounding lakes, the hot springs of Hakone, Lake Ashi-no-ko and the Izu peninsular. The park includes a great variety of geographical elements such as natural hot springs, coastline, mountains, lakes and more than a thousand volcanic islands, as well as different species of vegetation.

There are plenty of tourist attractions in the area around the volcanic Lake Ashi-no-ko. Starting at Gōra (1), the Hakone-Tozan funicular for Sōunzan (2) is the essential way to move easily between the ryokan and the numerous neighbouring hot spring centres. From Sōunzan you take the cable car to see the sulphur vents at Ōwakudani (3), a volcanic valley with active sulphur vents and hot springs created with the lake about 3,000 years ago, following the eruption of the Hakone volcano. This singular stop is today a popular tourist site for its panoramic views, volcanic activity and the local speciality, kuro-tamago or black hot spring eggs. The mile-long path through the hot springs was closed in 2015 due to an increase in volcanic activity.

Following the cable car's route, you reach Tōgendai port (4), north of Lake Ashi-no-ko. Here, the 3 pirate vessels are Hakone's icon besides being a means of panoramic transport between the tourist ports of Hakone-machi (5) and Moto-Hakone (6), this last near Hakone-jinja Shrine (8) surrounded by tall cedars and famous for the torii with foundations immersed in the lake, Heiwa-no-torii. Getting ashore at Hakone-machi port, you can take an enjoyable walk in the ancient wood along the old Tōkai-dō Road (7), which used to link Tōkyō to Kyōto. The peak of Komaga-take (10), on which sits Hakone Mototsumiya Shrine, is one of the slopes of Mount Hakone accessible by cable car from Hakone-en (9) and is a good observation point for Mount Fuji-san.

Further north, in autumn the Sengokuhara promontory (11) fills with pampas grass, a feast for the eyes of all lovers of autumnal nature, just to the west of the complex of museums (12) with exhibitions for all interests.

Finally, Mount Ashigara–yama (13) is the national park's highest slope and offers some tough trekking through the wilds: in recompense, once at the top the bold trekker can admire Mount Fuji–san from a unique position.

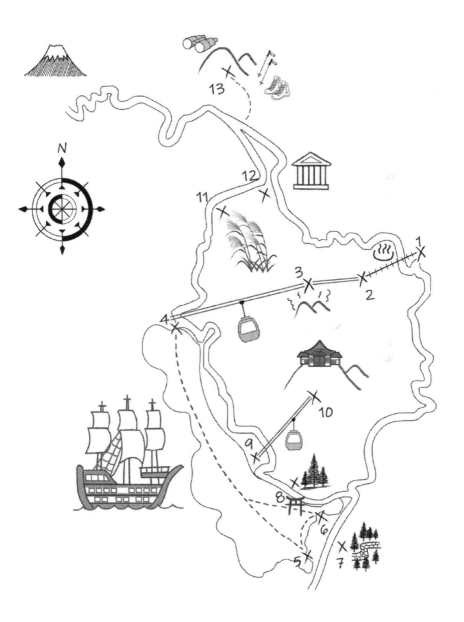

of seeing the ring of mountains encircling the print of blue water, we find the mist comes in to soften the horizon, cladding in secrecy the profile we're so dying to see. I manage to persuade Gabry out of his stubborn desire to simply wait for the timid mountain king, and he follows me, a wee bit grumpily, along the crest's snaking gravel path.

At the foot of Hakone Mototsumiya Shrine, which is crowned by a massive steel lightning conductor, a streamlined red *torii* rises upwards like a flame against the smokey sky, purifying the travellers preparing to enter. The surreal landscape here is almost lunar, with clumps of dwarf bamboo and purple-scarlet flowers poking out from among the white rocks, inseparable from the silence flooding over everything.

The only sound on Mount Komaga-take is the wind, accompanied by a whispering that seems to be coming from the enormous holy rock near the shrine, a living presence that appears to be scrutinizing us carefully, crouched in its sacred cord embroidered with bolts of lightning, and imperturbable in the eternal guard it keeps over this place. Japan makes the most expert traveller feel somewhat inadequate faced with a millennial stone guardian.

Hakone Mototsumiya Shrine's exterior of wood shows the marks of battle with the harsh elements up here on the ridge. Inside, despite a bit of dust and the odd spider's web, we find objects and textiles used during the *matsuri* that happens once a year, the sign of someone's tender loving care given to the ancient building so far from civilisation.

A cairn of piled rocks gathered by a previous visitor keeps company to two old men sitting on the ground, a small step from one of the mountain's craggy slopes. We don't need to ask the reason for the placid expectancy as they stare rapt into the wall of clouds and mist devouring the surrounding mountains, but from the relaxed look of their bodies, we are aware of the meditation of the moment.

The certainty, imposed by familiarity, of what will be revealed after an unknown period of time. Time I'd like to take hold of and expand to infinity to give Gabry the chance to remain mesmerized in front of the sacred mountain. So that the days, like these instants, stop running away so fast.

Here is the sacred mountain,
unveiling majestically,
unexpected but always anticipated,
teaching us daily of beauty,
reminding us we cannot manage without
living and awaiting that sight.
On the train everyone looks up,
waiting for his re-appearance,
so I'll come back here
and wait to admire it undemandingly
one more time

A deep breath in the mountains, filled with colours that will light up when we are too far away. From Gōra, the Hakone-Tozan line, now infused with a touch of sadness, takes us back to Odawara.

I look out the window on our last *shinkansen* trip here in Japan, reassured by the clean smell of the train, by the landscape of fragile blue-roofed houses, fields of rice, ploughed or yellowing, that has accompanied me over the days, welcoming me once again, even knowing that the time for another separation would inexorably arrive.

Blinking back the emotion filling my eyes; I swallow the painful lump in my throat that I know only too well, clutching at one powerful promise. To come back again.

***

Tōkyō
東京

At the end of these travels through places and steps in life,
I'm back where it all began just a few years ago.
I'll never cease to thank Tōkyō for seizing me
from the violent deluge of my existence,
fortified by a wonder I didn't think existed,
nurtured by new emotions and hopes.
And I will always thank her for showing me
how in fact it is easy to build happiness,
one of those things in life they say are
hardest to come by...

Ploughed fields caressed by the muted afternoon sun, dotted with white houses and their anthracite blue roofs, are to my eyes like the warm embrace of returning home on a winter's evening, something we must go back to and then never leave.

I think over the beauty of our trip, the care and love with which we chose and planned the various stops, including the last: Tōkyō.

We couldn't miss Tōkyō, and perhaps it could never have had a role other than being the city to close an unforgettable experience. This city, whose every crossroads I seem to know as if I'd lived there in a past life, always manages to show me something unexpected to feed my love for it. A reciprocal love, feelings built on what we know to be beautiful and what is new that we find to rekindle the desire to stay longer. I believe I love this city just as one might a person who is important in one's life, but feeling a gratitude that it would be hard to feel for someone who hasn't cured me in every possible manner. Above all in heart and soul.

Tōkyō appeared, in the summer rain of a few years ago, as the home I'd been missing in a world I was finding it hard to make sense of. Since then, it has burrowed deep into my existence, filling the space with culture and language, in short, a whole country.

"Are you pleased we're going back to Tōkyō?" Gabry asks, holding my hand. He's not a lover of the place, its futuristic aspect, ordered crowds, neon lights, distance from the countryside, and the untiring, pulsating life going on uninterruptedly in its streets every day. He doesn't like the solitude of the inhabitants, so many of them, so close but so distant, the skyscrapers full of minuscule apartments and the metro choc full but always silent. He doesn't like the businessmen so dedicated to their job at a screen that they forget the value of time and the seasons. Outside Tōkyō the seasons change and colour the countryside and mountains, bringing festivals and typical dishes, while people share the beauty of nature, teaching it and passing it down, perhaps slightly more than in this artificial organism.

Tōkyō always seems unchanged in its western garb, almost insensible to nature's changes if not through the red plastic leaves strewn around the alleyways in autumn, or the cherry blossom in the more famous parks and avenues in spring. He sees it as a place indifferent to human relationships and the cure of time that is always too short, always too fast and sucked in by the back and forth of the metros on their inextricable tracks.

I understand he, like many other travellers, can't see the soul that makes this city different from every other place in the world, its voracity in wanting to shape and chase after beauty of the new and the old in its own way. Because in her roads that never slow down, the people who pass by without looking their neighbour in the eye, Tōkyō nonetheless lives in the wonder of indiscreet and silent altars you find turning a corner, in the peace beneath the autumnal leaves of Meiji-jingū Shrine far from the chaos, in the cherry trees reflected in River Sumida-gawa in the evening, when the Tōkyō Skytree whispers, glimmers in the pink clouds. There is order in chaos, elegance in excess. It doesn't matter if he's not transported by the complex and profound beauty of this city that is and is not Japan. I'm content with the tenderness he shows wanting to accompany me through the streets, to watch me become emotional when faced with her secrets, absurdities and surprises.

We stay at a business hotel like so many, with small, clean rooms and a panoramic *onsen* looking out over the historic station of Shinbashi, near Ginza. I know this neighbourhood by its flamboyant reputation of fashion district, with chic bars, luxury cars parked in reserved spaces, stores selling clothes with Italian and French labels. But once you're in its arteries, the area reveals a hidden world of old bars, *izakaya* and *rāmen-ya* beneath the red brick arches of the railway bridge, old style buildings crushed between one skyscraper and the next, newspaper vendors that seem to date from 50 years ago.

We've only just arrived and the district lights up in the dark quickly covering the city, while we are gulped down by Shinbashi station with its railway line gliding along the ocean towards Odaiba.

I want to take Gabry to the famous island in the Bay of Tōkyō, where besides the city's beach, the shopping centres and attractions of various types, for some months there has been a gigantic statue of the robot Gundam Unicorn on show, a substitute for the famous statue of Gundam that became the island's symbol. Odaiba, an island built on reclaimed waste, has all the characteristics of a separate planet on which to land and enjoy all the peculiarities it has to offer.

Even the journey to get there is an adventure, for instance aboard the futuristic boat along River Sumida-gawa, embarking at Asakusa, or on the Yurikamome train which crosses the bay on tracks suspended over the water… with no driver. Although travelling along the river at night is a little like sliding along black velvet sparkling with the lights of skyscrapers and hanging bridges, the Yurikamome line moves us comfortably and speedily to our destination.

In the artificial white light of the train carriage, bursting through the edge of darkness, I move in close to Gabry, liking the familiar smell of his clothes mixed with the equally intimate smell of city trains. Outside the windows, Tōkyō quickly transforms itself into a skyline of sparkling parallelepipeds, a little universe made up of geometric elements throbbing with energy that reminds me of complex circuits on the electronic card of a computer.

Even Rainbow Bridge, which appears on the horizon once we reach Daiba station, shines out in the night like a molten wire, a bridge of energy in that wonderful electromagnetic system.

We travel up the wide avenue that leads into the little world of Odaiba, with the smell of a still mild ocean filling our nostrils. We go past the Fuji Television studios and cross the West Park road bridge, along a pedestrian walkway under which a road of several lanes winds, as full of traffic as a large motorway artery, not exactly what we were expecting to find on an island built on waste. For Tōkyō is this: a continuous impulse of life invested in every corner and surface, even the most improbable and absurd.

I don't recall precisely where the predecessor of the current Gundam was located, but I pin my trust on my inexplicable memory of the city that leads us to the enormous box of cement that is DiverCity Tōkyō Plaza. We hold our breath as we walk around the building, and there before us projected upwards is the silhouette of the Gundam Unicorn, an exact reconstruction of how one of the hundreds of robots that crowd Japanese *anime* might be in reality, as well as a fantasy for children. Elegant in white armour, the robot seems to us on the verge of coming alive from one moment to the next, lit from inside in an incandescent red escaping from every joint. We are seized by the beauty of the design details and by its grandeur, as we wander several times around those colossal robotic feet.

Further on, in Tōkyō's night sky, another out-sized attraction of Odaiba shines in the same way. The ferris wheel at the amusement and shopping centre Palette Town fascinates me every time, although it isn't as big as the much more famous wheel in Osaka, among the largest in the world. This year the alternating lightshows on its spokes are simpler, a dance of blue and purple that slightly outshines the memory of the magnificent rainbow when I first saw it two years previously.

I realize how my love for Tōkyō is changing with time, trip after trip, exactly as that for a person we're in love with would change as we spent hours, days and years together. The first time I saw the ferris wheel, like many things in this city, it was with a teenager's adoring gaze, more influenced by the exterior impact than the essence of a person. But time, daily life and maturity gradually supplant the initial shivers of closeness, the shyness of showing who we are, the excitement of an awkward kiss, and clarify who we have in front of us. Looking at Palette Town's ferris wheel after another year I realize how this wheel isn't the biggest, most beautiful and luminous you might come across in the course of a lifetime, in fact it is now a small wheel, in colours that aren't garish and with a radius that isn't too fine, and yet it's the symbol of a tie that can't be broken. Time has transformed that pounding heart into peaceful tenderness, that sudden, unbounded infatuation into a balanced, nourishing love: back at its feet, I let the colours embrace me without changing me, freeing my heart from the nostalgia of a neverending abstinence from happiness.

I tell Gabry about one of the many sights that struck me as we reach Megaweb Toyota City, with its futuristic cars and a small vintage automobile museum, to then dive back into the world of Venus Fort, the shopping centre that's just like an olden day Venice of grand palazzos and Renaissance fountains. Beneath the changing vault of the artificial sky that draws in hundreds of Japanese and tourists to Odaiba, I remember racing from one sixteenth century store to another, the excitement as I photographed the curved dome of the ceiling painted in wisps of clouds on a Botticelli blue, a trick of perspective and colour made more realistic by the lights that illuminate it and create sundown in the north wing and dawn in the west wing of the structure. Today we say a very brief hello to the ancient Italy of which Tōkyō, by means of its paradoxal pursuit of beauty, even manages to makes us feel we are missing.

We march quickly down the wide avenues of Odaiba, exaggeratedly large spaces filled with green flowerbeds, urban vegetable gardens and always a dearth of benches, that the city seems to disregard. A last trip to Aqua City, one of the island's largest shopping centres, and the similar Decks Tōkyō Beach and we are like any other citizen from Tōkyō spending the weekend here, like the young people who take an island break from study and work.

Daiba 1-chome-shōtengai survives on the fifth floor of

Decks, a shopping gallery with a picturesque Chinese bazaar that is off the beaten track, and every year from the first time I happened upon it, I only find it after getting lost on several floors and at different entrances to the building.

The first time I explored Tōkyō, I visited at least thirty shopping centres, on a breathless trip in which I felt every single store and commercial building was that gulp of air I had lacked until that moment. Although they all seemed a box of surprises unique in its way, I didn't become attached to any one mall in particular, except for the fifth floor of Decks.

With its kiosks flattened into a line under rivers of multicoloured Chinese lanterns, I had felt an immediate, deep affection which then grew through memories: the first trip was with my companion of the time, a good person who succeeded in having fun rootling around among the stupidest souvenirs you can find here; laughing with my sister and her boyfriend, squashed by the crowd between one stand and another or busy fishing for surprise gadgets; the lady who sold glass objects, an amazing *koi* [137] 「鯉」 carp, popped into my bag of purchases my first ever free gift of *origami* in Japan. Since then, like a ritual, every so often when I travel through Odaiba, I can't help going to the little Decks China Town, and am always beside myself with excitement to see the minuscule haunted house with a long queue of young people waiting to go in, a restaurant area selling *takoyaki* with soft toys in the shape of octopuses hanging from the ceiling, where the shop selling surprise boxes is always fit to bursting and where the lady's glass creations continue to sparkle in the windows.

I try to do the same thing this time, without imagining

---

[137] Coloured variety of fresh water, herbivorous carp. Large and in variable colours and patterns, it is very common in Japanese ponds and lakes

the result: an unknown space, full of ascetic neon lights, half-empty corridors and red and white lanterns hung almost too neatly from the ceiling. I ask myself what's happened to all the bazaars, the mass of customers crowding around the store windows so you can't get near them, under an excessively black ceiling decorated with rainbow garlands. I spot the haunted house, still there but with no one lining up excitedly outside, and I head in the direction of the lady's little glass shop. I pace up and down the corridor repeatedly, not wanting to resign myself to the disappearance of the kiosk shining with transparent coloured glass...

"If we don't want to be late for the restaurant we've booked, unfortunately we ought to be going..." says Gabry, in the tone of one who hasn't been able to experience the real Daiba 1-chome-shōtengai and see the fantastic place it used to be, now just an anonymous floor of any old shopping mall.

This is the cruel side of a Tōkyō that chases after novelty, changing from one day to the next to follow trends or simply construction investments, unscrupulously deleting memories and experiences by pitilessly substituting them with the new. It doesn't matter if the current is better or worse than what went before. It is nevertheless 'new'.

And this is also the vexing aspect that Tōkyō exercises on her adorers: it will let you love it without bounds, in a short time and in a way that creates a habit it is hard to shake off, and then when you least expect it, with no qualms the city denies and removes something, sweetening and consoling you with something else. One shouldn't become attached to Tōkyō, because there's no certainty that what is really there will remain so for any length of time. Which is the prerogative of memories.

You either love Tōkyō or you hate it, the way it

continually changes, betraying expectations but letting you in on something new, being in the present when it is already the future.

I have my photo taken, as in the past, under a surreal Statue of Liberty of almost human proportions, that soars in bluish victory on a nocturnal Daiba beach. And while Gabry takes shots of similar but different moments, behind my smile I reflect on how time can transform things, even those most loved, into something that can please in the same way, but also slightly less. Often, we find it easy to defend ourselves from something's absence, in part through nostalgia, in part through the memories that resurface, although living it is not the same as before, and it can be painful to think of what was and inexplicably is no more.

In this Tōkyō I see the metaphor of my life, of my relationship that lasted more than seven years and the difficult acceptance of how time and the inevitable changes in existence transformed a feeling, and us too, into something else. However, brimming with unforgettable memories and emotions, it was by this time impossible to recognise that past as something that could continue into the present and future.

The memories will always be there, unique, irreplaceable. While inevitably, we are different, mutable, a bit like the places of Tōkyō.

I say goodbye to Odaiba once again, letting myself be wooed by the image of boats on a dark ocean, blotting it in red and blue, little shards of colour sliding under Rainbow Bridge, the undisputed king of the night in Tōkyō Bay.

The city metro has the same colours, weaving in a rainbow tangle, and taking us in less than an hour from the island to Akebonobashi station, not far from the district of Shinjuku. Here we locate our evening meal: the Tai Shio

Soba Tōka *rāmen-ya*.

This little *rāmen* restaurant where you eat at the counter, makes an appearance in the documentary 'Rāmen Heads' directed by Koki Shigeno, a film that tells of the rise of the Japanese *rāmen* empire and the story of one of their best cooks, who has received a large number of national awards in recent years, Osamu Tomita of the Chūka-soba Tomita *rāmen-ya*. In the documentary, the maniacal personality of the chef and the stories of the great *rāmen* masters are intense and rich with content, giving viewers footage and stills in which food becomes poetry.

Several other famous restaurants appear in the film with their unique types of *rāmen*. And among them is Tai Shio Soba Tōka, a restaurant run by a team of young cooks who give their body and soul to preparing an exquisitely light sea bass and salt soup, to which tender *chāshū* is added. The soup is served in the *tsukemen* manner, separate from the noodles.

When we take our places inside the minuscule restaurant, we are quickly served by cooks on the other side of the counter, shy young people who try to pronounce some words in English and that seem light years from the fame won on the big screen.

Not long afterwards, before our eyes, a bowl of soup cheered by thin yellow petals, is accompanied by a plate overflowing with fat raw barley noodles topped with a boiled egg the colour of copper, proof of a perfect and delicious soy marinade. The balance between refined delicacy of taste in the soup and the substantial consistency of the tasty noodles is perfection, the exact representation of a culinary yin-yang that couldn't go unnoticed.

Our supper is over in the blink of an eye and heading back to Ginza I feel that sensation of peace and gratitude towards the umpteenth moment of simplicity that I've been offered through a bowl of *rāmen*.

Thanks to this trip, the value accorded to served food in Japan has become increasingly clear and more tangible to me: it's not just a question of the pleasure of eating, or that provoked by the taste of a dish and its ingredients, but the combination. It is the deep sense of respect felt for someone eating a meal, the great generosity of sharing a form of beauty and joy with your neighbour. The effort to elicit happiness in others.

There was beauty in the little restaurant of Tai Shio Soba Tōka, in the yellow flowers floating on the soup, in the noodles of just the right consistency, in the hesitant smiles of the young cooks. A beauty that stays with us as we leave the Akebonobashi *rāmen-ya*, on the metro and then under Ginza's vertical neon lights, under the covers in the hotel bed when the room's darkness can't contain our words.

Everything here in Japan seems created for this purpose, to induce a sense of beauty that remains while everything around is changing, and inevitably turns into a small slice of happiness.

Travel Notes

In Hakone, Lake Ashi-no-ko offers numerous tourist attractions besides the famous views of Mount Fuji-san. The quickest and most evocative way to move about on the lake is to take one of the pirate-themed boats included in the Hakone Free Pass. From Tōgendai port, sailing to Hakone-machi (30 min.) and immediately afterwards Moto-Hakone (15 min.) gives you truly unique views of the surrounding natural landscapes, as in the lake's symbol with Mount Fuji-san in the background and Heiwa-no-torii, the 'Torii of Peace' immersed in the water.

If you disembark at Hakone-machi, besides the imperial family's old summer residence, you can visit Hakone Checkpoint, a reconstruction of a checkpoint on old Tōkai-dō, the road between Tōkyō and Kyōto from the Edo period. Not far off, Onshi-Hakone-kōen is a park on a small peninsular from which you get a good view of the famous torii.

From here you can reach Moto-Hakone either on foot along an enchanting cedar path, or on the pirate boat to the next stop at the port. Having reached Moto-Hakone, on Jinja-dōri Street, there are various places to eat, lots of temples including Hakone-jinja Shrine with its majestic red torii at the entrance, the ancient and picturesque forest around it and right next door the small shrine of the 9 dragon heads, Kuzuryū-jinja, where on 31 July every year the Ashi-no-ko Kosui Matsuri is held, a festival to honour the spirit of a dragon that, according to legend, lives in the lake and protects the surrounding area.

On the evening of the event, a monk sails out to the centre of the lake on one of the pirate boats and throws offerings to the spirit while floating lanterns, tōrō-nagashi, light up the surface of the water, followed by a stunning firework display.

***

Built on a platform of recycled waste, the artificial island of Odaiba is located in the Bay of Tōkyō and is today one of the city's main places for entertainment and relaxing, attracting thousands of people at the weekends. You can reach the island in 20 minutes by the railway over the sea on the Yurikamome line from Shinbashi

Daiba, alternatively you can take the panoramic, futuristic ferry-boat on River Sumida-gawa that leaves Sumida Boat Terminal at Asakusa and takes about an hour.

At the Odaiba Marine Park, the terrace has an amazing view of Rainbow Bridge and you can have your photo taken beneath a re-duced replica of the Statue of Liberty. After which you can take in the shopping malls Decks and Water City, where among the hun-dreds of different stores, are attractions like Joypolis, a techno amusement park on floor 3F of Decks Tōkyō Beach shopping mall, or the Takoyaki Museum on the 4F floor of the same building. Nearby there is also a panoramic observatory belonging to Fuji TV. Opposite Diver City shopping mall is the 60ft statue of Gundam Unicorn, which lights up several times a day, and further on, past a suggestive park of hydrangeas and other seasonal flowers, there is a large museum area set up with sensory exhibitions. There is also a beach and several other recreational spaces on the island.

Day Trip:
* Take the cable car to Tōgendai port
* Travel by bus to Hakone-en
* Ascend Mount Komaga-take in the cable car for a view of Mount Fuji-san and visit Hakone Mototsumiya Shrine
* Take the train from Gōra to Tōkyō
* Visit the attractions of Odaiba
* Eat your evening meal at the famous Tai Shio Soba Tōka rāmen-ya

Alternative to Mount Komagatake:
* Take a pirate ship from Tōgendai port to Hakone-machi port
* Walk along the old Tōkai-dō Road, among ancient cedars
* Visit Hakone-jinja Shrine and Heiwa-no-torii

Typical Products and Souvenirs:
* Souvenirs from the Odaiba shopping malls
* Gadgets from 'The Gundam Base' store

Tōkyō
東京

Gliding between one quarter and another in Tōkyō
with the ease the metro lines slide
and crisscross on the map and in real life,
grabbing up people and lives and pulsating without stay
from the heart to the hinterland of this perfect organism.
The city enthralls me with that incessant rhythm,
and the thrill of taking part, as in the past,
stamping places and sights on my memory with a power
surviving time and distance

Ginza station is still whispering at six in the morning, when Tōkyō throbs with life that can't wait to burst out and run free through the streets and along the lines of the metro.

Taking the Hibiya line to Nakameguro and changing onto the Chiyoda line to Kashiwa, the map's coloured lines intermingle as we hold it in our hands, the carriage gently rocking and warming us, hot air blowing out from beneath the seats.

We get off at Matsudo, leaving silent carriages full of sleeping Japanese, their heads randomly leaning here and there like autumn leaves falling where they chance. Still half asleep, our hunt for that anonymous corner with the grey signs and two long wooden benches starts in this 'hood. We want to be there for our booking at all costs: to try chef Osamu Tomita's *tsukemen*.

Given the considerable daily influx into his establishment, he takes bookings in advance for a time to sit down.

351

Which is why the queue outside begins early in the day, with people stopping here on their way to the office with the aim of clinching one of the limited tickets to paradise. The anxiety of finding customers already waiting turns into excitement as we recognise the restaurant's shutters at the end of the road and then to our surprise a completely deserted pavement.

"Oh no, I can't believe they're closed! On the Internet it said it was open on Fridays!" Gabry is utterly crestfallen.

I have a go at reading a flier stuck to one of the lowered shutters, and as soon as I get the gist of it, I'm torn as to whether to tell him what it says or not.

"You know it's one of the *rāmen* festivals that Tomita is taking part in. On these days he's not at the restaurant..."

Incredulity turns into frustration, and then inability to give up. Armed with a translator we begin to decipher that cruel poster in lots of short phrases until we get to the magic word.

"Shinjuku! The event is at Tsukemen Expo, Shinjuku district, here in Tōkyō!"

It's ironic how sometimes life turns a bad situation into a glorious opportunity: the idea of meeting Tomita and other high profile *rāmen* chefs ready to take each other on to elect the country's best *tsukemen*! We don't need much convincing to see the snag as an unexpected boon. I call them little twists of fate, which here in Japan seem to occur frequently and always with a precise aim. Consequently, it is due to a muddle of unwanted situations and choices that I discovered memorable places I would never otherwise have known about, unfortunate developments that happened in the right place at the time it was important I be there and meet people I wouldn't otherwise have met.

If we'd known about the festival beforehand we might

not have crossed the entire city at dawn, but at least we are a little closer to the small town of Mito, in Ibaraki Prefecture. For Mito is home to the country's third most famous garden, Kairaku-en, celebrated for its central lake, perspective effects, cherry and plum blossom in spring and flame red acers in autumn. However, at Matsudo station, we find out there is work on the railway line pushing our departure to several hours later, we have to take the arduous decision to turn down this visit too.

"Today doesn't strike me as a lucky day..."

"Look at it like this: tonight we're going to eat the best *rāmen* in all Japan!"

The familiar pink of the Asakusa metro consoles us and accompanies us to the station of the same name. I take the north exit and find myself on that splinter of pavement on which, like a slice of shop cake, the station's historic building sits, looking like an unhappy experiment to reconcile ancient and modern.

Going on a few steps and I would be on Kaminarimon-dōri, the street with the humongous Thunder Gate with its massive lantern and where the top floor of the very elegant tourist information centre continues to hide from many unknowing visitors the splendid view from up there: on to Nakamise-dōri Street, with its carpet of tourists and rows of shops with turquoise roofs, appearing in all its archaic beauty, like the entrance road to the oldest temple in Tōkyō. Whereas I grab Gabry's hand and walk rapidly in the opposite direction, where I can smell the sea breeze channelling up River Sumida-gawa. I weasel round the building separating me from Azuma-bashi Bridge and all of a sudden it's there, just as I remembered it, like the sketch in my memory, engraved on my heart. The little harbour of Asakusa, boats sitting on the wide blue ribbon of river, the Asahi beer skyscraper that looks as though it is imitating a tankard with froth on top in a videogame with grainy pixels, and the weird golden thing on top of the building next door: a flame perhaps, or a cloud, or maybe whatever anyone wants to see in it. And then Tōkyō Skytree, the tower that is a mere babe next to the ancient city.

The relationship I have with this area of the city, whose name I love pronouncing with the 'u' that Japanese keep between their lips, is profound and has roots going back to the first time I ever set foot in Japan. Asakusa, in the way it perpetually merges the country's ancient face with the modern one, is to me the emblem of Japan itself and all the more the harbour of my new life, of my love at first sight for Tōkyō, starting from these very streets, which wrenched open my heart and filled it with a world of admiration.

At the time of my first trip, I had the good fortune to find a small apartment in a semi-traditional style house in the area of the new apartment buildings along the river, near Oshiage-Tōkyō Skytree station, terminus of the Asakusa line.

When the metro spat me out, still unaware of the world I would soon discover, the Tōkyō Skytree was the first thing I saw. I stood petrified in front of the beauty and perfection of that elephantine structure, and for no reason at all was magnetically, obsessively attracted to it from the start. In its elegance and potency, it seemed to me incomparable to anything I'd ever seen before, not the highest skyscrapers of New York or Brooklyn Bridge by night, nor the London Eye, Big Ben or the neon lights in Piccadilly Circus, nor all the sights that had struck me with wonder in my trips around Europe and Italy.

When, on arrival at my little apartment, I unexpectedly

found the tower standing magnificent and irresistible out-side the window, I realized I would be tied to it forever. For the next two weeks, I did little else but gaze at it, lying on the futon in front of the sliding door as I planned a new day's exploring.

I admired and photographed it at almost any hour I could, in any light: grey and metallic at dawn, or golden in the first rays of the sun; paled by fog, swallowed by clouds, devoured by two typhoons and invisible under the driving rain. Dusted with pink at sundown and indescribably, every evening, as it chose a new outfit, which I would amuse my-self guessing, sparkling purple, blue or white.

I couldn't sleep if I hadn't spent some time contemplat-ing it in its infinite shimmering, spellbound every time it chose to put on my favourite colour on the unreachable me-tallic bark of its trunk. Purple, associated with elegance, so-phistication, *miyabi* 「雅」 in ancient Japanese, in the ex-pression of the sensibility of beauty closely tied to the con-cept of *mono-no-aware* 「物の哀れ」 , the awareness of the transience of things that are more beautiful and refined.

Then I waited for midnight, when the great central body went dark while the tip continued to be run through with a white circular band. It was the sign that Tōkyō was half-closing its eyes, becalming itself for a few hours before ex-ploding with beauty again the next day.

In those days I saw the construction as the expression of what Japan had suddenly become in my life, and I never managed to formulate words to describe the moment in which, from a height of 1,500 feet, as the lift doors opened, I looked down on the world below, perceived its immense beauty and for the first time felt part of it, suddenly bursting into uncontrollable tears that couldn't contain the uncon-tainable.

By now I belonged to that tower, that city, that country.

Today I salute the symbol of that indissoluble tie from a distance and recognise the Tōkyō Skytree mascot drawn just outside Asakusa station: a soft toy with wavy fair hair and large blue eyes sitting at the top of the tower, by a strange twist of fate, it could be the Japanese caricature of me.

However, Asakusa isn't only the neighbourhood with the steel sequoia, it is also the place where one of the magical aspects of the city is most tangible, which is to say the titanic encounter and clash between modernity and the cult of the beauty of the new with Japanese historic tradition.

Along Nakamise-dōri, the straight road between the majestic red of Sensō-ji Temple and Kaminari-mon Gate, among tiny shops selling souvenirs and pastries, you can immerse yourself in a traditional Tōkyō that is no longer the one sucked up by skyscrapers and a network of interweaving roads, flyovers and metro lines. Here, surrounded by the nostalgic Japanese red of the holy buildings kept alive by continual restorations, you can lose yourself amongst the multitude of visitors flustering by the rows of kiosks, or by the smoke of the incense cauldron outside the main building of the temple.

It is a different river of people from that snaking along the youthful Takeshita-dōri Street at Harajuku, that inundates the crossing at Shibuya, or nonchalantly tramples everything in Shinjuku station because, in one way or another, it still holds traces of the pilgrim way it was in olden times. As in the past, the road trembles with life and souvenirs, and next to the more commercial and modern ones you find traditional objects like fans, *kimono* and *ukiyo-e*[138] 「浮世絵」.

---

[138] Artistic woodblock prints on paper from the Edo period

I pray on the temple's high steps and then peep at some of the hundreds of dubious *omikuji*[139] 「おみくじ」 left tied to the building's supports to drive away a difficult future, confining it to the temple, so that it won't happen. I still carry in my wallet the wish for happiness that I drew out three years ago. A message of hope and serenity that I am waiting to come true.

As Nakamise-dōri lives its autumn of people filing past beneath the fake orange maple branches, we dive into parallel streets selling manufacturing and craft products, where the activity is a bit less touristy. In memory of the past when it would welcome pilgrims from all over Japan, this area has maintained its love of tradition and there are many well-known stores preparing their own foodstuffs according to bygone recipes.

We decide to treat ourselves to a nice memory buying some sweet bread from Asakusa Kagetsudō, considered among the best pastry shops in Tōkyō in the preparation of traditional *meron pan*[140] 「メロンパン」. Outside the small shop with its simple interior, darkened by old wooden furniture, I am struck by a smell of childhood, summer evening walks with my parents, the smell of candy floss, roasted hazelnuts and of the rainbow of sweets on the stalls, the most wonderful thing we could stumble across.

This store isn't the only one here to sell nostalgia to taste. In the muddle of alleys there are pastry shops and restaurants making sweet breads and *tenpura* in the old manner. Like Chōchin Monaka, serving its monaka 「最中」 wafer

---

[139] Fortune-telling written on small strips of paper in Japanese, which you can purchase for a small donation. If the prophecy isn't positive, it is usual to leave the piece of paper tied to the area of the temple designed for this purpose

[140] Sweet bread covered in a thin layer of crisp biscuit that looks like a melon. Stuffed with cream or ice cream, today they can differ in pastry type and shape

Sensō-ji 浅草寺

Sensō-ji, the oldest and most famous Buddhist temple complex in Tōkyō, is situated in the historic area of Asakusa. The temple is also known as Asakusa Kannon, in that it is dedicated to Kannon Bosatsu, the Bodhisattva of compassion. It is said that in 628, when Nara was the capital of Japan and Asakusa only a small village, two fishermen on River Sumida-gawa caught a statue in their nets. Discovering that the statue was of Kannon Bosatsu, the head of the village decided to dedicate his life to her, founding the temple of Sensō-ji. Over the centuries, the various shōgun contributed to increasing the popularity of the place that today attracts more than 30 million tourists a year, making it the most visited Buddhist temple in the world.

From Asakusa metro you reach the complex through the majestic Kaminari-mon (1) or Thunder Gate, famous for its 13 foot paper lantern painted in red and black. The two statues guarding the entrance, protecting the temple from natural disasters, are Fūjin and Raijin, respectively the Kami of wind and thunder. Beyond the gate, Nakamise-dōri (2), once the pilgrims' way, is today full of workshops selling souvenirs and traditional objects, while the lateral roads have lots of confectionary shops and restaurants serving dishes made from historical recipes.

The street ends at a second impressive two story gate with three lanterns, the Hōzō-mon (3) or Treasure House Gate, watched over by two large Niō, the guardians of Buddha.

To the left, you can't miss the fabulous five story pagoda (4). Going straight on you reach the main building, Kannondō (5), in which the statue of Kannon is kept and opposite which are a large incense brazier, the fountain of the purification of the dragon and stalls selling amulets and omikuji.

There are other buildings scattered around, including the halls of Awashima-dō (6) and Yōgō-dō (7) with a little garden and the oldest stone bridge in Tōkyō, the Asakusa Shrine (11), where the three founders are worshipped and whose coat of arms portrays the nets used to catch the statue, and the side gate, Niten-mon (8), watched over by two Ten, the divinities Zochoten and Jiko-kuten respectively protecting the south and east. To the east of Hōzō-mon Gate you find Benten-dō Hall (9) with its enormous

Buddhist six hour bell, and to the west Denbō-in Temple (10), with a large garden that can be visited during annual events.

The main events at Sensō-ji are: Honzon Jigen-e (17 and 18 March), in honour of the goddess Kannon; Hana Matsuri (8 April) when the Buddha's birthday is celebrated among thousands of flowers; Sanja Matsuri in mid-May, one of the three largest Shinto festivals in Tōkyō with parades, music and dance in honour of the three founders; Shiman-rokusen-nichi (10 July), also known for the Hōzuki lantern plant market; Osame-no-Kannon Goenn-ichi (18 December) during which you can buy Hagoita, decorated wooden paddles that are lucky charms for the new year.

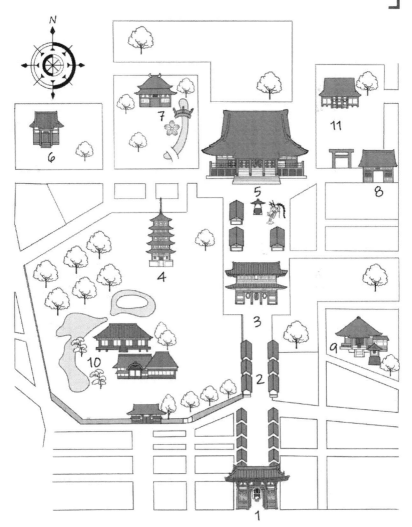

full of ice cream, or Kamejū, where you can taste the oldest *dorayaki* in Tōkyō, savouring the rough homemade consistency of its *azuki* jam.

Daikokuya Honten is known for its crunchy *tenpura* fried in sesame oil, while Sansada, with nearly 200 years behind it, is known to be one of the oldest *tenpura* restaurants in the country. Then you only have to look closely and ask the owners of local stores where you can flush out *soba, oden* and *unagi* restaurants that put down roots in the area a century ago and keep the atmosphere alive in this part of Tōkyō.

Kappabashi-dōgugai Street extends adjacent to Asakusa, but due to its outlying position it is easily left off the itineraries of less interested travellers. When we get there, we find ourselves in a wide avenue with arcades on either side, stretching for more than a mile and beyond belief, are stores selling every type of utensil, instrument and electrical appliance linked to the world of cooking, professional or not. Including shops selling costly reconstructions of food in resin, one of the singularities in Japan you come across when you encounter your first restaurant.

In this infinite museum of culinary art, there are also Japanese ceramics of every type and price range, shops bursting with every type of kitchen utensil, from modern stainless steel to traditional bamboo, dealers in professional appliances, and even shops offering an infinite array of *noren* or lanterns on which to print the name of your establishment.

We've hardly had time to work off our enthusiasm for buying in the first store, than we are drawn into the next, and then the next. Like Alice in Wonderland, we drift into a bazaar where it's hard to move in the narrow spaces between the shelves overflowing with the inconceivable, and we stop and gaze at the ceilings from which hang enormous bamboo plates, colanders the size of basketball nets, shining pots bigger than any I've ever seen and grills to strain *tenpura* of the most varied shapes, rather like the vault of a starry sky.

From centre table hot plates very much in fashion and straw bowls for *soba*, we even find an accessory Gabry has wanted for a while: a small Japanese cedar wood mold in which to make homemade *tōfu*. The joy on our faces when we walk out of the store with this little wooden cube reminds me again of how, in this country, even the simplest things acquire for us a value without precedent.

Kappabashi-dōgugai Street soon reveals itself as an amusement park without end where, as was to be expected, the shops with reconstructions of food are the main attraction. The windows explode with colour, bowls of *rāmen* and *udon, nigiri-zushi*[141] 「握り寿司」 and *uramaki*[142] 「裏巻き」 of every sort, rice topped with *tonkatsu, unagi* or *tenpura*. And then Japanese and western puddings, fruit from every part of the world, pizzas with toppings never tried before and even bowls overflowing with pasta and whimsical condiments.

All the foodstuffs and dishes are displayed in a highly orderly manner beneath lights that make the resin succulent, an army of soups and ingredients unperturbed by time that manage to defy gravity, poured or forked by cutlery ready to throw itself into the dish. Here food has become a sculpture to beguile, and every single detail is curated to

---

[141] Classic 'hand-pressed sushi', consisting in an oblong pile of rice forming an oval ball with a layer of raw fish, seafood or omelette on top. Usually accompanied by wasabi and soy sauce

[142] Commonly known as 'sushi-roll' and a western reinterpretation of the Japanese makimono, they are cylindrical in shape with rice on the outside and nori seaweed inside around a filling of fish, vegetables, etc

reach a perfection that is greater than reality.

As we stroll among fried prawns and appetizing cubes of Kōbe beef, I want to take that reality away with me too, not noticing the figures with three zeros stuck to every type of model on display. But in the end, two small prawn magnets wrapped in soft Japanese *tenpura* and a set of shiny golden dumplings bulging with an unknown filling, are the only fake items I manage greedily to feast on.

The only memory of a world that to my eyes never ceases to be fantastic.

Like *otaku* growing up watching *anime* while eating a plate of pasta cooked by grandma, Akihabara plucks us from the present to take us back to those years, when the world was created around anything amazing we came across during its perpetual exploration.

In the fluorescent streets of an eternally young part of town we feel a resounding nostalgia for the days when we didn't even know what happiness was simply because we were busy creating it. We were children busy being happy.

I remember as soon as I got off the metro train, shining as new, transported by the current of people so that I yield and am herded to the south exit of Akihabara station, like a sardine wedged into its counter. Here we encounter the necessity of dodging hordes of excited young people of all ages that dilute the tide of businessmen in jacket and tie. I remember too when the SEGA building with its blue and red neon lights appears overbearingly outside the station. It is he who kick-starts the games in the ageless district.

On the stage of the sky beginning to change from pale icy to dark blue, he parades this corner of Akihabara, which I would know in a million crossroads because of the wonderful silhouette of the skyscrapers, completely clad in signs, screens, lettering and billboards. Pink, blue, fluorescent reds along with heroes, heroines and robots following themselves in the mirrored windows of comic book stores with infinite floors, a *tsunami* of colour and moving images in which I want to lose myself every time.

This is the part of town where you go back to being a child, where you can shape your happiness setting out with an indistinct palette of voices, shades and shapes: all you need to do is let yourself be transported by crowded escalators between one dimension and the next, ascending supersonic skyscrapers in which you lose your focus among hundreds of shop windows about to explode with action figures, shelves smelling of the paper from the thousands of *manga* on display, of young people prey to the euphoria of finding themselves in a place where they feel more alive. And the happiness and lightness of perceiving anything is possible, when wonder supplants reality, and when past and future are simply present.

Here in Akihabara, we constantly tap into the excitement that comes from the chance to fantasize, to create and live in the world you want.

We struggle to find the model of the person we love, the one with whom we share values and with whom we identify. We hunt for them among the thousands we meet, with a frenzy we had in the treasure hunts with our friends as kids at school. Every skyscraper is an opportunity to win the spoils and at the same time a fount of other surprises.

We find ourselves shunning a queue of Dragon Ball fanatics waiting for the release of a new action figure in limited edition for which they are happy to curl around an enormous skyscraper for hours. Then, in a comic store, where youth stand immobile between the narrow lanes of black and white shelving like pawns on a chessboard, immersed in a recently released *manga*, practising what in Japan is called *tachiyomi*[143] 「立ち読み」.

It doesn't matter how quickly we walk down the main street in this part of the city, besieged by the enormous signs for *karaoke*[144] 「カラオケ」, by the incessant noise coming from the many *pachinko*[145] 「パチンコ」 and videogame rooms, from the high-pitched recorded voices of girls singing harrowing *anime* theme songs.

We don't stay long in the *otaku* zone, just long enough to locate some more pieces for our collection and then we bolt, trying to avoid the electronics area sucking us into its vortex of small stores with unimaginable electrical accessories or into the innumerable buildings belonging to Bic Camera and Yodobashi Camera, factories producing the world's cutting edge technology.

The neon lights are starting to flash in the twilight, resembling the thrills we have just left behind us. It is the simplest joy and we cultivate it unconsciously when we are young, to then, for some absurd reason, forget it.

'We should go back to being children' or 'They were the best years of our lives' are expressions of an inner human necessity not to take life too seriously. Because perhaps it's true that seriousness and rationality weigh us down. So we move further and further away from the possibility of being happy by seriously living a reality that is often not even what we wanted, preventing us from having the life that

---

[143] Term literally meaning 'to read on your feet'. Reading standing up is very popular in the bookshops and comic stores of Japan

[144] Buildings full of small sound-proofed rooms with microphones, tv's on which song lyrics appear, and tapes, reserved by the hour for people to sing their favourite songs with friends and colleagues. The word means 'without orchestra'

[145] Recreational arcade game like a vertical flipper, similar to western slot machines. Although cash gambling is illegal in Japan, its popularity and a specific legal loophole allow its existence

suits us best.

And if only we found ourselves, for example, on the streets of Akihabara more often, chasing after our favourite hero, driven by the power to define our existence and of that sensation of staggering wonder, perhaps we would be a little closer to that joy we persuade ourselves is unreachable. If we managed to be like children, to separate ourselves from reality in order to observe it and identify all its potential nuances, to shape it in such a way that we find that sense of perennial excitement in it, that pleasure of discovering and living, then we would find the way to build our road to happiness.

The metro resounds with the jingle indicating we are coming into Shinjuku. I wait anxiously for the female voice rhythmically announcing the stops in Japanese and English, which is one of those things that make me feel I'm at home here. I'd like to hear it more often, maybe lulling me in the background while the words of the novel I'm reading appear on the screen of my handheld device. As I have that thought, for an instant, just one, I am once again that dreaming child shaping her world, her happiness.

Shinjuku metro station, the most crowded and labyrinthine in the entire city of Tōkyō, is rather like a spider's web as far as I'm concerned: however many times I've tried, equipped with maps, satnav and online maps, once inside I end up trapped with no possibility of finding the right exit. So, trying to stay upright as yet another wave of commuters spills out of the train the second the doors open, we pray that the sign with the *kanji* for 'exit', 「口」, is the right one.

"Central East Exit! The north would have been better but that's not a bad result at all!" exclaims Gabry, who is much better and quicker than I am at reading the characters on signs.

At this exit we aren't that far from Ōkubo-kōen Park, the green area north of Shinjuku station that often hosts Tōkyō's culinary competitions. Today featuring Osamu Tomita and other renowned *rāmen* cooks from all over Japan.

At 5pm the queues at the individual stands still look manageable and the immense sign listing all the types of *tsukemen* competing seems to shine at the entrance to the park like the way in to an Eden of tastes. Having located Tomita's unmistakeable soup, we hurry to the curb by his stand. And there he is, leaping from one pan to the other, wearing the severe expression of the perfectionist.

Soon afterwards, on one of the long benches in the centre of the park, we sit in contemplation of the most famous *tsukemen* in Japan, whose aroma is evaporating under our very noses. Despite it being a dish prepared in the guise of a takeaway, the beauty of the deep, dense broth with the perfection of the soy-marinated egg and the noodles several millimetres thick leaves us speechless.

"*Itadakimasu!*"[146] Gabry takes a first taste, launching into a meal that, at the price of any other meal in Japan, is an explosion of sensations that should be tried at least once. It's hard to describe the consistency of a pork broth so thick that it's only a step from being a sauce, or the way it coats the chubby handmade noodles, mixing select flours chosen by Tomita in person, to bring that inimitable, compact roughness. The accuracy with which the chef prepares them is obvious not only in the consistency but also in the taste, because the noodle immersed in soup still tastes distinctive. And then the pork melts in the mouth, as does the egg, which Gabry and I open slowly so as to enjoy its ideally

---

[146] Expression generally translated as 'bon appétit', in fact it is thanks given for food and cook

cooked yolk, firm on the outside and creamy within.

As we warm each other by sitting close, the cool evening air, insinuating itself into a park now lively with lights and people, steals on a small part of the pleasure of our *tsukemen* which, eaten in a ceramic bowl in the warmth of the chef's premises might easily be someone's last wish. A dish that has transformed a poor tradition into a complexity of preparation and taste of unparalleled richness.

Before abandoning the arena of Japan's great cooks, we take a tour around the other stands to spot other 'Rāmen Heads' and decide where to go the next day when, more out of greed than sportsmanship, we will vote for another of the contestants.

The pulsing heart of Shinjuku is an agglomeration of skyscrapers and luminous signs, of nightclubs and *izakaya* frequented by youth and foreigners, of vast shops overloaded with artificial lights. From cute Godzilla sticking out from the roofs and leaning over the fluorescent junctions near the station, to glimpses of flyovers and shining buildings that the animator Makoto Shinkai reproduced in his *anime* films in the most poetic way possible. Shinjuku is loved for its particularly futuristic district dedicated to free time and amusements, be they simple or prohibited. It is a view of Tōkyō as the rest of the world generally knows it, homing in on the railway bridge hanging over a steel mesh or the backdrop of slender, incandescent skyscrapers in succession on Yasukuni-dōri Street.

And yet, even here there is something discreet and less conspicuous that catches the eye: the delightful, very narrow Golden Gai with its pubs and *izakaya*, sometimes with a mere three places to sit, where the laughter of Japanese who have drunk one too many *sake* rings out under a roof of autumn decorations, a sky of oranges and reds in the nighttime alleyway; or Kabuki-chō District at night, where, once through the unmistakeable ruby arch, it's interesting to wander around and form an idea of the intriguing dark side of red-light Tōkyō. Finally, the elegant, polyhedric sky-scraper belonging to the Tōkyō government with its two tall towers, the top floors of which you can visit free of charge to enjoy fabulous views over the city. Going up late in the afternoon, I admired a Tōkyō touched by the sinking sun, and between skyscrapers lit up like brass, caught sight of the hood of the mountain king, which is white, sugary or opaque depending on the season.

Before returning to the tentacular monster of Shinjuku station, our last stop in the area is at Artnia, a small café ex-travagantly shaped like a capsule a little further east of Ōkubo-kōen Park, near one of the *otaku* buildings best known by lovers of videogames. It is the skyscraper belong-ing to Square-Enix, the entertainment conglomerate that changed the world of videogames, responsible for the sagas Final Fantasy, Dragon Quest and Kingdom Hearts. The Art-nia café also has a view of a space where a trick cascade of water and lights encompasses a variety of thematic ele-ments that lovers of Final Fantasy wouldn't find it hard to recognise, as well as a sales point for a range of exclusive edition gadgets. From themed outfits to classic collector's pieces, we order the speciality of the house: exquisite pan-cake towers overflowing with fruit, cream and chocolate.

Laughing and mucking about like children, we sit down to a cup of Japanese coffee and a squishy, eatable sky-scraper. I'd like to stop time in this instant, modest and pre-dictable though it seems, but I can feel it forcibly filling my life. Like a child again, sitting at a table in a pastry shop with Dad made me feel on top of the world, as if I lacked nothing.

In the dark of the evening, heading down Central Road,

Shinjuku treats us to spectacular wall rainbows, animated screens and *kanji* dissolving along the buildings. Even the headlights of the armies of taxis and cars patiently wedged between one traffic light and the next, light up the streets by day and ensure that night never falls.

Everything here is permeated with light and colour, a universe so wonderful I could sink into it. In the gleaming metro that takes us back to Ginza I take hold of Gabry's hand, and I don't feel the least guilt if it appears childish, as if I were a kid hanging onto their parent's hand, the most important anchor of unexplored life.

I do it leagues from the west and its need to make me an adult - mature, absorbed in a career and covered in money – a west that imposes happiness as fruit of seriousness and schemes of a pre-arranged life in which there is suddenly no time to be childish, to laugh at a pudding, lose oneself in piles of comics or consider daily rules seen through play to be important. Because here the rules for the street, behaviour in the metro and public places or in the case of an earthquake, are given in infantile drawings, efficiently educating people through their most sensitive side, that of childhood.

I still don't know why it's necessary to travel 5,500 miles to feel as I want to always, in a world I want to live in and find the infantile side that turns out to be the best and most creative part of me. The part that finally makes me feel proud of the person I am and never out of place, that gives me a sense of realization and expels any feeling of failure.

In bed I cling to Gabry, looking for ingenuous, simple, pure affection. Because perhaps, just like a child, we need to fight monsters and demons in our lives to conquer our own world in which to be happy. To finally design and choose the best life for us.

And when I close my eyes in a Tōkyō pretending to sleep, I realise it's time to take in hand the new start that was a continent away until now.

I'll start to build my road to happiness here, with this Japan and this embrace.

Travel Notes

Despite being one of the most densely populated cities with its 14 million inhabitants, Tōkyō remains one of the safest and most livable metropoles in the world, boasting efficient services and leisure activities of every type. Although in constant transformation, the different neighbourhoods each have their own identities and unique characteristics.

Asakusa is the historic district, with Sensō-ji Temple, fascinating Nakamise-dōri and nearby shopping streets such as Hoppy-dōri and Denpōin-dōri. Beyond River Sumida-gawa is the Sumida district, where you find several Sumo gyms and arenas, and the modern, quiet area of Tōkyō Skytree, ideal for romantic walks along Kitajukken-gawa Canal or shopping for absolutely anything in Soramachi Mall at the foot of the Skytree. On the other side, in Taitō, you find Kappabashi-dōgugai Street, also known as Kappabashi-dōri or 'kitchen town' because it is entirely populated with shops selling restaurant equipment.

Akihabara is famous for technology, videogames, manga and anime culture: electronics shops are concentrated in the north of the station where, besides hundreds of small shops peddling components of every type, there are huge buildings belonging to the chains Yodobashi Camera, Bic Camera and Sofmap selling the most recent models of computer, mobile phones, cameras and a lot else, or Don Quixote, which sells good second-hand electronic devices; Mandarake, LAOX and Animate are the main shops for manga and anime, full of action figures, gadgets and comics of all the animated series, even the less well known; for lovers of videogames it would be impossible to resist the dozens of arcade cabinets in the Sega building or the Taito station games rooms, and the retro-gaming shop, Super Potato; there are numerous Maid cafés for a snack break, expensive tourist traps with alluring waitresses, and themed places such as the Final Fantasy Eorzea café.

***

Shinjuku has a futuristic style known for its sparkling neon streets, high skyscrapers and unstoppable night life, whose heart is around the immense underground metro station inhabited by hundreds of shops and restaurants. To the north of the station you get a first taste of the evening ebullience along Omoide-yokochō, narrow streets full of izakaya where you can sup on rāmen and beer in the typical pubs and eat yakitori in the famous alleyway dedicated to them. Not far off, Kabuki-chō includes the red light district and the central agglomeration of skyscrapers and neon lit Central Road with Godzilla's head lurching out, now the quarter's historic symbol, while heading east you find the Samurai museum and a second area of tight lanes and izakaya, Golden Gai. To the west of the station the massive Tōkyō Government Building stands out, and gives free access to the observation bridge on 45F of the south tower, worth it for the sunset panorama of Tōkyō and view of Mount Fuji-san.

Day Trip:
* Take the Jōban metro to Matsudo to book a midday meal at Chūka-soba Tomita
* Get back on the Jōban metro to the small town of Mito to visit Kairaku-en Garden
* Eat at Chūka-soba Tomita
* Visit Akihabara district in the early afternoon
* Snack in a themed café
* Visit Shinjuku district by night and for an evening meal

Alternative Trip to Kairaku-en Garden:
* Spend the morning wandering around Asakusa
* Visit Sensō-ji Temple and souvenir shops on ancient Nakamise-dōri Street
* Try meron pan, dorayaki and other specialities at the historical shops in the area
* Visit Kappabashi-dōgugai Street, the 'kitchen town'

Typical Products and Souvenirs:
* Omamori and omikuji at Sensō-ji Temple
* Goshuin at Asakusa-jinja Shrine
* Culinary souvenirs from Kappabashi-dōgugai Street
* Traditional sweets from Asakusa district
* Souvenirs from along Nakamise-dōri Street

* Nerd shopping in Akihabara district
* Sweets and gadgets in themed cafés

Tōkyō
東京

*Our last morning wading down
the crammed streets of Harajuku,
vibrant and impatient to usher in a new Halloween.
Our last shopping chance to tear away a part of Japan
and carry it back with us to Italy.
Our last meal fishing for slices of brilliant tuna
from the projectile dishes of Shibuya.
The final hours of a journey that has modelled
our crumpled and imperfect daily life,
transforming it into a beautiful origami.
Now at the close of these days
I still know nothing of the future,
and yet I certainly know the wonder of the present,
as Tōkyō never tires of reminding me,
bidding goodbye on a night lit up with flowers of fire.
Radiant corollas exploding and vanishing in an instant,
etching a memory that lasts forever.
Much like our travels.
Much like happiness*

On tiptoe at the close of a host of unforgettable days, I begin to think that perhaps happiness doesn't possess a definite form. At the most it might assume a colour, smell or taste that blossom on the instant or from a memory, a cutting of time impressed on the mind's eye, like a frame in a roll of film.

Happiness has no limits, it just happens, at the very

373

moment in which it is contained.

As I top up some suitcases before engaging in what I know will be a savage fight to close them, it occurs to me that this trip is made up of a kaleidoscope of happy moments now reduced to a single one of incredibly fleeting but crystal clear beauty.

"You know, I've never made a trip for a whole month, and it seemed eternal. While in fact it has gone in the blinking of an eye. The days have slid by so fast..." I wail, showing all the insatiability of the human being faced with good things. With joy.

"Don't think of it like that: think of it as the incredible journey around Japan you've had, of nearly a month. It's more than past trips. And besides, you're talking as though it has already finished. We've got another whole day ahead of us!"

'*Another treasure chest of happy moments in which to root around.*'

Breakfast in our not very sophisticated hotel in Ginza is straddled half way between east and west, and I enjoy a bowl of rice with grilled salmon and a steaming and delicious smelling *miso* soup, one of the things I will most miss on waking up back home.

Having taken our time this morning we find Harajuku already a river in spate of swaying bodies. Harajuku is another part of Tōkyō I am used to visiting every time I come, because although it fills a compact space with respect to its bulkier neighbours Shibuya and Shinjuku, it is a concentrate of extravagant *kawaii* things that make it a black swan sitting between two white ones.

You don't need to go far from the metro station to plunge into the thick of this zone, as Takeshita-dōri pullulates with so very many people it's almost impossible to walk down it at a normal speed. I stand at the top of the small street that descends in a blaze of protruding signs and small shops, and perform my ritual of holding up my camera as high as possible above the riot of moving heads, angling the lens to include the quirky luminous arch that frames the road itself. 'Takeshita Street' it says across the top, gleaming and slightly absurd like most of the things sold in the little shops here.

This street is the Tōkyō teenager ecosystem of overblown femininity and of youths falling on the most popular of the capital's fashion. From the shops selling clothes that are bizarre or dripping in bows and lace, to highly coloured cafés, to confectionery selling gigantic sticks of rainbow coloured candy floss, Takeshita-dōri provides everything most whacky and trendy you can find in Tōkyō.

Fulcrum of youthful fashion and the myriad outlandish styles that the city offers, in this small street I have always found something new, whether it be in charming boutiques full of lace and silk, designer labels hidden in the flanking lanes or the '100 *yen*' stores like Daisō, whose pink shop sign attracts its victims and then gives them no way out: in less than half an hour, the 100 *yen* you were spending morph into 10,000 and the total impossibility of getting it all into even the largest suitcase.

I listen to the incessant hubbub, I look at coloured backpacks and little bags in the form of a teddy bear or *Pokémon*[147] 「ポケモン」 crossing paths and I feel nostalgic for the first time I came here, with my sister. Then there was the

---

[147] Series of globally successful videogames from the late '90s, on which anime, manga and films were based. The term Pokémon refers to fantastical creatures similar to animals that live with humans

amazement of being surrounded by *cosplay*[148] 「コスプレ」
girls and youths with absurd feminine pochettes, the excitement of buying gigantic crêpe cones full of every possible
delight, of trying hot and cold bubble tea and rushing fre-
netically from one clothes shop to another was enough to
transform this impossible walk into something easy and
thrilling.

"Shall we move on to something else this time, what do
you think?" Gabry suggests, appalled like me at the idea of
spending too long in a trap that now, in a jungle of black
and orange festoons and shop windows thronging with
pumpkins and ghosts, feels like a cauldron waiting to blow.

In the end taking a mid-morning walk down Takeshita-
dōri means spending at least two hours elbowing your way
and having people continually tread on your feet, and woe
unto you if your companion disappears, quite likely sucked
into the twists and turns of this human forest. Then imagine
walking down it around Halloween, when the road is mon-
strously adorned and getting ready to welcome all of
masked youth on the night of 31 October; it is utter mad-
ness.

So, despite having the opportunity to visit the street at
one of the most characteristic times of year, somewhat reluctantly I make do with a take-away McDonald's at the entrance to the street then head off towards another Harajuku
attraction, the Omotesandō.

This wide avenue striated with Japanese elms is lit day
and night by the store windows of famed international
brands, sparkling with little lights and flamboyant decorations nowhere near Christmas. Spilling into the avenue is
the maze of internal lanes branching off from Takeshita-

---

[148] Term deriving from the union of the two English words 'costume' and 'play', it
describes the art of dressing up as famous characters from manga or videogames

dōri, a group of roads with low, elegant houses and English looking boutiques for the most part belonging to famous Anglo-American labels.

I don't particularly like this little western enclave that represents one of the many successful imitations of world glamour outside Japan, which Tōkyō, in an attempt to be up-to-the-minute and trendy, obsessively follows, every year slightly more. All the same, alongside the iconic Cat Bar on several floors at the entrance to the avenue, I set off along its wide tiled pavements with the aim of taking Gabry to a couple of shops worth exploring.

Kiddy Land is one of the city's most popular toyshops and with several floors of displays not only sells modern gadgets but also typically traditional Japanese toys now hard to come by. Once inside, whatever age the client, you feel like a child in never-never land. Here you find another Japanese obsession, that of small things. From the Nanoblock, like Lego but smaller, to do-it-yourself models in paper and the most disparate materials, the Japanese re-produce famous historical shops, attractions and religious monuments in as miniaturized a format as possible. They are not really toys, but more like works of art, pocketable beauty for a people strongly attached to detail and with a limitless and inexplicable love of small things.

In the wake of the art of *bonsai* and reproduction of min-iature landscapes one comes to see how 'small' is synony-mous for beauty to the extent that, in Japanese model-mak-ing where fulfilment of the eyes is also of the heart, each re-construction is so detailed that its assembly can take whole days. Notwithstanding the arduous experience I go through every time I make a d.i.y. model, I find it hard to resist the contents of the display cabinets: *rāmen* workshops, *takoyaki* and green tea shops, Japanese houses, with all the details in fabric, wood and rice paper identical to the ones that stir the heart every time I explore this country. Here the marvels met travelling sit in the palm of your hand.

Continuing along Omotesandō Avenue, we go over the junction of the characterful Cat Street, a long street of low houses in pastel colours, rows of parked bicycles and busy young people that winds through the whole quarter cutting across Takeshita-dōri and stretches towards Shibuya.

So we arrive at the Oriental Bazaar, a store on several floors recognisable by a façade like the entrance to a large temple of a lurid red colour. This enormous building sells souvenirs ranging greatly in price and value, both home-made and commercial, which makes it hard not to pick up something to take home once you are inside.

By the end of our trip, we are overloaded with Japanese ceramics, but on the lower floor, avoiding the severe old lady who chases clients around advising them on their pur-chases, we buy some really fantastic and original t-shirts with Japanese prints on them.

Saying goodbye to this part of the city we visit a place I have great affection for. Immediately behind the Harajuku station, hidden by the vegetation of Yoyogi-kōen Park stretching between Shibuya and Shinjuku, is the first *torii* in Meiji-jingū Shrine, a solid wooden portal covered in carv-ings and finished in gold at the entrance to a woody path.

I recall the summer I first found myself looking at this gate, unforeseen and colossal, so elegant in the awe and rev-erence it inspires. A way into the world of the *Kami*: so it appeared as I admired the beauty of the compact wood that seemed to run after the sky. I recall running my hand over the surface, dented by time's fissures, spontaneously bow-ing my head, and then setting off through the wood to the temple.

It was the first time I had been struck by the magnificence of a Japanese *torii* and then even more by the song of the crickets who lived there, a rhythmic, croaking riff which is deafening in the wood, monopolizing everything, densely clothing every meander through the trees exactly as the humid heat did.

A second vivid memory of that day remains: I walked along the avenue in the park, completely drowned in the cool shade of the trees' fronds, and I imagined taking the same steps in a different season, when red and yellow leaves danced in the air, the smell of moss and roasted chestnuts blew across the park, of the cool air swelled in the early dusk of the afternoon.

The image was powerful enough to create a film of me sitting on one of the benches between a couple of trees, the worn iron bench supports sinking into a bed of leaves, a book sitting next to me, a slim laptop sitting on my knees. Maybe a previous life, maybe a future one. And yet I felt the film close in to become my *ikigai*, my 'raison d'être', my perennial instant of happiness.

On that first trip, after the purification beneath the high wooden *torii* among the trees of the wood, I, the crickets and the other me took one of our most important decisions: I would come back, and somehow that place and that country, would inevitably become part of my life; in one way or another, sooner or later I would see the leaves fall in Meiji-jingū Shrine park.

"Move slightly to your left..." Gabry directs me so that the lens includes the two of us and part of the immense *torii*.

I smile, and technology does the rest, reproducing the joy I can feel plastered across my face into millions of pixels. I wonder, when I look at that photo in the future whether I will retrieve the emotion of the moment, bewildering like the absence of cricket song in autumn.

We take the first avenue into the park and I recognise a colourful wall of *sake* flasks donated to the shrine by various prefectures. The leaves aren't completely kindled, but they have decided that the time has come for a last dance.

The bench should be around here somewhere, but there's no time to look for it, nor do I want to hold up our itinerary for that. I attempt to see myself in the film that has been with me so long it feels like an eternity and I weep inside myself, thanking the *Kami* for allowing me to come back here, in autumn, in a gentle drizzle of leaves. I thank them from the heart, aware that the film, like the happiness linked to it, is not yet complete. Perhaps I knew that already.

'*Not yet.*'

"Do you imagine yourself writing the book of this trip? Knowing you, this place in autumn could inspire your best words..." Gabry breaks the silence of my thoughts and in a flash the film crystalises.

In a flash it is me, autumn, '*that*' book. In a flash it is all it should be. It isn't yet, but it already is.

I sigh as I look at him, then bury my head in his warm coat, which smells of him, to quickly dry that thin trickle of salt water teetering on my eyelids. This is the effect of a moment of happiness.

At Genki Sushi there's a queue at all hours. I forget this on every trip, when while visiting Shibuya, which is only one metro stop from Harajuku, I go to one of the places I can eat a quick, good quality *sushi* at a reasonable price and above all outside mealtimes.

In fact, unlike minor cities or those typically from the Japanese countryside, in Tōkyō there's no problem eating out of hours, and over time, chains like Sushi Zanmai and Ippūdō Rāmen have become established with continuous opening hours. Shibuya, like Shinjuku, is a notably lively district attracting many tourists and it offers a large number of alternatives even for a meal in mid-afternoon or late at night.

At the popular Genki Sushi, besides the reasonable prices, you can enjoy a special *kaiten-zushi*[149] 「回転寿司」: once you have a seat, two levels of belt transport the dishes you have chosen straight to where you are sitting, skyrocketing out of the kitchen and speedily moving round the restaurant. Equally out of the ordinary are the cooked meat *sushi* served here, balls of rice topped with little hamburgers or chicken croquettes, a perfect solution for anyone, like Gabry, who isn't a fan of raw fish.

Another of the best alternatives if you want to eat in this area are the different floors of the Shibu-building, renamed by the young as 'Graffiti Palace', a huge antiquated building completely covered by graffiti that houses a large number of *rāmen-ya* each with its own inimitable style of *rāmen*. However, in the end, on this marvellous culinary journey around Japan I felt I merited some *sushi* in the simple and essential Japanese way.

Having eaten just the right amount, we let ourselves be transported by the tireless crowd moving through the nearby streets, and a few blocks away we find another of the places I always feel drawn to: the Shibuya crossing. We enjoy it at our leisure, waiting for late afternoon when at sunset it becomes a blaze of neon and animation screens.

Under a darkening sky, the great big shopping centre, Shibuya109, frequented by the beautiful girls of Tōkyō,

---

[149] Restaurants that serve sushi and other dishes on little plates on a belt that moves in front of customers

stands out in an angular skyscraper, while at the crossing hundreds of signs take up battle. Signs for shops like Forever21 and H&M, and the huge Tsutaya bookshop in whose belly Starbucks resides looking out on the most famous view in the world.

Every year I've spent a few hours shopping inside the shimmering cylinder of Shibuya109, bearing in mind that, despite my almost non existent affinity with the world of fashion and the disastrous lack of attention I pay to dressing myself, here I always manage to find something that makes me feel happy in myself, and at the same time, feminine in a way I don't manage to be on the other side of the ocean.

I've always felt admiration for the girls of Tōkyō, for being tremendously attractive in all simplicity, with a fine and delicate elegance. They don't need fur coats, stiletto heels or high fashion items to feel sure of themselves and attractive, they just put on low necklines with simple, linear garments, or clothes in soft, muted tones with a bow in the right place to appear the most beautiful girls in the world. Less conspicuous outfits they combine with an embellishment in the Japanese manner, with lace and bows giving the girls of the Rising Sun an even more angelic and innocent look.

This image of a classic Tōkyō girl is yours from Shibuya109, a cake with narrow layers full of boutiques where you are assisted by stunning models who are so friendly and kind they could almost be robots. Nevertheless, in their concise outfits draped by their long dark perfectly-styled hair, there is something very charming about the discreet way they look after clients, without any vanity or ostentation, in the way they invite you to come into the shop with a piping 'Irasshaimase', or accompany you to the door, carrying your bag and bowing with thanks. I adore the succession of gestures, from the moment the assistant invites you to take off your shoes to go into the changing room, to when you are about to pay and she holds up the brand new outfit straight from the warehouse, because the one in the shop is only for trying on and isn't sold. This is followed by the impeccable wrapping of your purchase, including a plastic bag in case it should rain, and finally the solicitude shown over filling in the various tax-free receipts and attaching the tax exemption to your passport.

The colours Shibuya dresses in at night are as excessive as the lace on the dresses just tried on. The mob at the main crossing is in turmoil, and before I know it I am sucked into a centrifuge jumbling up everything in that part of the city. After all, it's hard not to be caught up by the ordered chaos swallowing the centre of the universe.

Walking through Shibuya crossing for the first time was a moment of inner renaissance, just before the more important experience of Tōkyō Skytree. In fact it was the day I understood I was finally in the right place.

I can still remember the wall of people through which I passed as I came out of the metro station, opposite the statue of Hachikō, surrounded as always by his ring of visitors and flash photographers. I remember the spontaneous reflex of holding my bag tight to my chest, a habit I grew up with but that here is out of place. I recall the growing sensation of fear and discomfort, the feeling that had always kept me away from crowded spaces, even when I might spend an evening socialising with friends.

I knew I should be defined misanthropic, someone extremely ill at ease with other people: my difficulty socialising with other children at a young age grew into insecurity of not being accepted and escalated into the bullying I suffered in secondary school. Because if being ourselves isn't easy then being with others is even less so.

That first day at Shibuya, on the pavement at the biggest crossing in the world, all my anxieties and fears rapidly came to the fore and I got to the point of wanting to run back into the metro station. Then, suddenly, everything changed with an unexpected and powerful naturalness.

The green traffic light, the variegated wall of people teetering on the pavement, and the urge to escape that trap of threatening bodies without succeeding.

Amber. Taxis and cars coming to a halt, bit by bit the crossing clearing, turning into an enormous deserted piazza painted with a crazy grill of white stripes all pointing in different directions.

Then finally, red.

Like a dam being opened for a few seconds, or a corral of wild mustangs thrown open towards grassland, suddenly the human wall poured onto the crossroad's striped lines and began advancing like a river in spate, like a herd finally set free, splitting up into the many individuals that comprised it. And I too participated in the fragmentation, I too broke away and began to walk forward, driven by an unconscious and primordial force.

Momentarily I saw the wall coming from the opposite direction break up in the same way. A brief moment to realise that I should stop there, in that precise instant, almost at the centre of the crossing. A moment to prepare for the impact. Two waves piercing through each other to become one. There were no blasts or frothing puffs, just a single ocean subsuming everything. And I was in the middle of that ocean, a drop with thousands of others.

It was the sensation of finding myself in the centre of the universe as much as that of feeling part of it that fired my heart, and made me feel as I had never felt before. Overcome by an inexplicable euphoria, I began to move back and forth in the crossing until the last possible second.

Wallowing in happiness in that sea of humanity and loving every single person there, every single face that appeared before my eyes. I felt alive exactly as they were, busy living their lives, moving from one place to another in that unique spot in the world. And I went on wanting to feel it until, just as the wave had taken form, it began to fall away increasingly rapidly to then reunite in two armies along the pavements.

That day, in the middle of Shibuya crossing, I became aware of myself in the world, of my identity and of the place I occupied in the pounding ocean of humanity.

Now I take the crossing under the bright lights of the skyscrapers, over tarmac gleaming with autumn rain, and as then, I feel wonderfully alive.

The shop windows shining out along elegant Dōgen-zaka Slope, the tree-lined road climbing gently beside Shibuya 109, and the luminous arch marking the entrance to Centre Gai are already palpitating with the hordes beneath, prelude to a night life that will soon be activating vigorously among its restaurants and clubs. Since then, I haven't had the opportunity to walk along these streets, stop for coffee at Starbucks, go up to the top floor and stand there entranced by the rhythmic movement of that heart of people contracting and relaxing at every beat of the traffic lights, but today, every video and photo taken from that elevated position, I find beautiful in a unique way, and all different, just like the ocean's waves: different and unique from all the others.

"We must go, or we won't make it..." Gabry reminds me that Tōkyō never stops giving me gifts like the one I received at the Shibuya crossing or the top of Tōkyō Skytree.

And I sense that what there is in store for this evening, on the eve of our departure, will be a goodbye we won't forget.

Hachikō nods goodbye encircled by his indefatigable audience of fans, in recent years tickled by the presence of a cat that spends much of the day curled between the metal paws of the loyal dog. Because that too happens in Tōkyō, and although I try to struggle against my fatalist spirit, I can't help but think fate brought the cat to live there, just as firework night at Chōfu this evening, was a mere happy coincidence on our itinerary.

Much like the lantern evening at Fukuoka, the little event at Chōfu suddenly barged into our travel plans, a few weeks before leaving, boldly taking charge of the final hours of our Japanese trip.

Riding the vibe, at 4.30pm we are on the Keiō line taking us from Shinjuku to Chōfu in about half an hour, not aware of the existence of Keiō-Tamagawa, the next stop on River Tama-gawa. The fireworks are released from the riverbed for the autumnal *hanabi*, not well known despite going on for an entire hour, which seems an eternity to us. We quickly exit a station that rarely sees such a flow of people, in a climate of unrivalled excitement and expectation that pretty well infects us as well.

Unlike me, Gabry has already had the chance to go to important festivals, like Sanuki Takamatsu Matsuri, known throughout the world for the beauty of the pyrotechnics put on for citizens and tourists. Which is why I feel all the more tenderness for his trepidation, the thrill a child feels before an hour of wonderment with no thought for the final burst bringing it all to an end.

So, on the heels of lovers holding each other by the hand, groups of shrieking kids, tender old couples and happy families all heading in the direction of the river, we set off down the unexplored streets of Chōfu, under what is now a dark sky.

We might have got distracted by scenes of Japanese life that enter the heart and memory with ease, such as the entire family eating outside on the veranda of their house, waiting to enjoy the spectacle with a tray of pot-bellied *onigiri*, or we may have underestimated the distance to the riverbank and one of the paying entrances. In any case, less than 10 minutes before the start of the show, we are still sneaking through the crowds, as they become increasingly thick, on neverending Hoikusho-dōri Street.

When the opening bang reverberates among the neighbourhood's small houses, we've still got a long way to go before getting to the central reserved area with standing room and food stands. As we decide what to do the first fireworks bursts open in the sky.

"We should have bought tickets in advance at a *konbini*..." I whimper trying to catch my breath.

"And we should have got off the metro at Keiō-Tamagawa. This was much further! Let's find a good place to watch from the road, otherwise we'll miss the whole show!"

Disappointed by not being able to reach the actual viewing area and tired from hurrying, we make do with various views along the avenue rather than miss even 15 minutes of delight. Stopping at a junction with a smaller road where the houses open out in the direction of the river, and armed with cell phone and camera, I delude myself that I can harness what will burn up in front of our eyes over the next hour, during which time faces are powdered with the colours released into the night and reality melts slowly into new hues.

The noise of the crowds quickly dissolves, even Gabry's voice seems miles away as, unaware, he is repeating 'wow...'

Chōfu Hanabi 調布花火

Chōfu is a small town in the metropolitan area of Tōkyō, easily reached in 40 minutes by metro from Central station. As a result, it is lived in by commuters who daily pour into offices in the capital. The town is known mainly for its annual hanabi of over 10,000 fireworks held along River Tama-gawa, which attracts over 300,000 spectators every year.

During the festival, access to the river area is by entry ticket that you can buy at kiosks in konbini all over Japan. Usually there are two areas, one sitting and one with standing room only, each with independent access. The cost of seats can vary between 30 and 50 Euros depending on whether you are reserving a single seat, a rug or a table, while the cost of entering the standing area, in which there are stands selling street food and gadgets, is around 20 Euros.

For anyone wanting to admire the fireworks free, on the south bank of the river there is a cycle way and pedestrian path. An alternative view, although not ideal, is along Sakurazutsumi-dōri Street, adjacent to the north bank. The closest metro station to the 3 areas reserved for the event is Keiō-Tamagawa on the Sagamihara line. The show generally begins between 6pm and 6.30 and lasts an hour, but it's best to arrive early given the huge number of people in the zone for the event.

The town is also home to the Jindai botanic garden, open to the public, the first botanic garden to be built around Tōkyō and inside which you can find many species of vegetation, including varieties of plum, sakura, peony, rose and wisteria. In the mid-1500s, the garden provided the capital with thousands of trees to be planted along the main streets.

Jindai-ji is also located here. Tōkyō's second oldest Buddhist temple, immersed in the forest of Chōfu, it is a destination for many local people during Daruma Matsuri in March and right next to an ancient village full of craft shops and soba restaurants.

on a loop. The explosions of the fireworks taking turns in the sky merge into a continuous muffled, distant sound, and everything suddenly seems superfluous, accessory to the single firework sparks that in seconds show a beauty that seems eternal.

I don't think there is a nation on earth that has managed to name things as appropriately as the Japanese. *Hanabi* is a composite word made up of the *kanji* for flower and fire, and expresses, without any doubt, the unequivocal aspect of a firework. But, like everything here in Japan, it's not sufficient to stop at the words or images they give life to, you also have to nurture the meaning.

Like *sakura*, the Japanese flower par excellence that blooms so briefly but displays a beauty to live on in the memory of anyone lucky enough to enjoy it, so a firework explodes in the sky, those few seconds that make the spectator's heart jump, gaze in wonderment, be moved and print the image in their memory. A few instants later and the night has already swallowed it all. It doesn't matter what form it took, nor how big the incandescent blue sphere sent up there, how many purple, green or vermilion rays crossed over each other to make a fabulous design. Seconds later it is already a memory.

Suddenly, my umpteenth leap in surprise: a white trail rises in the sky and opens into perfectly aligned red petals. I'm convinced it's a *higanbana*, the flower of the autumn equinox whose blood red colour is seen all over Japanese lawns in this season. Then, Mount Fuji-san lights up behind the skyline of houses, a silhouette with flaming edges that remains incandescent for minutes.

The sound of '*sugoi!*' [150] echoes among the crowd,

---

[150] Exclamation of awe translatable as 'incredible!'

anticipating even greater stupor at the final battery of fire-works, when the sky is dusted with gold and a continual whirlwind of star fragments. Then everything goes silent, an hour has gone by in an instant, everything around me starts up again and reality becomes distinct.

Once again, Tōkyō is taking its leave by leaving me something immense. Something learnt on this trip, the end and beginning of a journey that, setting out from a present made uncertain by both past and future, has gained consistency and assurance here, in the country that has shown me my *ikigai*.

Whether it is the instant of a firework, the hour-long display in Chōfu, or these three weeks devoured by autumn advancing and turning everything gold and ruby, it is nothing if not beauty. It can bloom in a single moment and fill existence.

Another, different *tsukemen* in Ōkubo-kōen Park. New tastes released on an evening that couldn't be more incredible than it was, and has left us dazed.

Despite it being late and us leaving tomorrow, I escape to the top floor of our Tōkyō hotel-skyscraper, in its artificial *onsen*, as though piping hot water could seal the memories in my body like wax on a letter.

In the silence of an empty pool, I rest my head on the stone side, raise my eyes to the skylight and give myself up to yet another gift of places in which my life has started again.

I'm going to write about them and how they taught me happiness. I'll recount this autumn moon, jewel of an irresistible world.

Happiness has no shape, it is a moment, an instant of pure astonishment that can issue from the unexpected red of a maple in early autumn or a firework in Chōfu. Engulfing you in a night of love on a *futon* in Takayama or in the sight of the autumn moon in Hakone. Leaving a memory of trembling lanterns in the dark of Fukuoka or the night steam of an *onsen* in Beppu.

And if life is nought but a composition of many diverse instants, then could living it as much as possible imbued with joy be the key to happiness?

Travel Notes

Located between Shinjuku and Shibuya, Harajuku is a small neighbourhood famous for excessive and whacky youth fashion, as well as cosplay and desserts. Just outside Harajuku metro station, the long descent of crowded Takeshita–dōri Street is full of clothes shops, from underground to 'Lolita' and 'Kawaii' styles with lots of lace and bows. Between one purchase and another, you can stop at one of the numerous cafés with fantastical interiors, at kiosks selling bubble tea or crêpes with fillings, and pastry shops. Among these, Totti Candy Factory is famous for its giant rainbow candy floss.

Parallel to Takeshita–dōri runs Omotesandō, the wide shopping avenue where you find the Oriental Bazaar, two floors of crafts, souvenirs, t–shirts and kimono, and Kiddy Land, one of the city's most famous toyshops, where you can find retro toys and several departments for model making. Crossing the neighbourhood widthwise, you get to Cat Street, an elegant lane with a more sober atmosphere and lots of designer clothes shops.

Near Harajuku station, you cross Jingū–bashi Bridge to access the biggest wooden torii in the world, 40 feet high and 55 feet wide. Beyond that is the forest of Meiji–jingū Shrine where, in summer, the song of the Japanese crickets is deafening. Inside, sheltered from the city's hectic pace, is the famous shrine's complex and other points of interest such as the great iris pond. Vast Yoyogi–kōen Park is nearby: with areas of different plants, ponds and fountains, it attracts a large number of people from the capital at the weekend and in the cherry blossom season.

***

Shibuya is one of the most dynamic zones in Tōkyō and also has the heaviest traffic. The Hachikō exit (A8) from the metro station leads straight to the statue of Hachikō, the dog that became famous for showing great loyalty to its master: after the latter's sudden death, every day for nearly ten years the dog made its way to Shibuya station, from where the man had daily left and returned. From here you can cross the largest pedestrian junction in the world, overrun with massive screens on the surrounding skyscrapers that create a truly amazing atmosphere at night. Stopping for coffee at Starbucks inside Tsutaya book store, there is a great view of the crossing and the rhythmic movement of the pedestrians. From the crossing you can see the arch at the entrance to the neighbourhood's main shopping street, Centre Gai, with a mass of restaurants and shops of every sort, like the enormous Disney store. Along the way you can take fun Japanese style passport photos at Purikura-no-mecca and eat at one of the many restaurants for economical sushi at kaiten-zushi in Genki Sushi, Japanese curried rice at the Curry House CoCo Ichiban or a hot rāmen at the Ippūdō Rāmen chain or in one of the rāmen-ya in 'Graffiti Palace', aka the Shibu Building.

After walking down the grand avenue Dōgen-zaka Slope, or along Bunkamura-dōri Street, you can find Japanese women's fashion at the symbolic mall Shibuya109 or male fashion and trending gadgets by Magnet at Shibuya.

Day Trip:
* Visit happening places in Harajuku, like Takeshita-dōri Street, Cat Street and Omotesandō Avenue
* Go for a walk in Meiji-jingū Park and admire the torii
* Visit Shibuya to walk over the largest crossing in the world and go shopping at Centre Gai and around there
* Enjoy a meal of sushi or rāmen in a local restaurant
* Take the metro from Shibuya to Keiō-Tamagawa to buy tickets for the firework display at Chōfu (also available in advance at a konbini)
* Enjoy Chōfu Hanabi display from 6pm by River Tama-gawa

Typical Products and Souvenirs:
* Female clothes shopping at Shibuya109 or male clothes from Magnet at Shibuya
* Kawaii gadgets, sweets and clothes from Harajuku
* Soba-pan and soba-inari, soft buckwheat sandwiches and snacks from Chōfu
* Akakoma, handmade straw horses at Jindai-ji temple in Chōfu

Epilogue

Gazing out of the plane window I see a world that isn't Japan anymore; where the ploughed rice fields dotted with sky-blue and grey-blue roofs gradually become less distinct until they melt into the mist. The lakes are little iridescent mirrors and the mountains a series of haphazardly emerging dark outlines.

A world that has lost every detail familiarly loved until the night before, except one: Mount Fuji-san is the guardian watching over the country, unavoidable even when you are a long way from its woods and rivers; even when the continent of land turns into clouds and you can no longer tell what is hidden underneath. There it is, protruding from the edge of the sky, unreachable in the final cone as it looks out over the white valleys of ocean vapours, that perfect, colossal silhouette jutting out over the hidden world to enshrine the identity of a unique place. It grants you a viewing, suddenly, as always, and accepts a last, appreciative salute.

"Look how much snow there is now..." Gabry points to the first eruption of white flowing down the crests, just scuffing the surface for now, before shrouding the whole area.

More beautiful than a few weeks ago, but I imagine increasingly so in the winter season.

"One day I'd like to climb it, and maybe - why not - wait at the peak for the sun to come up. But we'd need to wait for summer..." his voice catches at my throat like the last image of Mount Fuji-san before the plane turns definitively, exactly as in the past.

I swallow, hoping to swallow the tears too, concentrating hard on the sweetness of Gabry's words and the hope they are full of. The desire to continue cultivating these places and the happiness he derives from them.

"Although..." he whispers, just enough to make me turn to face him "... I've heard Japanese snow has a unique consistency in the world and I've always wanted to learn to snowboard, so... what do you say to taking a few lessons this year?"

I look at him as my face fills with a smile of immense gratitude. There's no need for him to finish his thought, or to ask whether I intend to come back again.

'Together'. In a different season, covering Japan in soft, floury snow, luminous decorations, a time of anticipation and celebrations for the new year.

I will nurture this autumn trip in the memories and dreams I have put aside, writing of a happiness that can be grasped. And I will nurture this love, fruit of inner growth and a new beginning. I will return in wintertime, to discover new wonders, to share and tell of its simplicity, and in this Japan of the present and future, I will narrate the incredible adventure to win your own place in the world. Some pages will already have been written and others are still to come, about the journey so rich with surprises and beauty that is life.

For a long time I pursued a happiness thought unattainable, the very thing these places showed me to be simple, daily, inherent in what surrounds us, in those little things that are often taken for granted. The fear of a future without it slowly turned into living in the present with the awareness I could fill it with joy. The joy of grasping and of creating it where it isn't.

When my life was all messed up, I found a new

beginning here, learning to be myself in a world where it is hard to do, and to appreciate the inexorable beauty of nature like past and present affection, to give importance to simplicity and to value time.

This 'Japan' of mine exists for all of us: whether it is a physical place or something else, it is simply through the courage to listen to our heart and to seek out the wonder around us that we can find it and be happy.

Autumn leaves -

at the end of the trip

spark a beginning

Valentina Sgambato

If you enjoyed reading my book, I would be very grateful if you could leave a review on Amazon.

For those who publish with their own resources, every single review means a lot!

Here is the QR code that will bring you to my website and then to the Amazon page of your country where you can review the book.

Thank you so much!

Acknowledgements

When I started writing this book, I never thought I would hold in my hands, in those few centimetres of paper, the fruit of a dream that I had cultivated since I was a child and that Japan motivated me to make concrete. Even more, I never imagined that it could one day be translated into another language. I will not dwell on the thanks that filled the final pages of the Italian version, but I think it is right to mention those who made it possible to bring this 'guide-novel' to other places in the world. Because even translation, like writing, is filled with that tenacity and spirit of sacrifice that I have learned is necessary to achieve one's dreams.

And maybe it was the tenacity in wanting to see this book in an equally beautiful guise that made me meet Sophie Henderson, the translator who made all this possible. To her go my most grateful thanks, for the incredible love and professionalism with which she was able to give confidence to the translation of an unpublished text, for the sensitivity and attention with which she adapted the text keeping intact the soul of every thought and reflection. Sophie arrived at a very delicate and precious moment in my life, when I was overwhelmed by the birth of my son Takumi and working on the winter volume. It may have been fate or maybe not, I could not have wished for a better 'voice' than hers, a translator of emotions and feelings beyond words.

Other essential thanks go to all those who, eager to read these pages in English, have supported this translation project through the Kickstarter platform. Their support has arrived from all over the world and for this reason I want to thank: Patrizia Vannini, Sergey Kochergan, Kento Suzuki, 'LauraLoveJapan', Roberta Napoleoni, Katherine Fischer,

Sharon Bussey-Reschka, Iyo, Samii, Luke Gvnn Centamore, Cris, Kylie Walker, Debbie Clark, Charles I. N. Venn, Joseph Whelan, Luca, Claire Ferguson-Smith, Ilaria Bianchi, Susanne, Erin Valenciano, Joy Cerqueira, James Reason, Kevin Villwock, Dragonsteel Entertainment, Fletcher Christensen, Rosemary, Sam, Alexander Bennett, Peter Graham, T. Hise, Tsubaki, Célia, Jessica, Ray, Tracy 'Rayhne' Fretwell, Joe Ou, Kevin Khong, Carollynne Pray.

The winter English book will also be launched through a Kickstarter campaign with another translation project. So, if you liked this first autumnal book, just stick around and I'll take you to Japan once again!

Finally, another big thank you goes to all the supporters of Onigiro's projects on Patreon.com. Scan the following QR code to learn more.

'Don't be afraid, ashamed, or hesitant
to do what you do.
You don't have to be when you create
and add beauty to the world'

(One of my first supporters)

Valentina Sgambato was born in Rome in 1989.

Being a lover of nature and science, she studied Biological Sciences at university, specialising in Environmental Biology, exploring botany and dedicating her free time to her passion for vegetable and flower gardens.

Continual contact with nature brought her closer to a culture that had fascinated her from a young age, through manga, anime and zen philosophy; that of Japan, and at 26 she set out on a trip to spend a fortnight in the metropolis of Tōkyō. The impact with a world and people so different from her own, and with which she feels she shares values and sensibility is so strong that she goes back every year.

Accumulated savings from part-time work didn't allow her to study in Japan so, in the meantime, she enrolled on a language course at the Japanese Institute of Culture in Rome, where she met Gabriele. Together, between 2018 and 2020, they made several trips outside Japan's customary destinations, experiences that would put them in contact with a genuine and rural Japan where they have developed their knowledge of cultural, anthropological and culinary aspects.

In 2020 they set up Onigiro.com, the international website of themed itineraries and insights into the Land of the Rising Sun. At the same time, Valentina is following her dream, spending all her free time on writing in order to share her path of personal growth alongside her love for Japan.

Storyline

First of four guide-novels, 'Four Seasons in Japan – Autumn' is the story of a fascinating journey made in the Land of the Rising Sun.

Struggling at a delicate moment in her life, Valentina sets out for the beloved country where, just like nature in autumn, she must 'throw off the old' sorrows and insecurities by taking a path in search of happiness and its meanings.

Alongside her inner journey of reflection, thoughts and emotions, is the engaging narration of a trip in the season celebrating colour, a diary gathering information about famous cities and places that are less known, often hidden from the traveller's eyes. So, the novel turns into a guidebook revealing less touristic destinations, delicious local foods and dynamic festivals on a journey to discover the more characteristic aspects of the country in autumn.

It is above all the 'lost places' that Valentina wants to recount, with her approach full of sensitivity and love, seen in the beauty of discovered details, the wonders hidden behind every corner and the experiences and people who live there, as she leads the reader down country roads, along streets and into temples, in the setting of an advancing autumn. Day by day, the adventure is revealed as the path to a rebirth, the journey towards an awareness of happiness, the courage to take hold of her own existence and dreams and to make them into the best journey ever.

To enrich the chapters of the novel, further information is provided on cultural aspects and places, maps and day trips, as well as travel notes, advice, and multimedia content accessible through QR codes.

Printed in Great Britain
by Amazon